MEMOIRS OF LIFE
AND LITERATURE

Books by W. H. MALLOCK

Memoirs of Life and Literature

The Limits of Pure Democracy   *5th Edition*

Religion as a Credible Doctrine

The Reconstruction of Belief

Novels

The Individualist   *3rd Edition*

The Heart of Life   *3rd Edition*

A Human Document   *9th Edition*

ALGERNON CHARLES SWINBURNE

MEMOIRS OF
LIFE AND LITERATURE

BY
W. H. MALLOCK
AUTHOR OF
"RECONSTRUCTION OF RELIGIOUS BELIEF" ETC.

ILLLUSTRATED

HARPER & BROTHERS PUBLISHERS
NEW YORK AND LONDON
MCMXX

CONTENTS

CHAPTER I

PAGE

FAMILY ANTECEDENTS I

The Mallocks of Cockington—Some Old Devonshire Houses
—A Child's Outlook on Life

CHAPTER II

THE TWO NATIONS 20

The Rural Poor of Devonshire—The Old Landed Families—
An Ecclesiastical Magnate

CHAPTER III

A PRIVATE TUTOR DE LUXE 39

Early Youth Under a Private Tutor—Poetry—Premonitions of Modern Liberalism

CHAPTER IV

WINTER SOCIETY AT TORQUAY 53

Early Acquaintance with Society—Byron's Grandson, Lord
Houghton—A Dandy of the Old School, Carlyle—Lord
Lytton, and Others—Memorable Ladies

CHAPTER V

EXPERIENCES AT OXFORD 68

Early Youth at Oxford—Acquaintance with Browning,
Swinburne, and Ruskin—Dissipations of an Undergraduate
—The Ferment of Intellectual Revolution—*The New
Republic*

V

CONTENTS

PAGE

CHAPTER VI

THE BASIS OF LONDON SOCIETY 92

Early Experiences of London Society—Society Thirty Years Ago Relatively Small—Arts and Accomplishments Which Can Flourish in Small Societies Only

CHAPTER VII

VIGNETTES OF LONDON LIFE 113

Byron's Grandson and Shelley's Son—The World of Balls—The "Great Houses," and Their New Rivals—The Latter Criticized by Some Ladies of the Old Noblesse—Types of More Serious Society—Lady Marian Alford and Others—*Salons* Exclusive and Inclusive—A Clash of Two Rival Poets—The Poet Laureate—Auberon Herbert and the Simple Life—Dean Stanley—Whyte Melville—"Ouida"—"Violet Fane"—Catholic Society—Lord Bute—Banquet to Cardinal Manning—Difficulties of the Memoir-writer—Lord Wemyss and Lady P—— ——Indiscretions of Augustus Hare—Routine of a London Day—The Author's Life Out of London

CHAPTER VIII

SOCIETY IN COUNTRY HOUSES 142

A Few Country Houses of Various Types—Castles and Manor Houses from Cornwall to Sutherland

CHAPTER IX

FROM COUNTRY HOUSES TO POLITICS 168

First Treatise on Politics—Radical Propaganda—First Visit to the Highlands—The Author Asked to Stand for a Scotch Constituency

CHAPTER X

A FIVE MONTHS' INTERLUDE 194

A Venture on the Riviera—Monte Carlo—Life in a Villa at Beaulieu—A Gambler's Suicide—A Gambler's Funeral

CONTENTS

CHAPTER XI

"The Old Order Changes" 209

Intellectual Apathy of Conservatives—A Novel Which Attempts to Harmonize Socialist Principles with Conservative

CHAPTER XII

Cyprus, Florence, Hungary 226

A Winter in Cyprus—Florence—Siena—Italian Castles—Cannes—Some Foreign Royalties—Visit During the Following Spring to Princess Batthyany in Hungary

CHAPTER XIII

Two Works on Social Politics 255

The Second Lord Lytton at Knebworth—"Ouida"—Conservative Torpor as to Social Politics—Two Books: *Labor and the Popular Welfare* and *Aristocracy and Evolution*—Letters from Herbert Spencer

CHAPTER XIV

Religious Philosophy and Fiction 270

The So-called Anglican Crisis—*Doctrine and Doctrinal Disruption*—Three Novels: *A Human Document, The Heart of Life, The Individualist*—Three Works on the Philosophy of Religion: *Religion as a Credible Doctrine, The Veil of the Temple, The Reconstruction of Belief*—Passages from *The Veil of the Temple*

CHAPTER XV

From the Highlands to New York 292

Summer on the Borders of Caithness—A Two Months' Yachting Cruise—The Orkneys and the Outer Hebrides—An Unexpected Political Summons

CONTENTS

PAGE

CHAPTER XVI

POLITICS AND SOCIETY IN AMERICA 308

Addresses on Socialism—Arrangements for Their Delivery
—American Society in Long Island and New York—
Harvard—Prof. William James—President Roosevelt—
Chicago—Second Stay in New York—New York to Brittany—*A Critical Examination of Socialism*—Propaganda in
England

CHAPTER XVII

THE AUTHOR'S WORKS SUMMARIZED 335

A Boy's Conservatism—Poetic Ambitions—The Philosophy
of Religious Belief—The Philosophy of Industrial Conservatism—Intellectual Torpor of Conservatives—Final
Treatises and Fiction

CHAPTER XVIII

LITERATURE AND ACTION 343

Literature as Speech Made Permanent—All Written Speech
Not Literature—The Essence of Literature for Its Own Sake
—Prose as a Fine Art—Some Interesting Aspects of Literature as an End in Itself—Their Comparative Triviality—No
Literature Great Which Is Not More Than Literature—
Literature as a Vehicle of Religion—Lucretius—*The Reconstruction of Belief*

INDEX 373

ILLUSTRATIONS

ALGERNON CHARLES SWINBURNE . . . . *Frontispiece*

ROBERT BROWNING . . . . *Facing p.* 30

THOMAS CARLYLE . . . . " 64

JOHN RUSKIN . . . . " 86

OUIDA . . . . " 126

CARDINAL MANNING . . . . " 134

HERBERT SPENCER . . . . " 266

THEODORE ROOSEVELT . . . . " 318

MEMOIRS OF LIFE AND LITERATURE

MEMOIRS OF LIFE AND LITERATURE

CHAPTER I

FAMILY ANTECEDENTS

The Mallocks of Cockington—Some Old Devonshire Houses—A Child's Outlook on Life

"MEMOIRS" is a word which, as commonly used, includes books of very various kinds, ranging from St. Augustine's *Confessions* to the gossip of Lady Dorothy Nevill. Such books, however, have all one family likeness. They all of them represent life as seen by the writers from a personal point of view; and in this sense it is to the family of Memoirs that the present book belongs.

But the incidents or aspects of life which a book of memoirs describes represent something more than themselves. Whether the writer is conscious of the fact or no, they represent a circle of circumstances, general as well as private, to which his individual character reacts; and his reactions, as he records them, may in this way acquire a meaning and unity which have their origin in the age—in the general conditions and movements which his personal recollections cover—rather than in any qualities or adventures which happen to be exclusively his own. Thus if any writer attempts to do what I have done myself—namely, to examine or depict in books of widely different kinds such aspects and problems of life—social, philosophical, religious, and economic—as have in turn engrossed his special attention, he may venture to hope that a memoir of his own activities will be taken as representing an age, rather than a personal story, his personal story being little more than a variant of one which many readers will recognize as common to themselves and him.

Now for all reflecting persons whose childhood reaches back to the middle of the nineteenth century, the most remarkable feature of the period which constitutes the age for themselves cannot fail to be a sequence of remarkable and momentous changes—changes alike in the domains of science, religion, and society; and if any one of such persons should be asked, "Changes from what?" his answer will be, if he knows how to express himself, "Changes from the things presented to him by his first remembered experiences, and by him taken for granted," such as the teaching, religious or otherwise, received by him, and the general constitution of society as revealed to him by his own observation and the ways and conversation of his elders. These are the things which provide the child's life with its starting point, and these are determined by the facts of family tradition and parentage. It is, therefore, with a description of such family facts that the author of a memoir like the present ought properly to begin.

The Mallocks, who have for nearly three hundred years been settled at Cockington Court, near to what is now Torquay, descend from a William Malet, Mallek, or Mallacke, who was, about the year 1400, possessed of estates lying between Lyme and Axmouth. This individual, according to the genealogists of the Heralds' College, was a younger son of Sir Baldwyn Malet of Enmore, in the county of Dorset. His descendants, at all events, from this time onward became connected by marriage with such well-known West Country families as the Pynes, the Drakes, the Churchills, the Yonges of Colyton, the Willoughbys of Payhembury, the Trevelyans, the Tuckfields (subsequently Hippesleys), the Strodes of Newnham, the Aclands, the Champernownes, and the Bullers. Between the reigns of Henry VII and Elizabeth they provided successive Parliaments with members for Lyme and Poole. One of them, Roger, during the reign of the latter sovereign, found his way to Exeter, where, as a banker or "goldsmith," he laid the foundations of what was then a very great fortune, and built himself a large town house, of which one room is still intact, with the queen's arms and his own juxtaposed on the paneling. The fortune accumulated by him was, during the next two reigns, notably increased by a second Roger, his son, in partnership with Sir Ferdinando Gorges, military governor of Plymouth, who had somehow become possessed of immense territories in Maine, and was a prominent figure in the history of English trade with America.

The second Roger, about the year 1640, purchased the Cockington property from Sir Henry Cary, a Cavalier, who appears to have been a typical sufferer from his devotion to the royal cause. Roger Mallock was, indeed, so far Royalist himself that he entered a protest against the execution of Charles; but both he and his relatives also were evidently in sympathy otherwise with the Parliamentary party; for, during the Protectorate, Elizabeth Mallock, his cousin, married Lord Blayney, an Irishman, who was personally attached to Cromwell; while Rawlin Mallock, this second Roger's son (who had married Susannah, Sir Ferdinando Gorges's daughter), was Whig member for Totnes, twice Whig member for Ashburton, and was one of the small group of peers and country gentlemen who welcomed William of Orange when he disembarked at Brixham. Rawlin's heir was a boy—beautiful, as a picture of him in the guise of a little Cavalier shows—who died a minor in the year 1699, but who, during his brief life, as a contemporary chronicler mentions, had distinguished himself by an accomplishment extremely rare among the young country gentlemen of his own day—indeed, we may add of our own—that is to day, a precocious knowledge of Hebrew.

The young scholar was succeeded by a third
Rawlin, his cousin, a personage of a very different
type, who, in concert with his next-door neighbor,
Mr. Cary of Torre Abbey, added to the pursuits of
a Squire Western the enterprise of a smuggler in a
big way of business. He was, moreover, a patron
of the turf, having a large stud farm on Dartmoor,
with results which would have been disastrous for
himself if the wounds inflicted by the world had not
been healed through his connection with the Established Church. He was fortunately the patron of
no less than sixteen livings, or cures of souls, by the
gradual sale of most of which he managed to meet,
as a Christian should do, the claims of his lay
creditors. Of the bottles of port with which he
stocked the Cockington cellars two, bearing the date
of 1745, still remain—or till lately remained—unopened. Through the successor of this typical
Georgian the property passed to my grandfather, of
whom my father was a younger son.

Like many other younger sons, my father, to use
a pious phrase, suffered himself to be "put into the
Church," where two of the livings still owned by
his family awaited him. These, to his temporal
advantage, he presently exchanged for another.
His health, however, since I can remember him,
never permitted him to exert himself in the performance of divine service. Indeed, his ecclesiastical interests were architectural rather than pastoral. He
accordingly, after a brief acquaintance with his new

2

parishioners, committed them to the spiritual care of a stalwart and well-born curate, and bought a picturesque retreat about ten or twelve miles away, embowered in ivy, and overlooking the river Exe, where he spent his time in enlarging the house and gardens, and in planting slopes and terraces, about a quarter of a mile in length, with what were then very rare trees. He was subsequently given for life the use of another house, Denbury Manor, of which I shall speak presently, which I myself much preferred, and with which my own early recollections are much more closely associated.

My mother was a daughter of the Ven. Archdeacon Froude, and sister of three distinguished brothers—Hurrell Froude, prominent as a leader of the Tractarian movement, Antony Froude the historian, and William Froude, who, though his name is less generally known, exercised, as will be shown presently, an influence on public affairs greater than that of many cabinet ministers. The Archdeacon of Totnes, their father, was a Churchman of a type now extinct as the dodo. Born in the early part of the reign of George III, and inheriting a considerable fortune, he was in his youth addicted to pursuits a proficiency in which is now regarded by no one as absolutely essential to a fitness for Holy Orders. He was famous for his horses, and also for his feats of horsemanship, one of these being the jumping of a five-barred gate without losing either of two guinea pieces which were placed at starting between his knees and the saddle. To the accomplishments of an equestrian he added those of a dilettante. He was an architect, a collector of pictures, a herald and archæologist, and also (as Ruskin declared, to whom some of his drawings were exhibited) an artist whose genius was all but that of a master. Like other young men of fortune, he made what was then called the "grand tour of Europe," his sketchbooks showing that he traveled as far as Corfu, and subsequently, when he settled for life as the vicar of Dartington parish, he was regarded as one of the most enlightened country gentlemen of the district, active in improving the roads, which, till his time, were abominable, and in bringing poachers to punishment if not to repentance.

Within a short walk of the parsonage, over the brow of a wooded hill, is another house, which in the scenery of my childhood was an object no less familiar—Dartington Hall, the home of the Champernowne family, with which, by marriage and otherwise, my father's was very closely connected. Yet another house—it has been mentioned already as associated with my childhood also—is Denbury Manor, with its stucco chimneys and pinnacles, its distance from Dartington being something like eight miles. These four houses—Denbury Manor, Dartington Parsonage, Dartington Hall, and Cockington Court—all lying within a circle of some twelve miles in diameter, represent, together with their adjuncts, the material aspects of the life with

which I was first familiar. Let me give a brief
sketch of each, taking Denbury first.

Denbury Manor at the end of the eighteenth
century was converted and enlarged into a dower-
house for my mother's grandmother, but was occupied when first I knew it by my great-aunt, her
daughter, an old Miss Margaret Froude. To judge
from a portrait done of her in her youth by Down-
man, she must have been then a very engaging
ingénue; but when I remember her she looked a
hundred and fifty. She was, indeed, when she died
very nearly a hundred, and her house and its surroundings now figure in my recollections as things
of the eighteenth century which, preserved in all
their freshness, had hardly been touched by the
years which by that time had followed it. The
house, which was of considerable antiquity, had
been, for my great-grandmother's benefit, modern-
ized or Elizabethanized under the influence of Horace
Walpole and Wyat. It was backed by a rookery
of old and enormous elms. It was approached on
one side by a fine avenue of limes, and was otherwise surrounded by gardens with gray walls or
secretive laurel hedges. Here was a water tank
in the form of a Strawberry Hill chapel. Here was a
greenhouse unaltered since the days of George II.
Everywhere, though everything was antique, there
were signs of punctilious care, and morning by
morning a bevy of female villagers would be raking
the gravel paths and turning them into weedless

silver. The front door, heavy with nails, would be opened by an aged footman, his cheeks pink like an apple, and his white silk stockings and his livery always faultless. Within were old Turkey carpets, glossy, but not worn with use, heavy Chippendale chairs, great Delf jugs with the monogram of George II on them, a profusion of Oriental china, and endless bowls of potpourri. On the shelves of whatnots were books of long-forgotten eighteenth-century plays. In one of the sitting rooms was a magnificent portrait by Reynolds of Miss Froude's mother. It represented her playing on a guitar, and on a table beneath it reposed the guitar itself. Here and there lay one of the ivory hands with which powdered ladies once condescended to scratch themselves. There were shining inkstands whose drawers were still stocked with the wafers used for sealing letters in the days of Lydia Languish. In another room, called "the little parlor," and commonly used for breakfast, an old gentleman by Opie smiled from one of the walls, and saw one thing only which he might have seen there in his boyhood—a small piano by Broadwood, always fastidiously polished, as if it had just come from the shop, and bearing the date of 1780. Many houses abound in similar furnishings. The characteristic of Denbury was that it contained nothing else. These things were there, not as survivals of the past, but as parts of a past which for the inmates had never ceased to be the present. They were there as the natural appurtenances of a lady who, so far as I knew, had never been near a railway till a special train was run to convey mourners to her funeral.

Miss Froude matched her surroundings. During her later years she was never visible till midday, by which time she would, in an upstairs drawing room, be found occupying a cushionless chair at a large central table, with a glass of port at her right hand and a volume of sermons at her left. On either side of her stood a faithful attendant, one being a confidential maid, the other a Miss Drake—an old, mittened companion, hardly younger in appearance than herself—both of whom watched her with eyes of solicitous reverence, and seemed always ready to collapse into quasi-religious curtsies. Here she would receive such visitors as happened to be staying in the house, and subsequently reverential villagers, who appealed to her for aid or sympathy.

Dartington Parsonage was in one sense more modern than Denbury, having been for the most part constructed by the Archdeacon himself. Originally a diminutive dwelling—a relic of medieval times —he enlarged it to the dimensions of a substantial country house, surrounding a court, and connected with a medley of outbuildings—servants' offices, stables, barns, and coach houses, one of these last containing as a solitary recluse a high-hung yellow chariot, lined with yellow morocco, in which the Archdeacon had been wont to travel before the battle of Waterloo, and in which his grandchildren were never weary of swinging themselves. If the parsonage and its appurtenances can in any sense be called modern, they represented ideas and conditions which are far enough away now. There was nothing about them more modern than the early days of Miss Austen. The dining-room sideboard, with its long row of knife boxes, whose sloping lids when lifted showed a glimmering of silver handles, would have seemed familiar to Mr. Knightly, Mr. Woodhouse, and Sir Thomas Bertram. Opposite the dining room was a library, very carefully kept, the contents of which were a curious mixture. Besides great folio editions of the classics and the Christian Fathers, were collections of the ephemeral literature of the days of Charles II, notable among which were lampoons on Nell Gwyn and her royal lover—works which the Archdeacon certainly never bought, and which must have come to him through his mother from the Cavalier family of Copplestone. In the hall was a marble table bearing a bust of Demosthenes. In the drawing-room were water-color drawings by artists such as Prout and Stansfield; a group of Dutch paintings, including a fine Van Ostade; sofas, on which Miss Austen might have sat by the Prince Regent; and scrap-work screens on which faded portraits and landscapes were half eclipsed by quotaticns from *Elegant Extracts*. From the drawing-room windows, in my mother's earlier days, might often have been seen the figure of an old head gardener and factotum,

George Diggins by name, bending over beds of geraniums, who was born in the reign of George II, who had passed his youth as a charcoal burner in woods not far from Ugbrooke, the seat of the Catholic Cliffords, and who often recounted how, on mysterious nights, "four horses and a coach, with the old Lord Clifford inside it, would come tumbling out of the woods into the road like so many packs of wool."

Dartington Hall—very well known to architects as the work of John Holland, Duke of Exeter, in the reign of Richard II—passed by exchange to the Champernownes in the reign of Henry VIII, and was originally an enormous structure, inclosing two quadrangles. A large part of it, as may be seen from old engravings, was falling into ruins in the days of George II, but its principal feature was intact till the beginning of the nineteenth century. This was one of the finest baronial halls in England, seventy feet by forty, with a roof resembling that of the great hall at Westminster. The roof, however, at that time showing signs of impending collapse, it was taken down by my grandfather in the year 1810, and only the bare walls and the pointed windows remain. The inhabited portion, however, is still of considerable extent, one of its frontages— two hundred and thirty feet in length—abutting so closely on a churchyard that the dead need hardly turn in their graves to peer in through the lower windows at faded wall-papers, bedroom doors, and endless yards of carpet. The interior, as I remember it, did not differ from that of many old country houses. There were one or two great rooms, a multitude of family portraits, and landscapes, marbles and coins brought from Italy by a traveled and dilettante ancestor. It was a great rendezvous for numerous Buller relations. It was, as was the parsonage also, a nest of old domestics, all born in the parish, and it included among its other inmates a ghost, who was called "the Countess," and who took from time to time alarming strolls along the passages.

It remains to add a word or two with regard to Cockington Court. At the time when my father was born in it, it was the heart of a neighborhood remotely and even primitively rural, and fifty years later, when I can first remember it, its immediate surroundings were unchanged. A few miles away the modern world had, indeed, begun to assert itself in the multiplying villas of Torquay, but on the Cockington property, which includes the district of Chelston, few dwellings existed which had not been there in the days of Charles II. Torquay, which at the beginning of the Napoleonic wars was nothing more than a cluster of fishermen's huts, owed its rise to the presence of the British fleet in Torbay, and the need of accommodation on shore for officers' wives and families. My grandfather built two houses, Livermead House and Livermead Cottage, in answer to this demand. Both were for

personal friends, one of them being the first Lord
St. Vincent, the other being Sir John Colbourne,
afterward Lord Seaton. But though elaborate plans
were subsequently put before him for turning the
surrounding slopes into a pretentious and symmetrical watering place, the construction of no new
residence was permitted by himself or his successor
till somewhere about the year 1865, when a building
lease was granted by the latter to one of his own
connections.

Meanwhile, on adjacent properties, belonging to
the Palks and Carys, Torquay had been developing
into what became for a time the most famous and
fashionable of the winter resorts of England, Cockington still remaining a quiet and undisturbed
Arcadia.

But the real or nominal progress of five-and-forty
years has brought about changes which my grandfather, blind to his own interests, resisted. To-day,
as the train, having passed the station of Torre, proceeds toward that of Paignton, the traveler sees,
looking inland at the Cockington and Chelston
slopes, a throng of villas intermixed with the relics
of ancient hedgerows. If, alighting at Torquay
station, he mounts the hill above it by what in my
childhood was a brambled and furtive lane, he will
find on either side of him villas and villa gardens,
till at length he is brought to a ridge overlooking
a secluded valley. For some distance villas will
still obscure his view, but presently these end.

Below him he will see steep fields descending into a quiet hollow, the opposite slopes being covered or crowned with woods, and against them he will see smoke wreaths straying upward from undiscerned chimneys. A little farther on, the road, now wholly rural, dips downward, and Cockington village reveals itself, not substantially changed, with its thatch and its red mud walls, from what it had been more than two hundred years ago. Its most prominent feature is the blacksmith's forge, which, unaltered except for repairs, is of much greater antiquity. It is said that, as a contrast between the old world and the new, few scenes in England have been more often photographed than this. Passing the blacksmith's forge, and mounting under the shade of trees, the road leads to a lodge, the grounds of Cockington Court, and the church which very nearly touches it.

The house as it now stands—a familiar object to tourists—is merely a portion of what once was a larger structure. It was partly built by the Carys in the year of the Spanish Armada. Roger Mallock reconstructed it some seventy years later. It formed in his days, and up to those of my grandfather, one side of a square, entered between two towers, and was surrounded by a deer park of four or five hundred acres. Toward the end of the eighteenth century, however, agricultural land then rising in value, my grandfather, who threw away one fortune by refusing to have a town on his property, had been shrewd enough to get rid of his deer, and turned most of his parkland into farms. He also destroyed the forecourt of his house and a range of antique offices, considerably reducing at the same time the size of the main building by depriving it of its top story and substituting a dwarfish parapet for what had once been its eight gables. The interior suffered at his hands to an even greater extent. A hall with a minstrels' gallery was turned by him into several rooms as commonplace as it is possible to imagine. Indeed little of special interest survived him but some fine Italian ceilings, the most curious of which exists no longer, a paneled dining-room of the reign of William and Mary, a number of portraits dating from the days of James I onward, and a wall paper representing life-size savages under palm trees, which was part of the plunder of a French vessel during the time of the Napoleonic wars. To this meager list, however, up to my father's time might have been added another item of a more eloquent and more unusual kind—namely, a gilded coach, in which, according to village tradition, an old Madam Mallock (as she was called) used to be dragged by six horses along the execrable lanes of the neighborhood for her daily airing in the early part of the reign of George III. It is a great pity that, of all the appliances of life, carriages are those which are least frequently preserved. The reason doubtless is that they take up a good deal of room, and become absurdly old-fashioned long before they become interesting. The old coach of which I speak was bequeathed, with other heirlooms, to my father, who, I may say without filial impiety, proved altogether unworthy of it. He left it in a shed near a pond, into which it subsequently fell, its *disjecta membra* being presumably at the bottom still.

But whatever the house may have lost in the way of hereditary contents, the church contained, in my childhood, other symbols of the past—they have now likewise vanished—which spoke of "the family" rather than the mysteries of the Christian faith. The family shrouded its devotions, and sometimes its slumbers, in a pew which was furnished with a large fireplace, and eclipsed with its towering walls something like half the altar. All the panels of the western gallery were emblazoned with coats of arms and quarterings, and all the available wall space was dark with family hatchments. One afternoon, some five-and-forty years ago, a daughter of the house, who happened to be alone indoors, was alarmed by a summons to show herself and receive the Queen of Holland, who was then staying at Torquay, and who wished to inspect an old English house and its appurtenances. My cousin, who took her into the church, and who was somewhat confused by the presence of so august a visitor, explained the hatchments, with regard to which the queen questioned her, by saying that one was put up whenever a member of the Mallock family married.

As for myself, these solemn heraldic objects

vaguely imbued me with a sense, of which I took long in divesting myself, that my own family was one of the most important and permanent institutions of the country. They were otherwise associated in my memory with a long succession of Christmases, when holly berries enlivened their frames and peeped over the walls of the pew where my elders drowsed, and my coevals were sustained during the sermon by visions of the plum pudding and crackers which would reward them in a near hereafter. I can still remember how, before these joys began, we would group ourselves in the dining-room windows, peering at distant woods, in which keepers still set man traps, or watching the village schoolchildren on their way from church homeward, making with their crimson cloaks a streak of color as they followed one another across slopes of snow.

The feelings excited by a landscape such as this bore a subtle resemblance to those produced in myself by the heraldrics which thronged the church. From the windows, indeed, of all the houses of which I have just been speaking the prospect was morally, if not visually, the same. They all looked out, as though it were the unquestioned order of things, on wooded seclusions pricked by manorial chimneys or on lodges and gray park walls, while somewhere beyond these last lurked the thatch of contented cottages, at the doors of which, when a member of "the family" passed, women and children would curtsy and men touch their forelocks.

Here some persons may be tempted to interpose the remark that the aspect which things thus wore for ourselves was in one respect quite illusory. They may say that the idyllic contentment which we thus attributed to the cottagers was the very reverse of the truth, and that the thatch of their dwellings, however pleasing to the eye, really shrouded a misery to which history shows few parallels. Such an objection, even if correct, would, however, be here irrelevant; for I am dealing now not with things as they actually were, but merely with the impressions produced by them on childish minds, and more particularly on my own. Nevertheless, the objection in itself is of quite sufficient importance to call, even here, for some incidental attention; and how far, in this respect, our impressions were true or false will appear in the following chapter.

CHAPTER II

THE TWO NATIONS

The Rural Poor of Devonshire—The Old Landed Families—An Ecclesiastical Magnate

OUR impressions of the cottagers, to which I have just alluded—and for us the cottagers represented the people of England generally—were not, it is true, derived from our own scientific investigations; they were derived from the conversation of our elders. But the knowledge which these elders possessed as to the ways, the temper, and the conditions of the rural poor was intimate, and was constantly illustrated by anecdotes, to which we as children were never weary of listening. The descriptions so often given of the misery of the agricultural laborers and the oppression of the ruling class from the beginning of the nineteenth century up to the abolition of the Corn Laws may be correct as applied to certain parts of the kingdom; but, in the case of Devonshire at all events, they are, it would appear, very far from the truth. The period more particularly in question, including the decade known as "the hungry 'forties," is precisely the period with which these elders of ours were most closely acquainted; and, though we occasionally heard of disturbances called "bread riots" as having occurred in Exeter and Plymouth, no hint reached us of such outbreaks having ever taken place in the country, or of any distress or temper which was calculated to provoke protests of any sort or kind against the established order. On the contrary, between the rural poor and the old-fashioned landed aristocracy, lay and clerical alike, the relations were not only amicable, but very often confidential also.

This fact may be illustrated by the case of old Miss Froude, the "Lady Bountiful" of her immediate neighborhood, who was constantly appealed to by its inhabitants, not only for material aid, but for religious guidance as well, and appreciation of their religious experiences. Thus on one occasion an old woman was ushered into Miss Froude's presence who had evidently some fact of great importance to communicate. The fact turned out to be this: that she had spent the whole of the previous night in a trance, during which she had ascended to heaven, and been let in by "a angel." "Well," said Miss Froude, "and did they ask you your name?" "No, ma'am, not my name," was the answer; "they only asked me my parish." "And do you," Miss Froude continued, "remember what the angel's name was?" The old woman seemed doubtful. "Do you think," said Miss Froude, "it was Gabriel?" "Iss, fay (yes, i' faith)," said the old woman. "Sure enough 'twas Gaburl." "And did you," said Miss Froude,

finally, "see anybody in heaven whom you knew?"
The old woman hesitated, but caught herself up in
time, and solemnly said, "I seed you, ma'am."

Had all Miss Froude's dependents been of an
equally communicative disposition, there would indeed in the confessions of two of them have been
matter of a less peaceful character. It had for some
time been whispered among her indoor servants—
this is before I can remember—that horses, after
days of idleness so far as carriage work was concerned, would on certain mornings be found covered
with sweat, and other signs of mysteriously hard
usage. It was ultimately found out that an enterpris-
ing coachman and groom had been riding them peri-
odically to Teignmouth, and playing a nocturnal
part in the landing of smuggled cargoes, these being
stowed in the cellars of a decaying villa, which for
years had remained tenantless owing to persistent
rumors that it was haunted by a regiment of exceedingly savage ghosts. The only other approach
to anything like rural violence which reached our
ears through the channel of oral tradition was an
event which must have occurred about the year
1830, and was reported to the Archdeacon by George
Diggins, his old factotum. This was the plunder
of a vessel which had been wrecked the night before
somewhere between Plymouth and Salcombe. The
Archdeacon asked if no authorities had interfered.
"I heard, sir," said George Diggins, "that a revenue
officer did what he could to stop 'un, but they

hadn't a sarved he very genteel. This statement meant that they had pushed him over the cliffs.

Otherwise the stories of rural life that reached me, though relating to times which have in popular oratory been associated with the rick-burnings and kindred outrages "by which the wronged peasant righted himself," were pictures of a general content, broken only by individual vicissitudes, which were accepted and bewailed as part of the common order of nature. Of such individual afflictions the larger part were medical. The women, even the most robust, would rarely confess to the enjoyment of anything so uninteresting as a condition of rude health. The usual reply made by them to the inquiries of any lady visitant was, "Thankee, ma'am, I be torrable" (tolerable); but, if conscious of any definite malady, their diagnosis of their own cases would, though simple, be more precise. One of them told my mother that for days she'd been terrible bad. "My inside," she said, "be always a-coming up, though I've swallowed a pint of shot by this time merely to keep my liver down."

In cottage households, though occasionally there might be some shortage of food, there were no indications of anything like general or chronic want. Indeed, if delicacies which the inmates had never seen before were brought them as a present from this or from that "great house," they would often eye them askance, and make a favor of taking them. That the ordinary diet of the Devonshire cottagers

of those days contented them is shown by the dinner prepared for a man who worked at a limekiln
by his wife, which she complacently exhibited to
my mother as at once appetizing and nutritious.
It was a species of dumpling with an onion, instead
of an apple, in the middle of it, the place of the cus-
tomary crust being taken by home-baked bread.

On the whole, however, the cottagers, no less than
their richer neighbors, were preoccupied by interests
other than those of mere domestic economy. Their
gossip would accordingly take a wider range, as
when one of them announced to an aunt of mine
that a son and a daughter who had emigrated to the
United States had "got stuck in the mud just outside America."

Often their discourses would relate to domestic
discipline and theology. There was a certain Mrs.
Pawley whose dwelling was widely celebrated as the
scene of almost constant strife between herself and
her husband, and who, on being asked by one of her
lady patronesses if she could not do something to
make matters run more smoothly, replied: "That's
just what I tries to do, ma'am. I labor for peace,
but when I speak to he thereof, he makes hisself
ready for battle direckly."

Another good woman again had acquired an un-
enviable fame by some petty act of larceny which
the magistrates had been bound to punish, and was
explaining in tears on her doorstep to some lady's
sympathetic ears that she had done the unfortunate

24

deed merely because she was "temp'ed," on which a neighbor, who had no need for repentance, promptly appeared on the scene and said to her: "My dear crachur (creature), why be you temp'ed to do sich thing? I be never temp'ed to do nothing but what's good."

Passing one day through an orchard, Mr. Froude the historian encountered a man who was contemplating a heap of apples. The man looked up as though about to speak of the crop, but instead of doing so he gave vent to the following reflection: "Pretty job, sir," he said, "there was about a apple one time. Now the De-vine, He might have prevented that if He'd had a mind to. But com', sir, 'tis a mystery."

Moral theology would sometimes take a more skeptical turn. A certain Mr. Edwardes—a most amusing man—used to describe a call which he paid one Sunday afternoon to a farmer near Buckfastleigh, whom he found reading his Bible. Mr. Edwardes congratulated him on the appropriate nature of his studies. The farmer pushed the book aside, and, pointing to the open pages, which were those containing the account of the fall of Jericho, said: "Do 'ee believe that, sir? Well—I don't." Mr. Edwardes, with becoming piety, observed that we were bound to believe whatever the Scriptures told us. "Well," the farmer continued, "when I was a boy they used to bake here in the town oven, and whenever the oven was heated, they sounded a sheep's horn. Some of the boys Sundays would get hold of that horn, just for the fun of the thing, and blaw it for all it was worth. If that there story was true, there wouldn't be a house in Buckfastleigh standing."

Independent, if not skeptical, thought was represented even by one of the members of Archdeacon Froude's own domestic establishment—a house carpenter, who was a kind of uncanonical prophet. He would see in the meadows visions of light and fire like Ezekiel's, and convert his commonest actions into means of edification. On one occasion, when he was constructing a bedroom cupboard, a daughter of the house remarked, as she paused to watch him, "Well, John, that cupboard is big enough." "It," said the prophet, reflectively, "is immense, but yet confined. I know of something which is immense, but not confined." On being asked what this was he answered, "The love of God."

Yet another story told by Mr. Antony Froude illustrates rural mentality in relation to contemporary politics. Mr. Froude was the tenant of a well-known house in Devonshire, and had come to be on very friendly terms with Mr. Emmot, his landlord's agent, a typical and true Devonian. One day Mr. Emmot came to him in a condition of some perplexity. He had been asked an important question, and was anxious to know if the answer he had given to it was satisfactory. It appeared that a cottager who had a bit of land of his own had been saying to him, "Look here, Mr. Emmot: can you tell us rightly what the difference be between a Conservative and a Radical?" "Well, Mr. Froude," said Mr. Emmot, "I didn't rightly knaw the philosophy of the thing, so I just said to 'un this: 'You knaw me; well, I be a Conservative. You knaw Jack Radford—biggest blackguard in the parish—well, he be a Radical. Now you knaw.'"

Chance reminiscences such as those which have just been quoted will be sufficient to indicate what, so far as a child could understand them, the conditions and ways of thinking of the rural population were, and how easy and unquestioning were the relations which then subsisted between it and the old landed families. These relations were easy, because the differences between the two classes were commonly assumed to be static, one supporting and one protecting the other, as though they resembled two geological strata. In slightly different language, society was presented to us in the form of two immemorial orders—the men, women, and children who touched their hats and curtsied, and the men, women, and children to whom these salutations were made.

I am not, however—let me say it again—attempting to write a chapter of English history, or to give a precise description of facts as they actually were so much as to depict the impressions which facts, such as they were, produced on children like myself through the medium of personal circumstances. At the same time, in the formation of these impressions we were far from being left to our own unaided intelligence. Our impressions, as just depicted, were sedulously confirmed and developed by carefully chosen governesses. One of these, young as she was, was a really remarkable woman, for whom English history had hatched itself into something like a philosophy. Her philosophy had two bases, one being the postulate of the divine right of kings, the other being her interpretation of the victory of the Normans over the Anglo-Saxons. Charles I she presented to our imaginations as a martyr; and, what was still more important, she seriously taught us that the population of modern England was still divided, so far as race is concerned, precisely as it was at the time of the completion of the Domesday Book; that the peers and the landed gentry were more or less pure-blooded Normans, and the mass of the people Saxons; that the principal pleasure of the latter was to eat to repletion; that their duty was to work for, that their privilege was to be patronized by, Norman overlords and distinguished Norman Churchmen; and finally, that of this Norman minority we ourselves were distinguished specimens. All this we swallowed, aided in doing so by books like *Woodstock* and *Ivanhoe*. But grotesque as such ideas seem now, they were not more grotesque than those shadowed forth in some of the novels of Lord Beaconsfield, and more particularly in *Sybil, or The Two Nations*. Had we indeed been set to compose an essay on the social conditions, as we ourselves understood them, "The

Two Nations" would have been the title which we could most appropriately have selected for it.

When, however, forgetting our general principles, we gave our attention to the adult relations and connections who, through personal acquaintance or otherwise, constituted for us what is commonly called society, our respect for many of them as "Normans" was appreciably tempered by a sense of their dullness as men and women. They were nearly all of them members of old Devonshire families, beyond the circle of which their interests did not often wander. But certain of them in my own memory stand out from the rest as interesting types of conditions which by this time have passed away. Of these I may mention four—Emma and Antony Buller, son and daughter of Sir Antony Buller of Pound; Lord Blatchford, a Gladstonian Liberal, and the celebrated Henry Philpotts, the then Bishop of Exeter.

Antony Buller, who was my godfather, was vicar of a parish on the western borders of Dartmoor. In the fact that "remote from towns he ran his godly race" he resembled the vicar described in "The Deserted Village," but except for his godliness he resembled him in little else. A model of secluded piety, he was educated at Eton and Christchurch; unquestioning in his social as well as his Christian conservatism, and expressing in the refinement of his voice and the well-bred quasi-meekness of his bearing a sense of family connection, tempered by a scholarly recognition of the equality of human souls. Lord

29

Blatchford, his not very distant neighbor, was in many ways an Antony Buller secularized. His piety, polished by the classics and Oxford chapels, was what was in those days called Liberal, rather than Tory. What in Antony Buller was a conservative Christian meekness was in Lord Blatchford a progressive Christian briskness; but his belief in popular progress was accompanied by a smile at its incidents, as though it were a kind of frisking to which the masses ought to be welcome so long as it did not assume too practical a character or endanger any of the palings within the limits of which it ought to be confined.

Emma Buller, too, was typical, but in a totally different way. She was a type of that county life which railways have gradually modified, and by this time almost obliterated. She was a woman remarkable for her vivacity, wit, and humor. At county balls she was an institution. At country houses throughout Devonshire and Cornwall she was a familiar and welcome guest, and to half of her hosts and hostesses she was in one way or another related. Among her accomplishments was the singing of comic songs, in a beautifully clear but half-apologetic voice, so that while gaining in point they lost all trace of vulgarity, her eyes seeming to invite each listener on whom she fixed them to share with her some amusement which was only half legitimate. At the Duke of Bedford's house, near Tavistock, she exercised this magic one evening on Lord John

ROBERT BROWNING

Russell. The song which she sang to him was political. It began thus, each verse having the same recurring burden:

> "Come, listen while I sing to you,
>   Lord John, that prince of sinisters,
> Who once pulled down the House of Lords,
>   The Crown and all the ministers.
>   That is, he would have if he could,
>   But a little thing prevented him."

For many years she spent a large part of every winter with Lady (then Miss) Burdett-Coutts, who had in those days a large villa at Torquay, generally filled with visitors. Emma Buller's allusions to these, many of whom were notabilities, enlarged, as I listened to them in my childhood, my conception of the social world, and made it seem vaguely livelier and more fruitful in adventure than the hereditary circle with which alone I was so far familiar.

This result was accentuated by the stories told in my hearing of another personage well known to my family likewise, to which I listened with a yet keener appreciation. Bishop Philpotts—for it is of him I speak—holding till the day of his death a "golden stall" at Durham, the emoluments of which amounted to £5,000 a year, interested me rather as a lay magnate than as a clerical. Among the many villas then rising at Torquay the Bishop built one of the largest. This agreeable residence, in the designing of which he was helped by my father, and which overlooked extensive glades and lawns sloping down toward the sea, enabled him to enjoy a society more entertaining than that of his own cathedral close; and the anecdotes current in my family as to his ways and his mundane hospitalities were as familiar to me as those of any character in the novels of Miss Austen—a writer whose social discrimination delighted and appealed to me before I was ten years old.

The Bishop was renowned for his suave and courtly manners, his charming voice, and the subtle precision of its modulations; and the following stories of him are still fresh in my memory.

At one of his luncheon parties he was specially kind to a country clergyman's wife, who knew none of the company, and he took her out on a terrace in order to show her the view—a view of the sea shut in by the crags of a small cove. "Ah, my lord," gasped the lady, "it reminds one so much of Switzerland." "Precisely," said the Bishop, "except that there we have the mountains without the sea, and here we have the sea without the mountains."

He was somewhat less urbane to an ultra-fashionable lady, his neighbor, who had developed a habit, in his opinion objectionable, of exhibiting his views to her visitors by way of passing the morning. This lady, with a bevy of satellites, having appeared one day in his drawing room about the hour of noon, the Bishop, with the utmost graciousness, took them into a conservatory, showed them some of his plants and then, opening a door, invited them to go outside. As soon as they were in the outer air, he himself retreated, saying, as he closed the door, "We lunch at one."

On another occasion at a dinner party a shy young lady was present, whose mother, with maternal partiality, admitted that her daughter sang. After dinner the Bishop had candles placed on the piano, and begged the shrinking vocalist to give them an exhibition of her skill. The luckless victim protested that she could not sing at all, but presently, despite her objections, she was blushing on the fatal music stool, and was faltering out a desperate something which was at all events intended to be a song. "Thank you," said the Bishop, benignly, as soon as the performance was ended. "The next time you tell us you cannot sing we shall know how to believe you."

On yet another occasion two intrepid females, armed with guidebooks, and obviously determined to see whatever they could, had entered the Bishop's carriage drive, and were considering which way they would take, when their ears were caught by a sound like that of an opening window. They discovered, on looking about them, that the drive was commanded by a summerhouse, and, framed in an open window, was the visage of the Bishop himself. "Ladies," he said, blandly, "these grounds are private, as the gate through which you have just passed may in part have suggested to you. The turn to the left will bring you in due time to the stables. If you should go straight on you will presently reach the house. Should you inspect the house, may I mention to you that in one of the bedrooms is an invalid? You will perhaps pardon my servants if they do not show you that. Good morning."

But my boyish appreciation of the Bishop's mundane qualities was equaled by my faith in the sacrosanctity of his office. I never for a moment doubted that men like Henry of Exeter were channels through which the Christian priesthood received those miraculous powers by their exercise of which alone it was possible for the ordinary sinner to be rescued from eternal torment. Of the structural doctrines of theology which were then the shibboleths of English Churchmanship generally, I never entertained a doubt. That the universe was created in the inside of a week four thousand and four years before the birth of Christ, and that every word of the Bible was supernaturally dictated to the writer, were to me facts as certain as the fact that the ear this globular or that the date of the battle of Hastings was 1066. They belonged to the same order of things as the "two nations"; and the attempts of certain persons to discredit the former and to disturb the reciprocal relations of the latter represented for me a mood so blasphemous and absurd as not to be worthy of a serious man's attention.

And yet in certain ways by the time I was twelve years old I was something of a revolutionary myself. Like the majority of healthy boys, I had tastes for riding and shooting, and to such things as rooks and rabbits my rifle was as formidable as most boys could desire. But long before I was conscious of any passion for sport I found myself beset by another, which was very much more insistent—namely, a passion for literary composition—I cannot say a taste for writing, for I dictated verses to the nursery-maids before I could hold a pen. As soon as I was able to read I came across the works of Fielding, whose style I endeavored to imitate in a series of lengthy novels, deriving as I did so a precocious sense of manhood from the eighteenth-century oaths with which I garnished the conversation of my characters. My ambitions, however, as a writer of fiction were on the whole less constant than those which I entertained as a poet. By governesses and other instructors, Wordsworth and Tennyson were obtruded on me as models of beauty and edification. Wordsworth I thought ridiculous. Tennyson seemed to me unmanly and mawkish. The poets I found out for myself were Dryden and, more particularly, Pope; and when I was about fourteen I imagined myself destined to win back for Pope, as a model, the supremacy he had unfortunately lost, while the sentimentalities of Tennyson and his followers would disappear like the fripperies of faded and outworn fashions.

When my father and his family migrated from the banks of the Exe to Denbury these literary projects found fresh means of expanding themselves. Opposite the front door of the Manor House was a large

and antique *annexe*, once occupied by a bailiff who
managed the home farm. This my grandfather had
intended to connect with the main building, by
which means the Manor House would have been
nearly doubled in size. His scheme was not carried
out. The *annexe*, covered with increasing growths
of ivy, remained locked up and isolated, and for
many years stood empty. But on the Archdeacon's
death, and the removal of his household from
Dartington, a use was at last found for it. The
upper rooms were converted into a temporary store-
house for his library—large rooms which now were
lined with shelves, and in which fires were frequently
lighted to keep the volumes dry. In a moment of
happy inspiration I obtained permission to look
after the fires myself. The key was placed in my
possession. Day by day I entered. I locked myself
in, and all the world was before me.

I had often before been irritated, and my curiosity
had been continually piqued, by finding that certain
books—most of them plays of the time of Charles II
—would be taken away from me and secreted if I
happened to have abstracted some such stray volume from a bookcase; but here I was my own
master. My grandfather's library was, as I have
said already, particularly rich in literature of this
semiforbidden class, and rows of plays and poems
by Congreve, Etheridge, Rochester, Dryden, and
their contemporaries offered themselves to my study,
as though by some furtive assignation. Among

other wrecks of furniture with which the worm-eaten floors were encumbered was an old and battered rocking-horse, bestriding which I studied these secret volumes, and found in it an enchanted steed which would lift me into the air and convey me to magically distant kingdoms.

Inspired by these experiences, and fancying myself destined to accomplish a counter-revolution in the literary taste of England, I endeavored night by night to lay the foundations of my own poetic fame. My bedroom was pungent with the atmosphere of a pre-Tennysonian world. Its floor, uneven with age, was covered with a carpet whose patterns had faded into a dim monochrome, and its walls were dark with portraits of Copplestone forefathers in flowing wigs and satins. My bed was draped with immemorial curtains, colored like gold and bordered with black velvet. Close to the bed was a round mahogany table, furnished with pens and paper, and night by night, propped up by pillows, I endeavored to rival Dryden and Pope, by means of a quill wet with the dews of Parnassus—dews which, having sprinkled the bedclothes, would scandalize the housemaids the next morning by their unfortunate likeness to ink.

My father had originally meant to send me to Harrow, but, on the recommendation of one of the sons of the Bishop of Exeter, he first tried on me the effects of a school which had just been established for the purpose of combining the ordinary course of education with an inculcation of the extremest principles of the High Church Anglican party. I was, however, deficient in one of the main characteristics on which a boy's suitability to school life depends: I had an ingrained dislike, not indeed of physical exercise, but of games. Football to me seemed merely a tiresome madness, and cricket the same madness in a more elaborate form. Instead, therefore, of promoting me to Harrow, where two of his brothers had been educated, he took, after many delays, a step for which I sincerely thanked him—he transferred me, by way of preparation for Oxford, to the most congenial and delightful of all possible private tutors, at whose house I spent the happiest years of my life.

CHAPTER III

A PRIVATE TUTOR DE LUXE

Early Youth Under a Private Tutor—Poetry—Premonitions of
Modern Liberalism

THE tutor of whom I have spoken was the
Rev. W. B. Philpot, a favorite pupil of
Doctor Arnold's at Rugby, an intimate friend
of Tennyson's, and himself a devotee of the Muses.
His domed forehead was massive, his features were
delicately chiseled, and his eyes were a clear gray.
His back hair—the only hair he had got—showed a
slight tendency to assume picturesque and flowing
curves on the collars of his well-made coats; and,
having heard from my father that I, too, was a
poet, he declared himself eager to welcome me, not
only as a disciple, but also as a valued friend. Mr.
Philpot lived at Littlehampton, where he occupied a
most capacious house. It was the principal house
in a very old-fashioned terrace, which faced a sandy
common, and enjoyed in those days an uninter-
rupted view of miles of beach and the racing waves
of the sea. Mr. Philpot's disciples numbered from
ten to twelve. They had, for the most part, been
removed from Harrow or Eton, by reason of no
worse fault than a signal inclination to indolence;
and though, even under their preceptor's genial and

scholarly auspices, none of them except myself showed much inclination for study, we formed together an agreeable and harmonious party, much of its amenity being due to the presence of Mrs. Philpot, his wife, whose brother, Professor Conington, was then the most illustrious representative of Latin learning at Oxford.

We enjoyed, under Mr. Philpot's care, the amplest domestic comforts, and we enjoyed, under our own care, almost unlimited credit at every shop in the town. We had carriages, the hire of which went down in Mr. Philpot's account, whenever we wanted them for expeditions; and we would often drive out in the warm after-dinner twilights to a tea garden three miles away, where we lingered among the scent of roses till the bell of some remote church tower sounded, through the dewy quiet, its nine notes to the stars. We had boats on the Arun, a stream on which our oars would take us sometimes beyond Amberly, and not bring us back till midnight. On other occasions we would, like Tennyson's hero, "nourish a youth sublime" in wandering on the nocturnal beach, and, pre-equipped with towels, would bathe in the liquid moonlight.

The Littlehampton season, so far as visitors were concerned, was summer, and from the middle of May onward various ladies of ornamental and interesting aspect would make their appearance on the pavement of Beach Terrace, or, seen on the balconies of houses which had just unclosed their shutters, would trouble and enliven the atmosphere with suggestions of vague adventures. Some of these we came to know, as Mr. Philpot and his wife had many mundane acquaintances. Others—and indeed most of them—remained tantalizing mysteries to the end. At all events they filled the air with the subtle pollen of a romance which a closer familiarity with them might very possibly have destroyed.

The effect on myself of such influences was presently betrayed by the fact that poetry, as understood by Pope, no longer satisfied me. I gradually submitted to the dominion of Keats, Browning, and Matthew Arnold. Even at Denbury, in my most conservative days, I had so far escaped from the atmosphere of Pope's Pastorals that I had described a beautiful valley in which I would often sequester myself as a place—

> Where no man's voice, or any voice makes stir,
> Save sometimes through the leafy loneliness
> The long loose laugh of the wild woodpecker.

One of my fellow pupils, whose youth had an air of manhood, and who played with much expression on the cornet, confided to me, on returning from a summer holiday, his adventures on the Lake of Como, where, resting on his oars, he had agitated with his musical notes the pulses of a fair companion. "Now there," he said, "you have something which, if you tried, you might manage to make a verse about." I tried, and the result was this:

The stars are o'er our heads in hollow skies,
　In hollow skies the stars beneath our boat,
Between the stars of two infinities
　Midway upon a gleaming film we float.

My lips are on the sounding horn;
　The sounding horn with music fills.
Faint echoes backward from the world are borne,
　Tongued by yon distant zone of slumbering hills.

The world spreads wide on every side,
　But cold and dark it seems to me.
What care I on this charmèd tide
　For aught save those far stars and thee?

I accomplished, however, such feats of imagination, not on my friend's behalf only, but on my own also. Readers of *Martin Chuzzlewit* will remember how "Baily Junior," who was once bootboy at Mrs. Todger's boarding-house, imagined that Mrs. Gamp was in love with him, and that her life was blighted by the suspicion that such a passion was hopeless. I, in common with other imaginative boys, was frequently beatified by the magic of a not unlike illusion. My practical hopes for the future, so far as I troubled to form any, were to enter the diplomatic service as soon as I left Oxford, and it seemed to me that this or that distinguished and beautiful lady, old enough to be my mother, would meanwhile be blighted by some hopeless passion for myself, or else —what, in my opinion, was a still more exciting alternative—that I should, like another Byron, be blighted into renown through her treachery by a

42

misplaced passion for *her*. As I paced the sands at Littlehampton, I pictured myself as having discovered her faithlessness on the eve of my own departure for the Embassy at Constantinople, and I addressed to her the following epistle, which I could not, with all my ingenuity, manage to protract beyond the two opening stanzas:

> For you the ballroom's jaded glow—
> The gems unworthy of your hair.
> For me the milk-white domes that blow
> Their bubbles to the orient air.
>
> Your heart at dawn in curtained ease
> Shall ache through dreams that are not rest.
> But mine shall leap to meet the seas
> That broke against Leander's breast.

Such dreams are not more absurd than those of the French Jacobins, who thought themselves Gracchus or Brutus; and they were accompanied when I was at Littlehampton by the growth of other preoccupations, which related to matters very different from the romance of individual adolescence. Mr. Philpot, in his own tastes, and also in his choice of pupils, was fastidious to a degree, which perhaps would be out of date to-day, and had actually been known to apologize, under his breath, for the fact that one of his flock—a singularly handsome youth and heir to an enormous fortune—came of a family which "was still distinctly in business." But he betrayed, at the same time, strong Radical leanings.

43

Indeed, through him I first became aware that Radicalism meant more than some perverse absurdity of the ignorant. He completely bewildered and at the same time amused his pupils by taking in a paper called *The Beehive*, one of the earliest of the "Labor organs" of England; and from this mine of wisdom he would on occasion quote. To most of us the views expressed by him seemed no more than comic oddities, but they were to myself so far a definite irritant that I devised, though I never showed them to him, a series of pictures called "The Radical's Progress," in which the hero began as a potboy in a public house, and ended as an over-dressed ruffian, waving a tall silk hat and throwing rotten eggs at Conservative voters from a cart. A taste of Mr. Philpot's equalitarian sentiments was given to us one day at luncheon, the occasion being his wife's commendation of a celebrated Sussex bootmaker who had just called for orders. "I like that man," she said. "He is always so civil and respectful." "Mary Jane! Mary Jane!" said Mr. Philpot, clearing his throat, and speaking from the other end of the table, "that respectfulness of yours is a quality to which I myself attach very little importance." In view of this speech we felt considerable satisfaction when, a few hours later, the day being the 5th of November, a disturbance was made by some boys at the front door, and Mr. Philpot, snatching up a tall hat, went out to appease the storm by the serene majesty of his presence. He

44

was far from gratified when the immediate result of his intervention was to elicit the disrespectful cry of "Hit 'n on the bloody drum."

But, besides the novelty, as we thought it, of his vague democratic opinions, he exhibited what to me was at least equally novel—namely, a liberalism before unknown to me with regard to theological doctrine. He never obtruded this on us in any systematic way; but on not infrequent occasions he solemnly gave us to understand that dissenters enjoyed the means of salvation no less fully than Churchmen; that sacraments were mere symbols useful for edification according to varying circumstances; that sacerdotal orders were mere certificates of the fitness of individuals for the office of Christian ministers, and that everything in the nature of dogmatic authority was due to, and tainted with, the apostacy of Babylonian Rome. To myself all this was shocking in an extreme degree, and I began to ask myself the question, which might otherwise not have occurred to me, of whether the Church of Rome was not perhaps the one true religion, after all.

These movements of the spirit on my part led to the following incident. Among Mr. Philpot's pupils was a shy and very delicate boy, whose parents took a house at Littlehampton, and with whom he lived. His father was a fire-eating Irish baronet, who might have walked out of the pages of one of Lever's novels. His diet was as meager as that of an Indian fakir, though not otherwise resembling it. It consisted of rum and milk; and his favorite amusement was lying down on his bed and shooting with a pistol at the wick of a lighted candle. His wife—a lady of gentle and somewhat sad demeanor—one day took it into her head to join the Catholic Church; and Mr. Philpot hastened, as soon as he heard the news, to ask her, in the name of common sense and of conscience, what could have induced her to take a step so awful. Her answer, so he informed me afterward, was that I had told her that it was the best thing she could do. I had no recollection of having tendered to her any such momentous advice, and Mr. Philpot, who hardly could help smiling, acquitted me of playing intentionally the part of a disguised Jesuit. I must, however, have said something on behalf of the mystical Babylon, for not long afterward I was busy with a theological poem, prominent in which were the two following lines:

> Oh, mother, or city of the sevenfold throne,
> We sit beside the severing sea and mourn—

and by way of correcting such defects in my sentiments Mr. Philpot lent me a work by Archer Butler, a Christian Platonist, who would provide me, in his opinion, with a religious philosophy incomparably more rational than the Roman. This work had the result of directing me to certain old translations of Plotinus and other Neoplatonists of Alexandria; and my dominant idea for a time was that in Alexandrian mysticism Anglicans would discover a rock, firmly based, on which they would bring Rome to her knees, and conquer the whole world.

But such juvenile theologies, and the secret troubles connected with them, did not seriously interfere with the adventurous optimism of youth. They did but give a special flavor to the winds blown from the sea, to the suggestions of the sunsets on which the eyes of youth looked, and mixed themselves with the verses of Browning, Matthew Arnold, and Shelley. But a yet more successful rival to the speculations of Archer Butler and Plotinus was, in my own case, another and a new poet, who had at that time just made himself famous. This poet was Swinburne, who had recently given to the world his first *Poems and Ballads*. That volume, on the ground that it was an outrage on morals and decency, had been received, when originally published, with such a howl of execration that the publishers hastily withdrew it, and for some time it was unobtainable; but at length another firm found courage enough to undertake its reissue. To Mr. Philpot, who knew it merely by extracts, the mere mention of this volume seemed to be something in the nature of an indecency. But there is always an attraction in the forbidden. I dreamed of this volume, from which I had seen extracts likewise; and at last a chance came to me of securing an apple from the boughs of this replanted tree of knowledge.

Among our various dissipations were occasional excursions to Brighton, and on one of these I was accompanied by a fellow pupil whose family had a house there in one of the then fashionable squares. The family was absent, but the house was open, and my friend proposed that we should sleep there and make a night of it. We accordingly telegraphed to Mr. Philpot that we should be back next day by breakfast time, and arranged to dine early, and spend the evening at the play. As we walked to the theater we found the shops still open, and we paused to look for a moment at the windows of Treacher's Library. In a long row of volumes I saw one bound in green. Its gilt lettering glittered, and the gaslight revealed to me the reissued poems of Swinburne. I went in and bought it and entered the dress circle hugging this priceless treasure. The play, I believe, had something to do with racing, but I hardly looked at the stage. My eyes and attention were magnetized by the green object on my knee. I occasionally peeped at its pages; but the light, while the play was in progress, was too dim to render the print legible. Between the acts, however, I began to decipher stanzas such as the following, and notes new to the world invaded my ears like magic:

> The sea gives her shells to the shingle,
>   The earth gives her streams to the sea,

or again:

> As the waves of the ebb drawing seaward
>   When their hollows are full of the night.

When had words, I asked myself, ever made music such as this? I felt by the time I got back to my friend's door that:

> I on honeydew had fed,
> And drunk the milk of paradise.

This magic still remained with me when, my days at Littlehampton being ended, I went at length to Oxford. But meanwhile to my conditions at home a new element was added, by which the scope of my experiences was at once greatly enlarged.

I have mentioned already that, during the first sixty years of the growth of Torquay, the owners of Cockington had preserved their rural seclusion intact, having refused, during that long period, to permit the erection of more than two villas on their property. But somewhere about the year 1860 a solitary exception was made in favor of Mr. William Froude, my mother's eldest brother, to whom, by my paternal uncle, a lease was granted of a certain number of acres on the summit of what was then a wooded and absolutely rural hill. Here he erected a house of relatively considerable size, from which, as a distant spectacle, Torquay was visible beyond a tract of intervening treetops. It was nearing completion at the time when I was first under Mr. Philpot's care. My father, being a complete recluse, and my kindred, whether at Cockington Court or otherwise, confining their intimacies to hereditary friends and connections, I found few fresh excitements at their houses or his beyond such as I could spin for myself, like a spider, out of my own entrails. It was, therefore, for me a very agreeable circumstance that presently in Chelston Cross, while I was still under Mr. Philpot's care, I was provided with a second home during a large part of my holidays, and subsequently of my Oxford vacations, where the stir of the outer world was very much more in evidence.

Distinguished as a man of science, a mathematician, and a classical scholar, Mr. Froude possessed the most fascinating manners imaginable. His wife, the daughter of an old-world Devonshire notable who once owned the borough of Dartmouth, returning two members for it, he himself being always one, was a woman of remarkable intellect, of a singularly genial shrewdness, and of manners attractive to every one with whom she might come in contact. Indeed, no two persons could have been more happily qualified than Mr. and Mrs. William Froude, together with their daughter (subsequently Baroness A. von Hugel), to render their house a center of interesting and intellectual society, and their circle of friends was widened by two adventitious circumstances. Mrs. Froude, under the influence of Newman, who was her frequent and intimate correspondent, had entered the Catholic Church, her children following her example, and the freemasonry of a common faith resulted in closely connecting her and hers with various old Catholic

families and many distinguished converts; while
Mr. Froude, at the time to which I now refer, was
becoming, through his indulgence in purely accidental taste, a figure in the world of national, and
even of international, affairs.

His favorite recreation was yachting, and one of
his possessions was a sailing yacht. He was thus,
as a man of alert observation, led to pay special
attention to the relation of a vessel's lines to its behavior under different conditions in respect of its
stability and speed, and the project occurred to him
of testing his rough conclusions by means of miniature models, these being placed in some small body
of water and then submitted to systematic experiments. Accordingly, soon after he had settled himself at Chelston Cross, he proceeded to lease a field
which adjoined his garden, and constructed in it
a sort of covered canal, along which models of various designs were towed, the towing-machine recording the various results by diagrams. The discoveries
which Mr. Froude thus made soon proved so remarkable that Edward, Duke of Somerset (then First
Lord of the Admiralty), secured for him a government grant, in order that his operations might be
extended, the whole of the earlier expenses having
been borne by Mr. Froude himself. The enterprise
soon attracted the attention of other governments
also; Admiral Popoff, on behalf of the Tsar, having
come all the way from Russia to visit Mr. Froude
in connection with it. But the pilgrims to Chelston

Cross were not naval experts only. Torquay was at that time nearing its social zenith, and the rumor that Mr. Froude was conducting a series of mysterious experiments which bade fair to revolutionize the naval architecture of the world stirred interest in many men of mark—statesmen and others who were far from being naval experts, and also of ladies, many of them with charming eyes whose attention alone was, in my opinion at all events, sufficient to throw a halo of success round any experiment which excited it.

All of these, masculine and feminine alike, were sensible of the charm of Mr. William Froude and his family; and for many years, even in London, it would have been difficult to find a house more frequented than Chelston Cross by a society of well-known and entertaining persons, not only English, but continental and American also. Thus, during the years of my tutelage at Littlehampton and Oxford, which comprised but occasional and brief visits to London, I acquired a considerable acquaintance, and what may be called some knowledge of the world, before I had entered the world as my own master and on my own account. Of the persons with whom I became, during that period, familiar some idea may be given by a mention of the names, or by brief sketches, of a few of them—those being selected who, whether as types or otherwise, may still have some meaning and interest for the social generation of to-day.

CHAPTER IV

WINTER SOCIETY AT TORQUAY

Early Acquaintance with Society—Byron's Grandson—Lord
Houghton—A Dandy of the Old School—Carlyle—Lord Lytton,
and Others—Memorable Ladies

O F the men—the noteworthy men—with whom
I thus became acquainted before I had
escaped from the torture of my last examination at Oxford, most had a taste for literature,
while some had achieved renown in it. Of these,
however, the first with whom I became intimate
was one whose literary connections were vicarious
rather than personal. My friendship with him
originated in the fact that he was an old friend of
the Froudes, and, as soon as Chelston Cross was
completed, he would pay them protracted visits
there. This was the then Lord Wentworth, who for
me was a magical being because he was Byron's
grandson. Another acquaintance who brought with
him a subtle aroma of poetry was Wentworth's
remarkable brother-in-law, Wilfrid Blunt, then the
handsomest of our younger English diplomatists, a
breeder of Arab horses, and also the author of love
poems which deserve beyond all comparison more
attention than they have yet received. Others
again were Robert Browning, Ruskin, Carlyle, and

5   53

Swinburne. These I met either at Oxford or in London, but to those whom I came to know through the William Froudes at Torquay may be added Aubrey de Vere, the Catholic poet of Ireland, Lord Houghton, Lord Lytton, the novelist, and the second Lord Lytton, his son, known to all lovers of poetry under the pseudonym of "Owen Meredith." As figures then prominent in the winter society of Torquay, I may mention also a courtly cleric, the Rev. Julian Young, a great diner out and giver of dinners to the great, a raconteur of the first order, a very complete re-embodiment of the spirit of Sidney Smith, and, further, an old Mr. Bevan, who, sixty years before, when he occupied a house in Stratton Street, had flourished as an Amphitryon and a dandy under the patronage of the Prince Regent.

Of the ladies of Torquay who, together with men like these, were prominent in my social landscape as I to-day recollect it, it is less easy to speak, partly because they were more numerous, and partly because many of them impressed me in more elusive ways. I may, however, mention a few of them who were well known as hostesses—the Dowager Lady Brownlow, Mrs. Vivian, Lady Erskine of Cambo, Lady Louisa Finch-Hatton, Miss Burdett-Coutts, and Susan, Lady Sherborne. All these ladies were the occupants of spacious houses the doors of which were guarded by skillfully powdered footmen, and which, winter after winter, were so many social centers. Lady Sherborne, indeed, was far more than a hostess: she was unrivaled as a singer of simple English songs—songs which her low voice filled with every trouble of which the human heart is capable; and as such she was, under a thin disguise, celebrated by the first Lord Lytton in one of his latest novels. To these ladies might be added innumerable others whose claims on my memory do not in all cases lend themselves to very exact statement. Most of them were English, and some of them, then in the bloom of youth and beauty, have between that time and this played their parts in the London world and ended them. But not a few were foreign—vivacious Northerners from New York, with the sublimated wealth of all Paris in their petticoats; Southerners whose eyes were still plaintive with memories of the Civil War; Austrians such as the von Hugels; Germans such as Countess Marie and Countess Helen Bismarck; and Russians whose figures and faces I remember much more accurately than their names.

It is idle, however, to say more of these, whose charms are with the last year's snows. And yet of these there were two of whom I may, for purposes of illustration, say something in detail. The two were sisters—we may call them Miss X and Miss Y—whose invalid father, a cadet of a well-known family, rarely left Torquay, where for some months of the year his daughters, otherwise emancipated from parental control, stayed with him. Both of these sisters were beautiful, and, so far as the resident ladies of Torquay were concerned, they received what is incomparably the sincerest form of homage that extraordinary beauty can elicit from ladies who do not possess it. Each of them was labeled as possessing that mysterious thing called "a history," or a shadow on her reputation of some sort, which my imagination, as soon as I heard of it (I was then about sixteen), turned into a halo iridescent with the colors of romance. For me, in Swinburne's words, they were "daughters of dreams and of stories" before I knew either by sight, or had any prospect of doing so. Dreams, except unpleasant ones, do not often fulfill themselves, but an exception to this rule was one day made in my favor.

As I was going home for my holidays from Littlehampton to Devonshire, my compartment at Eastleigh Junction was invaded by a feminine apparition, accompanied by a French poodle, which she placed on the cushion opposite to her. Her dress, though I divined its perfection, was quiet and plain enough; but the compartment, as soon as she entered it, seemed to be filled at once with the kind of fugitive flash which sunlit water sometimes casts on a ceiling. Acting, I suppose, on the principle of "Love me, love my dog," I had the temerity to express a commendation, entirely insincere, of hers; and this being received with a graciousness not perhaps unmixed with amusement, we were very soon in conversation. She talked of Nice, of Baden-Baden, and London; then she got to literature—I cannot remember how—and a moment later she was vouch-safing to me the intimate information that she was a poetess, and had contributed an anonymous poem to a certain lately published collection. Then, having caught my name on a printed label, she said, with a smile, "Is it possible that you are on your way to Torquay?" I answered that I should be there shortly, and, while elaborating this proposition, I managed to inspect the French poodle's collar, on which was engraved the name of the fair owner. In a flash the personality of this "daughter of dreams" was disclosed to me. This was Miss X, the most talked about of the two wonderful sisters. As I gathered that she herself would be soon at Torquay likewise, I tried, when she got out at some intermediate station, to express a hope that, if we met in the street, she would not have wholly forgotten me; but my modesty would not allow me to find adequate words. On the Parade, however, at Torquay, a fortnight later we did meet. She at once welcomed me with a laugh as though I were an old acquaintance, and my intimacy with her lasted so long, and to so much practical purpose, that it wrung from me at last a poem of which the concluding lines were these:

> Pause not to count the cost;
> Think not, or all is lost—
> Fly thou with me.

But the "incident," in parliamentary language, was soon afterward "closed," partly because of her marriage to a very sensible husband, and partly because, having become acquainted with her sister, I began to look on the sister as the more romantic figure of the two.

The most successful rival, however, to the excitements of young romance is to be found by some natures in the more complex stimulations of society. In these the feminine element plays a conspicuous part; but a part no less conspicuous is that played by the masculine. Moreover, as the object of the social passion, unlike that of the romantic, is not identified with the vagaries of any one individual, society for those who court it is a corporation that never dies. It is for each individual what no one individual ever can be—namely, a challenge to faculties or acquirements which are coextensive with life. I will, therefore, turn from Miss X, and the lines in which I suggested an elopement with her as a project desirable for both of us, to some of the male celebrities whose names I have just mentioned, and describe how they impressed me when I first made their acquaintance.

Of the well-known visitors who wintered at Torquay none was more punctual in his appearance than Lord Houghton, who found an annual home there in the house of two maiden aunts. Through these long-established residents he had for years been familiar with my family, and from the first occasion on which I met him he exhibited a friendship almost paternal for myself. Lord Houghton was a man

who, as Dryden said of Shadwell, would have been
the wittiest writer in the world if his books had been
equal to his conversation. Certainly nothing which
he wrote, or which a biographer has written about
him, gives any idea of the gifts—a very peculiar
mixture—which made him a marked figure in any
company which his ubiquitous presence animated.
He knew everybody of note in the fashionable and
semifashionable world, and many who belonged to
neither, such as the Tichborne Claimant, and Cal-
craft, the common hangman; and his views of life,
from whatever point he looked at it, were expressed
with a weighty brilliance or a subcynical humor.
One day when lunching at Chelston Cross he was
asked by Mrs. William Froude if he was, or had
ever been, a Mason. "No," said Lord Houghton,
"no. I have throughout my life been the victim of
every possible superstition. I am always wondering
why I have never been taken in by that." He was
once sitting at dinner by the celebrated Lady E——
of T——, who was indulging in a long lament over
the social decadence of the rising male generation.
"When I was a girl," she said, "all the young men
in London were at my feet." "My dear lady,"
said Lord Houghton, "were all the young men of
your generation chiropodists?" Mr. C. Milnes
Gaskell of Thornes told me of a perplexing situation
in which he had once found himself, and of how he
sought counsel about it from Lord Houghton, his
kinsman. Gaskell's difficulty was this. A friend

for whom he was acting as trustee had, without imposing on him any legal obligations in the matter, begged him with his dying breath to carry out certain instructions. These seemed to Gaskell extremely unwise and objectionable, "and yet," he said to Lord Houghton, "of course a peculiar sanctity attaches itself to dying wishes. What would you do in such a situation as mine?" For a little while Lord Houghton reflected, and then answered, with an air of grave detachment, "I always tell my family totally to disregard everything I say during the last six months of my life."

Of his social philosophy otherwise he gave me in the days of my youth many pithy expositions, with hints as to what I should do when I entered the world myself. One of his pieces of advice was especially appropriate to Torquay. This was to make the acquaintance of old Mr. Bevan, a lifelong intimate of his own. Accordingly my introduction to this mysterious personage was accomplished.

Mr. Bevan lived in a large villa close to that which was occupied by Miss Burdett-Coutts. Its discreetly shuttered windows, like so many half-closed eyelids, gave, when viewed externally, the impression that it was asleep or tenantless; but to ring the front-door bell was to dissipate this impression immediately. The portals seemed to open by clockwork. Heavy curtains were withdrawn by servitors half seen in the twilight, and the visitors were committed to the care of an Austrian groom of the chambers, who, wearing the aspect of a king who had stepped out of the Almanach de Gotha, led the way over soundless carpets to a library. This was furnished with a number of deep armchairs; and I recollect how, on the first occasion of my entering it, each of these chairs was monopolized by a drowsy Persian cat. For a moment, the light being dim, these cats, so it seemed to me, were the sole living things present; but a second later I was aware that a recumbent figure was slowly lifting itself from a sofa. This was Mr. Bevan. His attire was a blue silk dressing-gown, a youthfully smart pair of black-and-white check trousers, varnished boots, and a necktie with a huge pearl pin in it, the pearl itself representing the forehead of a human skull. His hands were like ivory, his face was like a clear-cut cameo. With the aid of a gold-headed cane that had once belonged to Voltaire he gently evicted a cat, so that I might occupy the chair next to him, and said, in the language of Brummell's time, that he was "monstrous glad to see me." He pointed to objects of interest which adorned his walls and tables, such as old French fashion-plates of ladies in very scanty raiment; to musical clocks, of which several were presents from crowned heads; to sketches by d'Orsay, and to framed tickets for Almack's. "Whenever the dear lady next door," he said, with a glance at the seminudities of the French fashion-plates, and alluding to Miss Burdett-Coutts, "comes to have a dish of tea with me, I have to lock those things up. I fear," he said, presently, "I'm in a shocking bad odor with her now." Only last night, he explained, he had received from one of the French Rothschilds a magnificent *pâté de foie gras;* and, having himself no parties in prospect, he sent this gastronomical treasure to Miss Coutts, who was about to entertain, as he knew, a large company at luncheon. There was one thing, however, which he did not know—the luncheon was to be given to the members of a certain society which had for its object the protection of edible animals from any form of treatment by which they might be needlessly incommoded. What, then, were the feelings of the hostess when she suddenly discovered that a dish which, with Mr. Bevan's compliments, had been solemnly placed before her was the most atrocious of all the abominations which the company had assembled to denounce! "It was sent back to me," said Mr. Bevan, "as though it were the plague in person. It's a pity that you and I can't eat it together. I'd ask you to dinner if only I were sure of my new cook. My last cook was with me for twenty years. Shall I tell you what he wrote in a letter when he had left me to join the army during the Franco-German War? 'Alas! monsieur,' he said, 'I must now make sorties instead of *entrées.*'" The banquet, however, which Mr. Bevan had suggested—and it was followed by others—took place before many days were over. The guests numbered eight or nine. I cannot recollect who they were;

but the cooking, the wines, and the decorations of the table would have satisfied Ouida herself. The china, covered with royal crowns, was a gift from Louis Philippe. The wines, of which the names and dates were murmured by the servants who dispensed them, seemed all to have come from the cellars of a Rothschild or an Austrian emperor, while every dish was a delicacy unique in its composition and flavor, the last of them being a sort of "trifle," which the artistry of a *chef* had converted into the form of a pope's tiara. Mr. Bevan, in short, was a model of the ultrafastidious man of the world as he figures in the novels of Bulwer Lytton and Disraeli. I mentioned this impression of him some time afterward to Lord Houghton, and he said: "There's a very good reason for it. When Bulwer Lytton and Disraeli entered the London world, Mr. Bevan was one of their earliest friends. He privately helped Disraeli in social and other ways. To him Bulwer Lytton owed his first personal knowledge of the then world of the dandies; and Mr. Bevan," said Lord Houghton, "was the actual model from which, by both these writers, their pictures of the typical man of the world were drawn."

My acquaintance with Mr. Bevan, however, and even that with Lord Houghton, were but minor experiences as compared with another meeting of a similar yet contrasted kind. At the time of which I speak there was one British author whose influence as a philosophic moralist eclipsed that of any of his contemporaries. This writer was Carlyle. His fame was then at its highest, and the moral consciousness of ultrapolite drawing rooms was being stirred to its well-dressed depths by his attack on "the dandies" in his book, *Sartor Resartus*, which many earnest and ornamental persons were accepting as a new revelation. I was myself sufficiently familiar with its pages, and, though some of them roused my antagonism, I could not deny their genius. One morning, during a brief visit to London, I received a note from Mr. Froude the historian, asking me to come to luncheon, and I duly arrived at his house, not knowing what awaited me. I presently learned that he was going to introduce me to Carlyle, and, as soon as luncheon was over, he walked me off to Chelsea. In a fitting state of awe I found myself at last in the great philosopher's presence. When we entered his drawing room he was stooping over a writing table in the window, and at first I saw nothing but his back, which was covered with a long, shapeless, and extravagantly dirty dressing gown. When he rose to meet us his manners were as rough as his integument. His welcome to myself was an inarticulate grunt, unmistakably Scotch in its intonation; and his first act was to move across the room to the fireplace and light a "churchwarden" pipe by sticking its head between the bars. As I watched him perform this rite, I noticed that close to the fender was a pair of very dirty slippers. To me these things and proceedings were so many

THOMAS CARLYLE

separate shocks, the result of my reflections being this: If you represent fame, let me represent obscurity. But worse was still to come. It was presently proposed that we should all go out for a walk, and as soon as we were in the open air, the philosopher blew his nose in a pair of old woolen gloves. I here saw at once an illustration of the chapter in *Sartor Resartus* in which the author denounced what he christened "The Sect of the Dandies," as described and glorified by Bulwer Lytton in *Pelham*. Illustration could go no farther.

The very next famous man whom I met after this glimpse of Carlyle I met a little later at Torquay. The famous man was Lord Lytton himself. He was dining at Chelston Cross, and, owing to some lady's defection, I was actually his nearest neighbor. I saw in him everything which the spirit of Carlyle hated. I saw in him everything which was then in my opinion admirable. All the arts of appearance, conversation, and demeanor which in Carlyle were aggressively absent were in him exhibited in a manner perhaps even too apparent. I was indeed, despite my reverence for him, faintly conscious myself that his turquoise shirt stud, set with diamonds, was too large, and that his coat would have been in better taste had the cuffs not been of velvet. But it seemed to me that from his eyes, keen, authoritative, and melancholy, all the passions, all the intellect, and all the experiences of the world were peering. To have sat by him was an adventure; to have been noticed by him was not far from a sacrament.

Before very long, and likewise at Chelston Cross, I became acquainted with his son, "Owen Meredith," afterward Viceroy of India. Having heard that, like him, I was touched with the fever of the Muses, he at once showed me signs of an amity which ended only with his life. Treating me as though I were a man of the same age as himself, he would take my arm, when wandering in the Froudes' shrubberies, and describe to me the poems to the production of which his future years would be consecrated, or ask me to confide to him my corresponding ambitions in return. Like most poets, he was not without personal vanities; but never was a man more free from anything like jealousy of a rival. To praise others was a pleasure to him as natural as that of being praised himself.

To some of the celebrities associated with my youthful days I was introduced, as I have said already, not at Torquay, but at Oxford. There was one, however, whom, though essentially an Oxonian, I first met at Torquay. This was Jowett, the renowned Master of Balliol, to whose college I was destined to be subsequently either a disgrace or ornament. Jowett was frequently at Torquay, having a sister who lived there, and he was specially asked to luncheon at Chelston Cross to inspect me and see how I should pass muster as one of his own disciples. His blinking eyes, the fresh pink of his cheeks, his snow-white hair, and the birdlike treble of his voice, have been often enough described, and I will only say of them here that, when he took me for a walk in the garden, I subconsciously felt them —I cannot tell why—to be formidable. He inquired as to my tastes and interests with a species of curt benignity; but to my interest in poetry he exhibited a most disconcerting indifference, and I felt during the whole of our interview that I was walking with a mild east wind. In this he was a marked contrast to Ruskin, Robert Browning, and certain others— especially to "Owen Meredith"—men between whom and myself there was at once some half-conscious bond. There are no estrangements so elusive, and yet so insuperable, as those which arise from subtle discords in temperament. And yet in certain individual acts, to which I shall refer presently, Jowett treated me, when I was safely settled at Oxford, with much sympathetic good nature. But these and other Oxford experiences shall be reserved for another chapter.

CHAPTER V

Early Youth at Oxford—Acquaintance with Browning, Swinburne, and Ruskin—Dissipation of an Undergraduate—The Ferment of Intellectual Revolution—*The New Republic*

MY experiences at Oxford I may divide into two groups—namely, those belonging to the social life of an undergraduate, and those consisting of the effects—philosophical, moral, or religious—produced in an undergraduate's mind by the influence of academic teaching.

As to my social experiences, my recollections are, on the whole, pleasurable, but they are somewhat remote from anything that can properly be called scholastic. They are associated with the charm of certain cloistered buildings—with Magdalen especially, and the shades of Addison's Walk; with country drives in dogcarts to places like Witney and Abingdon; with dinners there in the summer evenings, and with a sense of being happily outside the radius of caps and gowns; with supper parties during the race weeks to various agreeable ladies; and with a certain concert which, during one Commemoration, was given by myself and a friend to a numerous company, and for which the mayor was good enough to lend us the Town Hall.

From the incubus of mere collegiate discipline I was perhaps more free than nine undergraduates out of ten. At the time when I matriculated there were within the college precincts no quarters available; and I and a fellow freshman who was in the same position as myself managed to secure a suite of unusually commodious lodgings. That particular partnership lasted only for a term, but subsequently I and two other companions took the whole upper part of a large house between us. We were never what is called "in college"; we rarely dined in Hall, having, besides a good cook, a very good dining room of our own, where we gave little dinners, much to our own contentment. We had, moreover, a spare bedroom, in which on occasion we could put up a visitor. One visitor who stayed with us for some weeks was Wentworth. Little things remain in the mind when greater things are forgotten; and one little incident which I remember of Wentworth's visit was this. Those were days when, for some mysterious reason, men, when they smoked, were accustomed to wear smoking caps. Wentworth had one of Oriental design, which he would somehow attach to his head by means of a jeweled pin. One evening when he was adjusting it the light caught his features at some peculiar angle, and for a fugitive moment his face was an exact and living reproduction of one of the best-known portraits of Byron.

Another incident belonging to this same order of memories occurred during one of the race weeks.

About half past ten one evening, accompanied by three companions, I was making my way along a rather ill-illuminated street. My three companions were feminine, and the dresses of two of them—triumphs of the latest fashion—were calculated to arrest attention as though they were so much undulating moonlight. Suddenly I was aware that a strange voice was addressing me. It was the voice of a proctor, who, attended by several "bulldogs," was asking me, with a sinister though furtive glance at the ladies, what I was doing, and why I was not in cap and gown. I could see in his eyes a sense of having very neatly caught me in a full career of sin. I explained to him that Mrs. L., wife of one of the greatest of the then university magnates, and her two charming daughters had just been so kind as to have had supper with me, and that I was seeing them back to All Souls'.

To return, however, to the first week or fortnight which saw me and my original housemate established as full-blown freshmen; I cannot for the life of me remember by what steps we entered on any course of formal instruction, but he and I were told with very surprising promptitude that we should, without loss of time, give a breakfast to the Balliol Eight. We did so, and never before had I seen on any one matutinal tablecloth provisions which weighed so much, or disappeared so rapidly.

Not many days later I found myself at another breakfast table of a very different character, in the capacity not of host, but guest. The host on this occasion was Jowett, who asked me to breakfast with him in order that I might meet Browning. Browning by some one or other—I think it was James Spedding—had been shown certain manuscript verses—precious verses of my own. He had sent me a message of a flattering kind with regard to them, and he now held out both his hands to me with an almost boisterous cordiality. His eyes sparkled with laughter, his beard was carefully trimmed, and an air of fashion was exhaled from his dazzling white waistcoat. He did not embarrass me by any mention of my own performances. He did not, so far as I remember, make any approach to the subject of literature at all, but reduced both Jowett and myself to something like complete silence by a constant flow of anecdotes and social allusions, which, though not deficient in point, had more in them of jocularity than wit. He was not, perhaps, my ideal of the author of "Men and Women," or the singer of "Lyric Love" as "a wonder and a wild desire"; but there the great man was, and when I quitted his presence and found myself once more in undergraduate circles I felt myself shining like Moses when he came down from the mount.

I was subsequently enveloped in a further reflected glory, due also to Jowett's kindness—a kindness which survived many outbursts of what I thought somewhat petulant disapproval. I received from him one day a curt invitation to dinner, and

presented myself, wondering mildly to what this
mark of favor could be due. But wonder turned to
alarm when, on entering the Master's drawing-room,
I discovered in the dim twilight no other figure than
his own. His manner, however, though not effusive,
was civil, and was certainly fraught with no menace
of any coming judgment on my sins. We exchanged
some ordinary observations on the weather and kindred topics. Then, looking over his shoulder, he
uttered a half-audible word or two, which, being
plainly not addressed to me, must have been addressed to somebody else. Presently, out of the
shadows, a somebody else emerged. This was a
person remarkable for the large size of his head, his
longish hair, his insignificant stature, and his singularly sloping shoulders. I was introduced to him
without catching his name. Dinner was announced
forthwith. It was evident that, except for myself,
this person was to be the sole guest. In the candle-
light of the dinner table I realized that this person
was Swinburne.

The dinner passed off pleasantly. Swinburne
showed himself an intelligent, though by no means
a brilliant, talker; and as soon as we had returned
to the drawing room, where we drank a cup of
coffee standing, Jowett, who had some engagement,
abruptly left us to finish the evening by ourselves.
On Swinburne the effect of the Master's disappear-
ance was magical. His manner and aspect began to
exhibit a change like that of the moon when a dim

cloud drifts away from it. Of what we discussed at starting I have not the least remembrance, but before very long Swinburne was on the subject of poetry. His observations at first consisted of general criticisms. Then he began to indulge in quotations from various poems—none of them, I think, from his own; but, however this may have been, the music seemed to intoxicate him. The words began to thrill me with the spell of his own recitation of them. Here at last I realized the veritable genius who had made the English language a new instrument of passion. Here at last was the singer for whose songs my ears were shells which still murmured with such lines as I had first furtively read by the gaslight of the Brighton theater. My own appreciation as a listener more and more encouraged him. If he began a quotation sitting, he would start from his chair to finish it. Finally he abandoned the restraints of a chair altogether. He began, with gesticulating arms, to pace the room from one end to the other, reciting passage after passage, and appealing to me, who managed to keep pace with him, for applause. "The most beautiful lines that Tennyson ever wrote," he exclaimed, "were these, from 'Maud':

"And like silent lightning under the stars
  She seemed to divide in a dream from a band of the blest.

"Yes," he went on, "and what did the dream-Maud tell her lover when she had got him? That the salvation of the world depended on the Crimean War and the prosecution of Lord Palmerston's policy." Finally he strayed into quotations from Sidney Dobell, a writer now hardly remembered, with one of which, describing a girl bathing, he made the Master's academic rafters ring:

> "She, with her body bright sprinkles the waters white,
>   Which flee from her fair form, and flee in vain,
> Dyed with the dear unutterable sight,
>   And circles out her beauties to the circling main."

He was almost shouting these words when another sound became audible—that of an opening door, followed by Jowett's voice, which said in high-pitched syllables, "You'd both of you better go to bed now."

My next meeting with Swinburne took place not many days later. He had managed meanwhile to make acquaintance with a few other undergraduates—all of them enthusiastic worshipers—one of whom arranged to entertain him at luncheon. As I could not, being otherwise engaged, be present at this feast myself, I was asked to join the party as soon as possible afterward. I arrived at a fortunate moment. Most of the guests were still sitting at a table covered with dessert dishes. Swinburne was much at his ease in an armchair near the fireplace, and was just beginning, as a number of smiling faces showed, to be not only interesting, but in some way entertaining also. He was, as I presently gathered, about to begin an account of a historical drama by himself, which existed in his memory only—a sort of parody of what Victor Hugo might have written had he dramatized English events at the opening of the reign of Queen Victoria. The first act, he said, showed England on the verge of a revolution, which was due to the frightful orgies of the Queen at "Buckingham's Palace." The Queen, with un-blushing effrontery, had taken to herself a lover, in the person of Lord John Russell, who had for his rival "Sir Peel." Sir Peel was represented as plead-ing his own cause in a passionate scene, which wound up as follows: "Why do you love Lord John Rus-sell, and why do you not love me? I know why you love Lord John Russell. He is young, he is beautiful, he is profligate. I cannot be young, I cannot be beautiful, but I will be profligate." Then followed the stage direction, "Exit for ze Haysmarket." In a later act it appeared that the Queen and Lord John Russell had between them given the world a daugh-ter, who, having been left to her own devices, or, in other words, to the streets, reappears as "Miss Kitty," and is accorded some respectable rank. Under these conditions she becomes the object of much princely devotion; but the moral hypocrisy of England has branded her as a public scandal. With regard to her so-called depravities nobody entertains a doubt, but one princely admirer, of broader mind than the rest, declares that in spite of these she is really the embodiment of everything that is divine in woman. "She may," he says, "have done everything which might have made a Messalina blush, but whenever she looked at the sky she murmured 'God,' and whenever she looked at a flower she murmured 'mother.'"

The vivacity and mischievous humor with which Swinburne gave his account of this projected play exhibited a side of his character which I have never even seen mentioned, and the appreciation and surprise of his audience were obviously a great delight to him. He lay back in his chair, tossed off a glass of port, and presently his mood changed. Somehow or other he got to his own serious poems; and before we knew where we were he was pouring out an account of *Poems and Ballads*, and explaining their relation to the secrets of his own experiences. There were three poems, he said, which beyond all the rest were biographical: "The Triumph of Time," "Dolores," and "The Garden of Proserpine." "The Triumph of Time" was a monument to the sole real love of his life—a love which had been the tragic destruction of all his faith in woman. "Dolores" expressed the passion with which he had sought relief, in the madnesses of the fleshly Venus, from his ruined dreams of the heavenly. "The Garden of Proserpine" expressed his revolt against the flesh and its fevers, and his longing to find a refuge from them in a haven of undisturbed rest. His audience, who knew these three poems by heart, held their breaths as they listened to the poet's own voice, imparting its living tones to passages such as the following—

This is from "The Triumph of Time":

"I will say no word that a man may say,
  Whose whole life's love goes down in a day;
For this could never have been, and never,
  Though the gods and the years relent, shall be."

This is from "Dolores":

"Oh, garment not golden but gilded,
  Oh, garden where all men may dwell,
Oh, tower not of ivory, but builded
  By hands that reach heaven out of hell."

This is from "The Garden of Proserpine":

"From too much love of living,
  From hope and fear set free;
We thank with brief thanksgiving
  Whatever gods may be
    That no life lives for ever,
    That dead men rise up never,
    That even the weariest river
  Winds somewhere safe to sea."

Then, like a man waking up from a dream, Swinburne turned to our host and said, nervously, "Can you give me another glass of port?" His glass was filled, he emptied it at a single draught, and then lay back in his chair like a child who had gone to sleep, the actual fact being, as his host soon recognized, that, in homely language, he was drunk.

Drink, indeed, was Swinburne's great enemy. He had, when I met him at Balliol, finished his own career there more than twelve years ago; but he had since then been a frequent guest of the Master's, who treated him, in respect of this weakness, with a watchful and paternal care. When I dined with him at the Master's Lodge there was nothing to tempt him but a little claret and water. The consequence was that afterward he was brilliant as the burning bush till he finally went in his sober senses to bed. He was not, I think, intemperate in the sense that he drank much. His misfortune was that a very little intoxicated him.

I associate my early days at Balliol with yet another memorable meeting. One of the most prominent and dignified of the then residents at Oxford was Sir Henry Acland, who, as a Devonshire man, knew many of my relations, and had also heard something about myself. He was a friend and entertainer of men of all sorts of eminence; and while I was still more or less a freshman he invited me to join at his house a very small company in the evening, the star of the occasion being a university lecturer on art, who was just entering on his office, and whose name was illustrious wherever the English language was spoken. He, too, knew something about me, having been shown some of my verses, and to meet him was one of my cherished dreams. Only half a dozen people were present, and from a well-known portrait of him by Millais I recognized his form at once. This was Ruskin. He had sent me, through Lord Houghton or somebody, a verbal message of poetic appreciation already. I was now meeting him in the flesh. The first thing in him which struck me was the irresistible fascination of his manner. It was a manner absolutely and almost plaintively simple, but that of no diplomat or courtier could be more polished in what was at once its weighty and its winning dignity. Such was his charm for the elect; but here again comes the question of temperament. Between Ruskin and Jowett there was a temperamental antipathy. An antipathy of this kind is a very different thing from any reasoned dislike, and of this general fact Ruskin and Jowett were types. I was myself another. Just as Jowett repelled so Ruskin attracted me. During my later days at Oxford I grew to know Ruskin intimately, and my sympathy with his genius never lost its loyalty, though for a long time certain of his ideas—that is to say, ideas relating to social politics—were to me barely intelligible, and though, when they became intelligible, I regarded them as perversely mischievous.

But beneath these social experiences, many of them sufficiently frivolous, and all of them superficial in so far as their interest related to individuals, Oxford provided me with others which went to the very roots of life. Of these deeper experiences the first was due to Jowett, though its results, so far as I was concerned, were neither intended, understood, nor even suspected by him.

The most sensational event which occurred during my first term at Balliol was the suicide of one of the undergraduates. He was a poor Scotch student of a deeply religious character, who had found, so his friends reported, that the faith of his childhood had been taken from him by Jowett's skeptical teachings, and who had ended by cutting his throat with a razor in Port Meadow. Jowett preached his funeral sermon—the only sermon which I ever, so far as my recollection serves me, heard preached in Balliol chapel by himself or by anybody else. Jowett, who on the occasion was obviously much moved, chose for his text the story of the woman taken in adultery, and of Christ's challenge to her judges, "Which of you will dare to assault with the first stone?" The course of his argument was curious. He began with examining the passage from the standpoint of verbal scholarship, the gist of his criticism being that its authenticity was at least doubtful. From this argument he diverged into one of wider scope, insisting on how much is doubtful in what the Gospels record as the sayings of our Lord generally, from which illuminating reflection he advanced to one wider still. It was as follows: Since we know so little of what Christ really said about God, how much less can we really know of the nature of God himself; of what he loves, condemns, or, in his infinite mercy, pardons?—the moral being that we ought to cast stones at nobody, and should in especial refrain from condemning our departed brother, who, for anything which we knew to the contrary, might be just as acceptable to God as any one of ourselves.

All my impressions of Jowett as a religious teacher were summed up in my impressions of that one sermon. Though his tone in delivering it was one of unusual tenderness, there lurked in it, nevertheless, a mordant and petulant animus against the Christian religion as a whole, if regarded as miraculously revealed or as postulating the occurrence of any definite miracle. It was the voice of one who, while setting all belief in the miraculous aside, on the ground that it had no evidence of a scientific kind to support it, was proclaiming with confidence some vague creed as unassailable, the evidence in support of which was very much more nebulous, or what many would describe as *nil*. A story used to be told about him by which his position in this respect is aptly and amusingly illustrated. He was taking a walk with an undergraduate, who confessed to him that his deepest trouble was his failure to find anything which accurate reason could accept as a proof of God's existence. Jowett did not utter a word till he and the young man parted. Then he said, "Mr. Smith, if you can't find a satisfactory proof of God's existence during the next three weeks, I shall have to send you down for a term." Had I been in the young man's place I should have retorted, "And pray, Mr. Jowett, what satisfactory proofs are you able to adduce yourself?"

But, in speaking of Jowett thus, I am not wholly, or even mainly, speaking of him as a single individual. I speak of him mainly as a type, exceptional indeed on account of his signal intellect, but otherwise representing a moral and mental attitude which was common not only to the teaching body of Balliol, but also to the age in general, in so far as its traditional temper had been influenced by scientific knowledge. Nearly all the Balliol dons—even those who never spoke of religion—seemed to start with the same foregone conclusion, that the dogmatic theology of the churches was as dead as the geocentric astronomy. They assumed this, just as Jowett did, on what purported to be scientific grounds, and yet when they sought, as he did, to put in the place of this some solemn system of quasi-scientific ethics, their attempts seemed to me to exhibit the same absurdity with which Jowett's constructive teaching had first made me familiar. Their denials of everything which to me had been previously sacred appalled me like the overture to some approaching tragedy. Their confident attempts at some new scheme of affirmations affected me like a solemn farce.

Some foretastes of the new gospel had, as I have said already, been vouchsafed to me at Littlehampton by Mr. Philpot. I now saw what logically the new gospel implied. The sense of impending catastrophe became more and more acute. I felt like a man on a ship, who, having started his voyage in an estuary, and imagining that a deck is by nature as stable as dry land, becomes gradually conscious of the sway of the outer sea, until, when he nears the bar, showers of spray fall on him, he perceives that the bows are plunging, and at last the percussion of waves makes the whole vessèl shudder.

Such, then, were the effects on me of the religious liberalism of Oxford, and in this respect, as I now see, looking backward, my condition was temperamentally the same as it had been when I was still under the tuition of superorthodox governesses. In those days any questioning of the verbal inspiration of the Bible and the miraculous events recorded in it seemed to me, as it did later, to be at once absurd and blasphemous. There was, however, even then, something which to me seemed no less absurd than "the infidel's" attack on the dogmas of Christian orthodoxy—for I knew that "the infidel" existed—and this was the manner in which the Anglican clergy defended them. I was always, when a child, looking forward each week to the Sunday sermon, in the hope of finding some portions of it which I could either mimic or parody. I remember one sermon in particular, which the preacher devoted to a proof of God's existence. My own mental comment was, "If anything could make me such a fool as to doubt this self-evident truth, your arguments and the inflections of your voice would certainly make me do so." I heard another preacher indulge in a long half-hour of sarcasm at the expense of "the shallow infidel, who pointed to the sky and said, 'Where are the signs of His coming?'" In those days we were required by a governess to write out the morning's sermon as a pious discipline in the afternoon. This sermon I reproduced with a series of pictures in the margin, one of which represented the "shallow infidel" exploring the sky through a telescope, which he did his best to steady by holding it against the stem of a palm tree. And yet so literally true did all orthodox doctrines seem to me that I believed a member of my family to have committed the sin against the Holy Ghost by kissing a New Testament and swearing that one of the nursery maids had mispronounced some word—an imputation which she had indignantly denied.

This dual mood, as renewed in me by Oxford influences, differed from its earlier and childish form in the fact that my sense of the absurdities distinctive of modern religious thought acquired a wider range and went deeper than I had at first anticipated. The absurdities of which I was conscious as a child were those of the arguments by which the orthodox clergy endeavored to defend doctrines which were then for myself indubitable. At Oxford I became conscious of an absurdity to which as a child I had been a stranger—namely, the absurdity of the arguments by which men who repudiated orthodoxy altogether endeavored to establish in its place some purely natural substitute, such as the "enthusiasm of humanity," a passion for the welfare of posterity, or a godless deification of domestic puritanism for its own sake. In addition to this second absurdity a third gradually dawned on me. This was the absurdity, common to all parties alike, of supposing that, if the cardinal doctrines of religious orthodoxy were discredited—namely, that the human soul is immortal, that the human will is free, and that a God exists who is interested in the fortunes of each soul individually—these doctrines, in disappearing, would take away with them nothing but themselves alone; the actual fact being that they are known to mankind generally not so much in themselves as in their indirect effects on that plexus of moral, emotional, and intellectual values on which all our higher interests in the drama of life depend.

Thus, in whatever direction I turned, I felt that, if I listened to the reasoning of liberal Oxford, I was confronted with an absurdity of one kind or another. Of the only liberal answers attempted to the riddle of life, not one, it seemed to me, would bear a moment's serious criticism; and yet, unless the orthodox doctrines could be defended in such a way that in all their traditional strictness they could once more compel assent, life, in the higher sense of the word, would—such was my conviction—soon cease to be tolerable.

The only human being at that time who held and publicly expressed views similar to my own, so far as I knew, was Ruskin. Of the riddle which I found so importunate, he did not profess to have discovered any adequate solution of his own. On the contrary, he confessed himself a victim of a tragic and desolating doubt, but he did boldly proclaim that until some solution was found the men of the modern world were of all men the most miserable. Take, he said, the belief in immortality, which, according to some men, is a matter of mild indifference. It is really a belief which affects our whole conception of the human race. Consider, he said, the carnage of war, with its pile of unnumbered corpses. It must make some matter to us whether, according to our serious belief, each man has died like a dog, and left nothing in the way of a personal existence behind him, or "whether out of every Christiannamed portion of that ruinous heap there has gone forth into the air and the dead-fallen smoke of battle some astonished condition of soul unwillingly released."

Here, it seemed to me, was the true voice of reason and challenging passion combined—a voice which would not say "peace when there was no peace," and which I missed altogether in Jowett and the Oxford liberals generally. Jowett always regarded me as a mere dilettante and an idler, who was bound to disgrace Balliol by coming to grief in the schools, and he was, I think, mortified rather than pleased when I won, in my second year, the Newdigate prize for poetry.

But mine was certainly no mere idler's mood; and whatever Jowett may have thought of me when he heard of my giving parties to ladies, of my driving them out to picnics, or of my concocting prize poems, my mental life at Oxford was far from being a life

JOHN RUSKIN

of idleness. On the contrary, from my second year of residence onward I was constantly engaged in tentative sketches of a book in which I hoped some day to give a comprehensive picture of the moral and intellectual condition to which my Oxford experiences had by that time raised or reduced me. That book was *The New Republic*, with regard to which in this place a few words may be apposite.

The form of nearly every book is more or less fashioned on some model or models. My own models in the case of *The New Republic* were *The Republic* of Plato, the *Satyricon* of Petronius Arbiter, and the so-called novels of Peacock. All these books introduce us to circles of friends who discuss questions of philosophy, religion, art, or the problems of social life, each character representing some prevalent view, and their arguments being so arranged as to have, when taken together, some general and coherent meaning. Many of Peacock's characters are taken direct from life, and in this respect I made myself a disciple of Peacock. My characters in *The New Republic* were all portraits, though each was meant to be typical; but the originals of some —such as Lady Ambrose, the conventional woman of the world—were of no public celebrity, and to mention them here would be meaningless. The principal speakers, however, were drawn without any disguise from persons so eminent and influential that a definite fidelity of portraiture was in their case essential to my plan. Mr. Storks and Mr.

Stockton, the prosaic and the sentimental material-
ists, were meant for Professors Huxley and Tyndall.
Mr. Luke was Matthew Arnold. Mr. Rose was
Pater. Mr. Saunders, so far as his atheism was concerned, was suggested by Professor Clifford. Mrs.
Sinclair was the beautiful "Violet Fane"; and
finally—more important than any others—Doctor
Jenkinson was Jowett, and Mr. Herbert was Ruskin.
All these people I set talking in polite antagonism to
one another, their one underlying subject being the
rational aim of life, and the manner in which a definite
supernatural faith was essential, extraneous, or
positively prejudicial to this.

To all the arguments advanced I endeavored to
do strict justice, my own criticisms merely taking the
form of pushing most of them to some consequence
more extreme, but more strictly logical, than any
which those who proclaimed them either realized or
had the courage to avow. Thus when Doctor
Jenkinson descanted in his sermon on the all-
embracing character of Christianity, I made him go
on to say that "true Christianity embraces all
opinions—even any honest denial of itself." By this
passage Browning told me that Jowett was specially
exasperated, and Browning had urged on him that
such a temper was quite unreasonable. I think myself, on the contrary, that Jowett had an excellent
reason for it, this reason being that Jowett's position
was false, and that my method of criticism had
brought out its absurdity. Here indeed was the

method employed by me throughout the whole book, except in the case of Ruskin, and there the method was inverted. Just as I sought to show that Jowett's principles, if carried far enough, ended in absurdity, so did I seek to show that Ruskin's principles, despite their superficial absurdities, ended, if carried far enough, in the nearest approach to truth which under modern conditions of thought and knowledge is possible. In my effort to give point to what were really my own underlying convictions, I wrote *The New Republic* six or seven times over, and in doing so it became clearer and clearer to me what my own convictions were. They ended in an application of the method of a *reductio ad absurdum* to everything; and this fact I finally indicated in the words of a Greek epigram which I placed as a motto on the title-page: "All is laughter, all is dust, all is nothingness, for all the things that are arise out of the unreasonable."

Such seemed to me the upshot of all the intellectual and moral teaching of Oxford, of the faintly hinted liberalism of Mr. Philpot's teachings which had preceded them, and of my own enlarging experiences of male and female society. That such a conclusion was satisfactory I did not for a moment feel, but here was the very reason which urged me on to elaborate it. The mood which expresses itself in a sense that life is merely ridiculous was, so my consciousness protested, nothing more and nothing better than a disease, and my hope was that I should get rid of it by expressing it once for all as pungently and as completely as I could, after which I would address myself to the project of finding a foundation for some positive philosophy of life which should indeed be fortified by reason, but against which reason should not prevail. When, however, *The New Republic* had been completed and given to the world, I felt that my sense of the absurdities of current liberal philosophy had not even yet exhausted itself; and I presently supplemented that work by another—*The New Paul and Virginia, or Positivism on an Island*, a short satirical story in the style of Voltaire's *Candide*. This is a story of an atheistic professor, such as Tyndall, who, together with a demimondaine, now the wife of a High Church colonial bishop, is wrecked on a desert island, and there endeavors to redeem her from the degrading superstitions of theism and to make her a partner with him in the sublime service of Humanity—of that "Grand Être," so he says to her, "which, so far as we are concerned, has come in the course of progress to consist of you and me." *The New Paul and Virginia* was followed some two years later by *Is Life Worth Living?* a formal philosophical treatise, in which the values of life and their connection with religious belief, the methods of fiction being abandoned, were submitted to scientific analysis. These three books represent the compound results produced by the liberalism of Oxford on a mind such as my own, which had been cradled in the conservatisms of the past. But meanwhile I had left Oxford behind me, and the death of my father and other family events which occurred about that time left me free to determine my own movements, the consequence being that thenceforward the months of what is called "the season" found me year by year in London from Easter till the approach of August. Of my early experiences of London, and of the kind of life I lived there, I will now give some brief account, not disdaining the humble aid of gossip.

CHAPTER VI

THE BASIS OF LONDON SOCIETY

Early Experiences of London Society—Society Thirty Years Ago Relatively Small — Arts and Accomplishments Which Can Flourish in Small Societies Only

COMPARING London society as it was when I first knew it with what it has since become, I should say that its two most distinguishing features were its then comparative smallness and its practically unquestioned position. Its position was mainly founded on the hereditary possession of land, its nucleus being the heads of more or less ancient families whose rent rolls enabled them to occupy London houses and play an agreeable and ornamental part in the business of entertaining and being entertained for the few months called "the season." Certain qualifications in the way of family being given, mere personal charm and accomplishment would often secure for their possessors a high place in its ranks. Indeed, such qualifications were by no means always necessary, as was shown in still earlier days by the cases of Moore and Brummell; but, on the whole, the social conditions then prevalent in London coincided with what, in the country, I had known and accepted, when a child, as part of the order of Nature. Of society as represented by a definite upper class, the basis was still inheritance in the form of inherited land.

This was no mere accident. It was a fact definitely explicable in terms of statistical history. At the time of the battle of Waterloo, outside the landed class there did not exist in England five hundred people whose incomes exceeded £5,000 a year. The landed class was typically the rich class of the country. The condition of things since then has in this respect been reversed. During the sixty years succeeding the battle of Waterloo business incomes exceeding £5,000 a year had increased numerically in the proportion of one to eight, while since that time the increase has been still more rapid. On the other hand, not only has the number of the large agricultural landlords shown no increase whatever, but since the year 1880 or thereabouts their aggregate rental has suffered an actual decrease, having fallen in the approximate proportion of seventy to fifty-two. This shrinkage in the fortunes of the old landed families, except those who were owners of minerals or land near towns, and the multiplication of families newly enriched by business, were, when I first knew London, proceeding at a rate which had never been known before. It was, however, slow in comparison with what it has since become, and the old landed families, at the time to which I am now alluding, still retained much of their old prestige and power, as is shown by the fact that the leaders of both political parties were still mainly drawn from the limited class in question. It is shown with even greater clearness by facts more directly presenting themselves to the eye of the ordinary observer.

One of these is the aspect which thirty years ago was presented by Hyde Park during the season at certain hours of the day. Thirty years ago, for an hour or two before luncheon and dinner, its aspect was that of a garden party, for which, indeed, no invitations were necessary, but on which as a fact few persons intruded who would have been visibly out of place on the lawn of Marlborough House. To-day this ornamental assemblage has altogether disappeared, and its place has been gradually taken by a miscellaneous crowd without so much as a trace even of spurious fashion left in it. Thirty years ago Piccadilly in June was a vision of open carriages brilliant with flowerlike parasols, high-stepping horses, and coachmen, many of whom still wore wigs. To-day these features have been submerged by a flow of unending omnibuses which crowds fight to enter or from which they struggle to eject themselves. Fashionable hotels have succumbed to the same movement. Of such hotels thirty years ago the most notable were commonly described as "private"—a word which implied that no guests were received who were not known to the landlord either personally or through fit credentials. Claridge's, until it was rebuilt, was an establishment of this description. An unknown and unaccredited stranger could, by the mere chance latchkey of wealth, no more obtain access to such hotels as these than he could make himself to-day a member of some exclusive club by placing the amount of the entrance fee in the hands of the hall porter.

But society, as it was in this relatively recent past, did not differ from that of to-day merely in the fact of having been absolutely less numerous and of less multifarious origin. It differed in the effects which a mere restriction of numbers, coupled with inherited wealth and a general similarity of antecedents, has on the quality of social intercourse itself. In societies which are small, and yet at the same time wealthy enough to secure for their members as a whole a monopoly of varied experience, and invest them with a corporate power which cannot be similarly concentrated in any other cohesive class, these members are provided, like the believers in some esoteric religion, with subtle similarities of tastes, behavior, and judgment, together with daily opportunities of observing how far, and in what particulars, individuals belonging to their class conform or do not conform to them. These are constant provocations to refinements of mutual criticism which give life and conversation a zest not attainable otherwise. Finally a society which is small enough to possess such common standards, and whose position is so well established as to pervade it with a sense that no standards are superior to its own, tends to make manners perfectly simple and natural which could otherwise be approached only by conscious effort or affectation.

The result of such conditions, in so far as they prevailed in London when London life became first familiar to myself, was that society, in the narrower sense of the word, was taken in a spirit more serious than that which it excites to-day. To say nothing of ambitious hostesses who vied with one another in the entertainment of guests whose very names had a ring of importance when printed in the *Morning Post*, society was, even for men of conspicuous talent—such, for example, as Lord Houghton, Augustus Savile, and Hayward—a matter as serious as politics, or any war not of the first importance. To men like Christopher Sykes and Kenneth Howard it was very much more engrossing. Thus, at a luncheon party which I remember, a lady who had just reached London from Scotland asked, by way of conversation, "What is going on to-night?" Lord Houghton, who was one of the guests, answered, with all the gravity of a judge summing up the evidence at a murder trial: "The only event of to-night is the ball at Grosvenor House. There's nothing else worth mentioning." "The ball of to-night," I heard him say on a similar occasion, "will be Lady Harriet ——'s. That is sure to be good, for Lady Harriet knows nobody, so she can't ask the wrong people, and her list of invitations is in the hands of Augustus Savile." One of the cleverest hostesses of that time, Lady G——, denounced to a friend the impertinence of a "society paper" which had ventured to describe one of her entertainments as "political"; and she had actually been to the trouble of writing to inform the editor that her parties were fashionable gatherings and not political menageries. The then Lord Orford, a man of the highest literary culture, who professed to despise society, and very rarely entered it, said that his own idea of real happiness was "to go nowhere, and yet to be asked everywhere."

The seriousness with which society was taken, and the fear of its judgments entertained even by many of its most conspicuous members, was illustrated in a way now oddly belated by the celebrated "Lady A.," as she was called, who occasionally lent her house in Hertford Street for the month of August to her niece, Mrs. Marcus Hare. To this act of kindness she attached one strict condition—namely, that the blinds of the front windows should always be drawn down, lest anyone should suspect that she —Lady A. herself—was guilty of remaining in London when the fashionable season was over. A well-known social philosopher, Lady E—— of T——, gave me in my early days an ultraserious lecture on the principles by which a young man should be guided when beginning to form acquaintances in a world like that of London. Her advice was almost identical with that which, in Bulwer Lytton's novel, *Pelham*, is administered to the hero by his mother. "You should be specially careful," said Lady E——

to me, "as to people with whom you dine. Some are remarkable for their *chefs*, some for the importance of their company. There are all sorts of differences which a young man has to learn. There are some evening parties," she said, "at which it will be enough for him to be merely seen; and, with very few exceptions"—this was her concluding counsel—"you should never be seen at a ball in a two-roomed house—a house, for example, like the houses in Eaton Place."

Another sort of social philosopher, in his own way equally typical, was Hamilton Aidé, who united to the life of society the cultivation of art, and was equally serious in his combined devotion to both. He was a musician, a poet, a singer of his own songs in a voice perfectly modulated. He was also as a painter in water colors one of the most distinguished amateurs of his time. His landscapes, indeed, and his sketches of old houses and gardens, Scotch castles, and the seclusions of Italian villas, were in themselves poems; and when he entertained the world—a world very carefully chosen—the attention of his guests was divided between his music and his great portfolios. His bachelor's quarters provided him with an appropriate background. His writing table was dominated by something resembling an altarpiece—namely, a large and ingenious rack, on which was arranged a battalion of invitations to balls and dinner parties; and his blotting book was flanked by two delicate volumes, one being a *libro d'oro* in the shape of a bulky visiting list, the other being a list of his engagements from day to day. He and his accomplishments were a finished work of art between them. But in a larger world his development would have been no more possible than the development of an orchid in the middle of a crowded street.

And the same is the case with regard to society generally. There are certain accomplishments which a small society tends to develop, and which a larger society does not. Among these the art of conversation is prominent, especially when it takes the form of wit, or becomes the vehicle of certain kinds of humor. I may further illustrate this general observation by mentioning a few individuals, of whom three at least are still well known by name, not to society only, but also to the world at large. These are Constance, Duchess of Westminster; Caroline, Duchess of Montrose, and the Duchess of Somerset, who, as Lady Seymour, was the heroine of the Eglinton Tournament. These ladies were all remarkable for the peculiar magic of their voices and for a peculiar sense of humor which their voices managed to indicate, and which gave its quality to their general views of life. They none of them laughed audibly, but the voice of each was a sort of laugh in solution, and this would produce a sense of laughter in others, even though in the words of the speaker herself there was no special felicity.

The Duchess of Montrose, by the mere tone in

which she mentioned a name, would often convey a whole criticism of the person named; and though her topics and language were not infrequently of a kind which caused austere censors to reprehend, and even to avoid, her, yet if such censors found themselves by chance in her company, they would one and all be listening to her before five minutes was over.

The Duchess of Somerset's voice had the same spell of ambushed laughter in it, but she was a far greater mistress of the actual arts of language, if "art" be a word appropriate to the exercise of natural genius. I was asked by her daughter, Lady Guendolen Ramsden, to help her in compiling a volume of family memoirs, which would, so we hoped, have comprised a number of the Duchess's letters; but most of these had to be discarded as not suitable for publication, because of the numerous sketches contained in them of various friends or connections, which were drawn with a wit and precision worthy of Miss Austen herself in her least merciful moments. One specimen, however, may be given without compunction. She was describing a visit paid by her to a well-known country house, and mentioned that among the company were a prominent statesman and his wife, the former of whom was dear to caricaturists on account of his superabundant figure. "Sir —— and Lady —— are here," she wrote. "She is expecting; but he shows it most."

Here are examples of conversational or descriptive art which, in a large and mixed society, would, even if possible, be hardly so much as perceptible. I may take as two other examples Sophy, Lady Roden, and Lady Dorothy Nevill. Unlike Lady Dorothy, whose chronicled sayings have made her a public character, Lady Roden was known only to a small circle of intimates. She was a daughter of Byron's celebrated friend Mr. Hobhouse, subsequently Lord Broughton, and had received something of a really classical education under the semipaternal auspices of Thomas Love Peacock. Hence her conversation had a certain natural crispness which enabled her to indicate by touches, however light, any oddities of demeanor or conduct on the part of friends or acquaintances to persons whose standards were more or less like her own. There was a silly young woman who, after several years of matrimony, was ambitious of pushing her conquests beyond the matrimonial limits; and with this object in view did her best to be visible driving about with a succession of guiltlessly apathetic admirers. "Poor Mrs. P——," said Lady Roden. "She takes far more trouble in attempting to ruin her reputation than most women do to preserve it; but all her attempts are vain."

Lady Dorothy's charm in conversation was due to an adventurous whimsicality, perfectly natural, which was absent from Lady Roden's. She saw everything through a medium of unexpected analogies. She was one day asked in my hearing whether she had enjoyed herself at a Marlborough House garden party. "My dear," she said, "half of the people there I had never seen before in my life, and of those whom I *had* seen, I thought that half had been safe in Kensal Green." On another occasion, having been at a fancy ball—balls were a kind of entertainment which she very rarely frequented—and having been asked by a friend for an account of it, she replied: "By far away the most remarkable figure was ——. There she was—I don't know what she called herself—Diana in front, and George the Second behind."

But of the conversational art which flourishes in small societies only I could find the best examples, not among women, but among the men of what was then an expiring generation—men whose manners had been formed in a society smaller still. Alfred Montgomery was a wit of this classical type, and may be taken as representing others, all of whom, when I knew them, were verging on old age. These men, though free from any trace of pedantry, were never guilty of slang, unless slang was used intentionally for the purpose of humorous emphasis. Their conversation, if taken down verbatim, would have afforded perfect specimens of polished yet easy English. A lady of great wealth (who has long since been dead, but who shall nevertheless be nameless) had been for a time under some sort of social cloud, many influential people having virtuously refused to notice her. Toward the end of her life, however, the most august of all possible influences had raised her to a position of such fashionable brilliance that a great ball given by her had been the chief event of a season.   Lady Roden asked Alfred Montgomery some question as to who had, and who had not, been there. "When a woman like Mrs.——gives a ball of that kind, it is," he said, "an act of revenge quite as much as an act of hospitality. She takes far more pleasure in thinking of the people she has *not* asked than in thinking of those she has."

Certain other examples of conversational art occur to me which I associate with a form of entertainment now a thing of the past. Of London life as it had been long before I knew it, a notable feature, constantly referred to in memoirs, had been the breakfast party. It had before my time nearly, but had not quite, disappeared. It was so far kept alive by Lord Houghton, at all events, that a breakfast at his house in Bruton Street is one of my own early recollections. The repast began at ten and lasted for half the morning. There must have been about twenty guests. Two of them were "lions," whose hair was more remarkable than their speech. The rest were men of some sort of social eminence, who seemed to find the occasion not wholly congenial; and, in spite of the efforts of the host, conversation had a tendency to languish till a topic turned up which was then attracting public notice. This topic roused one of the guests—a seasoned man of the world—from a mood of apparent apathy into one of such humorous animation that soon the rest of the company were holding their breaths to listen to him. The topic in question was a volume of scandalous memoirs which had lately been published by Rosina, wife of the first Lord Lytton, for the purpose of attacking a husband from whom she had long been separated. The guest to whom I am now alluding caught the attention of everybody by confessing to an intimate acquaintance with the ways of this caustic lady, and proceeded to illustrate them by a series of amusing anecdotes of which I recollect the following:

Bulwer Lytton, as he then was, was candidate for one of the divisions of Hertfordshire, and speeches were being delivered from the hustings by supporters of local influence—among others by Lord Cowper. Lord Cowper was still speaking when something appeared at his elbow in the likeness of the candidate's wife. "Now, Billy Cowper," she said, "we've listened to you long enough. Sit down, and let *me* speak. You propose, gentlemen, to send my husband to Parliament. I am here to tell you that Parliament is not the proper place for him. His proper place," she said, pointing to the ground, "is below; and when you have sent him there, he will learn something of what he at present knows nothing. That something is Justice."

On another occasion, speaking in more moderate tones, she observed to a circle of acquaintances: "My husband is a man who has been born out of his due time. He ought to have been born nineteen hundred years ago. Had he been born then, he would have been Judas Iscariot. He would have betrayed his Master; he would have taken the thirty pieces of silver; but then he would not have hanged himself—far from it. He would have sat down and written the Epistle to the Ephesians."

On another occasion she told the following story of him. He was, so she said, in London, and she, having been left in the country, had written to propose joining him. He had at once replied begging her not to do so, but to leave him a little longer in the enjoyment of philosophic solitude. "When I heard that"—so she confided to a friend—"I set off for London instantly; and there I found him with Philosophic Solitude, in white muslin, on his knee."

"Perhaps," added the narrator, "even less agreeable to the delinquent would have been, had he heard it, her description of his physical appearance. Alluding to the fact that his head was undoubtedly too large for his body, she said, 'My husband has the head of a goat, and he has the body of a grasshopper.'"

But of all the men who, in the way of conversational wit or otherwise, figure in my memory as types of a now vanished generation, the most remarkable still remains to be noticed. This was the second Duke of Wellington. Even to those who knew him only by sight he was memorable, on account of his astonishing likeness to the portraits or statues of his father. He had not, or he had not chosen to cultivate, the talents which mainly lead to distinction in public life, but by the small circle of those who were intimate with him during his later days he was known for a humor, a polished wit, and a shrewdness which made him, of all possible companions, one of the most delightful. I knew him intimately myself as far as my age permitted. I often stayed with him at Strathfieldsaye, not only when he had parties, but also when, as sometimes happened, we were together for a week alone. On these latter occasions I had all the mornings to myself, and every afternoon I took with him long walks, during which he poured forth his social or other philosophies, or else told me stories of his father so pointed and numerous that, had I written them down, I might then have compiled a life of him which would form a very interesting supplement to those which exist already. I never, in the course of these walks, experienced a dull moment.

The only great entertainment at which I ever encountered him was a dinner party of his own given at Apseley House. During one of such visits which I paid him at Strathfieldsaye he told me that very soon he would have to give a party in London in honor of the King of the Belgians. The party was to be a large dinner, and he asked me to be one of the company. The time arrived. The King of the Belgians for some reason failed to come, but everything had been arranged in an appropriate manner for his reception. As a spectacle the table was note-worthy. It was covered with gold plate—a his-toric monument to the great hero of Waterloo—which consisted of figures of soldiers, horses, palm trees, camels, artillery, and other military objects symbolical of his various campaigns; and gold plate at intervals all round the table was supplemented by triumphal wreaths. The duke told me afterward that all these decorations were due to his own for-getfulness. He had for years been accustomed to celebrate the anniversary of the battle of Waterloo by a banquet to certain officers who had been present at it, and who still survived; but the number of these had already been so reduced that he had de-termined to discontinue the celebration. In fixing, however, a day for the dinner now in question, he had entirely forgotten that the date ultimately chosen was none other than the day of the great battle. His servants had concluded that, in honor of Belgian royalty, he was giving one more repetition of the Waterloo banquets of the past. Everything had been arranged accordingly; and I was thus pres-ent at a function which will never take place again.

But it was not at such functions that his real character displayed itself. This only came out in intercourse of a much more private kind, as would happen at Strathfieldsaye when he entertained par-ties of not more than ten people. When I was present on such occasions I was usually the youngest —by far the youngest—member of the company.

Of the rest I may mention as examples Lady Dorothy Nevill, Alfred Montgomery, Sir Hastings Doyle, Lord Calthorpe, Sir St. George Foley, Lady Chesterfield, and Mr. Newtons, the courtly police magistrate, called by his friends "The Beak." And here—to repeat in substance the observation which I have made already—what always struck me was the far greater polish of manner that prevailed among these my elders than any which was cultivated among my own, the then rising, generation. In such an atmosphere the Duke's special gifts were at home. He never strained after effect. His words seemed to crystallize into wit or poignant humor before he had time to reflect on what he was going to say. But these qualities were perhaps seen at their best in tête-à-tête encounters or correspondence. At all events, it is from such occurrences that illustrations of them can be most readily drawn.

He had often spoken to me of his dislike of anything in the nature of jobbery, and this was once brought out in a very characteristic way by a passage at arms between himself and Lady St. Helier. Lady St. Helier had written to him to ask him if, as Lord Lieutenant of Middlesex, he would make one of her friends a magistrate. The duke promptly replied that her friend was an entire stranger to him, and that he never made appointments of that kind as a favor to some third party. There the matter rested for a week or two, at the end of which period she received the following note from him:

Dear Lady St. Helier.

You have treated me extremely ill. I have made inquiries about your friend, and I find he is part-proprietor of—here he named a certain place of amusement—which I learn is frequently used as a place for assignations of a very reprehensible kind.

Lady St. Helier's immediate reply was this:

My dear Duke.

I have nothing more to say. You are acquainted with such matters so much better than I am.

Not long afterward he met her on somebody's doorstep, and she, who was taking her departure, greeted him with some slight frigidity. He merely looked at her with a momentary twinkle in his eye, and said, "I think you had me there." Some days later she received yet another letter from him, which consisted of these words:

Dear Lady St. Helier.

The deed is done. God forgive me.

A further encounter took place of something the same kind—the duke himself told me of this—from which he emerged the victor. He had, he said, received a letter from Lady Herbert of Lee, in which she begged him to contribute £100 toward the total required for the restoration of some Catholic church, and his answer had been as follows:

Dear Lady Herbert.

I shall be very happy to give you the sum you name, for a purpose so excellent as yours. At the same time I may say that I am myself about to restore the Protestant church at Strathfieldsaye, and I do not doubt that you will aid me by sending me a similar sum. Only, in that case, I think no money need pass between us.

In a kindred vein was his answer to another application, addressed to him, in formal terms, by a committee of the inhabitants of Tiverton. When the first duke was merely known as a soldier, the Tivertonians had begun to erect, on a neighboring hill near Wellington, a monumental column in his honor; but subsequently, when he came to show himself to the British public, not as a great general, but as an obstinate and intolerable Tory, the Radical Tivertonians refused to carry on the work farther. The column was left unfinished, as it stands at the present day; and the second duke, many years later, was petitioned, for the credit of the neighborhood, to finish it at his own cost. His answer to the petitioners was, so he told me, this:

GENTLEMEN.

If I were to finish that monument it would be a monument to nothing. As it stands, it is a monument to your own ingratitude.

Strathfieldsaye may have been in old days the scene of many political incidents. The latest was one at which I myself was present. The heroine of it was Miss Meresia Nevill, Lady Dorothy's daughter, who afterward achieved renown as a luminary of the Primrose League. She was then in her novitiate only, and the duke one morning whispered to her that he would give her a lesson in oratory.

I was asked to be present at it, but otherwise it was to be strictly secret. Accordingly after breakfast she, I, and the duke met by appointment in the library. The doors were locked, and Miss Nevill, who had brought some memoranda with her scribbled on a half-sheet of letter paper, was told by the duke to take her stand on the hearth rug and give him a specimen of her powers by declaiming what she proposed to say, he himself being seated on a sofa watching her. "Now," he said, "begin." Bashfully consulting her notes, and speaking with apologetic rapidity, Miss Nevill began to murmur, "My lords, ladies and gentlemen." "No!" ejaculated the duke; "my dear young lady, no! Mouth it out like this: "My lords—ladies—and—gentlemen. Don't say it as if you were saying your prayers." In this humorous but most admirable advice there was no great verbal brilliance; but his tendency to verbal brilliance showed, on one occasion at all events, how capable it was of translating itself into the highest form of literary art. A favorite amusement of his was making translations from Horace. Among the passages which had specially provoked this enterprise was one the Latin of which is so terse and pungent that it has often been pronounced untranslatable. It is the passage in which Horace describes true happiness as that of the man who, looking back from to-morrow, is able to say, "I was really alive all yesterday." Dryden's pithy version of it is to the effect that the sole true happiness is that of the man:

> Who, secure at eve, can say,
> "To-morrow, do thy worst, for I have lived to-day."

The duke's version was on a yet higher level than this, embodying in it a concentrated pungency and a *curiosa felicitas* which were quite in the vein of Horace, but contain a thought not present in the original. They were comprised in these few words:

> Happy if only I enjoy
> My rival's envy for a day.

It is true this specimen of the duke's wit in literature does not bear directly on the question of wit in social conversation; and yet it may lead the mind to questions which are very closely akin to it. The felicity of the duke's translation has a very close resemblance to the *curiosa felicitas* of Pope—for instance, in his "Characters of Women" and his celebrated satire on Addison. Nearly all Pope's satires are addressed, if not to a small society, yet at all events to a small public, and outside that limited body they would have neither vogue nor meaning.

CHAPTER VII

VIGNETTES OF LONDON LIFE

Byron's Grandson and Shelley's Son—The World of Balls—The "Great Houses," and Their New Rivals—The Latter Criticized by Some Ladies of the Old Noblesse—Types of More Serious Society—Lady Marian Alford and Others—*Salons* Exclusive and Inclusive—A Clash of Two Rival Poets—The Poet Laureate —Auberon Herbert and the Simple Life—Dean Stanley— Whyte Melville—"Ouida"—"Violet Fane"—Catholic Society —Lord Bute—Banquet to Cardinal Manning—Difficulties of the Memoir-writer—Lord Wemyss and Lady P—— —Indiscretions of Augustus Hare—Routine of a London Day—The Author's Life Out of London

THE few portraits and anecdotes which I have just sketched or recorded are sufficient, let me say once more, to illustrate two general facts. They indicate the way in which society owes much of its finer polish to it. They emphasize the fact that, when I first knew it myself, it was very much smaller than it has since then become, and, though divided into sections even then, was very much more cohesive. Let me pass from this latter fact to some of my own experiences as connected with it.

For young men who are already equipped with influential friends or connections, a society which is relatively small and more or less cohesive is in some ways more easy of access than one which is more numerous, but in which, unless their means are ample enough to excite the competitive affection of mothers, they are more likely to be lost. In this respect I may look on myself as fortunate, for my circle of acquaintances very rapidly widened as soon as, having done with Oxford, I began to stay in London for more than a week at a time, and secured a habitation, more or less permanent, of my own. While I was first looking about for one which I thought would be suitable, Wentworth returned the hospitality which I had previously shown him at Oxford by putting me up for a fortnight at his house on the Chelsea Embankment, and during this visit an incident took place which, if merely judged by the names of the few persons concerned in it, might be thought picturesquely memorable.

Students of Robert Browning may recollect a short poem of his which begins with the following lines:

> And did you once see Shelley plain?
> And did he stop and speak to you?
> And did you answer him again?
> How strange it seems and true!

My own answer would be, I did not see Shelley plain, but I did the next thing to it. Sir Percy and Lady Shelley—the poet's son and daughter-in-law —were Wentworth's near neighbors, though he never had met either of them. Lady Shelley had been an old friend of my mother's, and I took him one day to tea with her. To the wife of Shelley's son I introduced Byron's grandson. What event could seem more thrilling to any one whose sentiments were attuned to the music of Browning's verses? What really happened was this: Lady Shelley said to me some pleasant things about my mother; we all of us lamented the prevalence of the east wind, and then, having recommended her crumpets, she discussed with Wentworth the various large houses lately built in the neighborhood. At this juncture the drawing-room door opened and the son of the author of "Prometheus Unbound" entered. He was a fresh-looking country gentleman, whose passion was private theatricals. Close to his own house he had built a little private theater, and the conversation turned thenceforward on the question of whether a license would be necessary if the public were admitted by payment to witness the performance of a farce in the interest of some deserving charity.

By the time I left Wentworth's roof I had arranged to share with two Catholic friends a suite of rooms at a private hotel in Dover Street. Both belonged to well-known Catholic families, and had ready access to the world of Catholic gayety, especially in so far as this was represented by balls. One of them, through his skill as a dancer and his buoyant vivacity in conversation, was in much wider request. By the agency of Augustus Savile and others—of "social fairies" (as Lord Beaconsfield called them), such as the Duchess of Sutherland, whom I had known well at Torquay—cards for balls and parties, in quickly increasing numbers, found their way to myself likewise; while in other directions doors were opened also which led to a world of a more serious aspect and character.

Of balls I need say little except to observe that I went to a great many, and so far followed the advice of Lady E—— of T—— that I did not often find myself at a ball "in a two-roomed house." For this the principal reason was that, even from my childhood, I was wanting in any inclination to dance, and thus preferred many-roomed houses in which persons who were so disposed could sit out and converse, the very fact that a ball was in progress being hardly so much as perceptible. In this connection I may observe that, during my earlier days, the principal balls were still to a certain extent those which were given in houses famous for their traditions and their magnitude, such as Devonshire House, Bridgwater House, Stafford House, and so forth; but already things were in this respect changing. Newly established families, or families in the act of establishing themselves, had begun to outdo the "great houses" in their lavish expenditure on this kind of entertainment. The center of social gravity was in this respect being shifted. As an illustration of this fact I remember some curt observations made by two ladies who were in the act of bringing out their daughters. Both belonged to families of historical and high distinction, but their means were not equal to their dignity. One of them said, "If

I want to take out my daughter, I have generally to go to the house of someone who is not a gentleman." Another said: "I don't care for London any longer. It seems that the only people who are giving balls to-day are people whose proper business would be to black my boots." Utterances of this kind, though of course greatly exaggerated, were straws which showed the direction in which the wind was blowing.

Let me turn from the world of balls to a *milieu* which is less frivolous, and take certain ladies as types of tendencies which then prevailed in it. It will be enough to mention four, whose houses represented society as, in some ways, at its best. I refer to Mrs. William Lowther, Lady Marian Alford, Louisa, Lady Ashburton (whom I thus group together because their isolated and commanding dwellings stood practically in the same row), and Lady Somers. All these were women of the highest cultivation. They were devoted to art. Mrs. Lowther was herself an artist. Mrs. Lowther and Lady Ashburton, though thorough women of the world with regard to their mundane company, were remarkable for a grave philanthropy which they sacrificed much to practice. Indeed at some of their entertainments it was not easy to tell where society ended and high thinking began. This could not be said of Lady Somers or of Lady Marian. Though in artistic and intellectual taste they equaled the three others, the guests whom they collected about

9

them were essentially chosen with a view to the social charm which wit, manners, or beauty enabled them, as if by magic, to communicate to the passing moment. And here it may be observed conversely that in a world like that of London the art of society depends not on choice only, but also, and no less, on an equally careful rejection, and is for that reason beset by peculiar and varying difficulties. Of these difficulties Lady Marian herself once spoke to me. They had, she said, been lately brought home to her by certain of her friends who had been urging her to give a ball—a suggestion which, for the following reasons, she found herself unwilling to entertain. "It is impossible," she said, "to give a successful ball in London without being very ill-natured to a large number of people. Many of those who would think they had a right to be asked would—though on other occasions no doubt welcome enough—be as much out of place in a ballroom as a man would be in a boat race who could not handle an oar." But she was, so she added, going to make an attempt at reviving a kind of entertainment to which no such difficulties would attach themselves. During the months of the coming winter she proposed to send out cards to all her more intimate acquaintances, announcing that she would always be at home after dinner on a certain day each week, and begging them to give her their company whenever, and as often as, they pleased. A certain number of people— all of them agreeable and distinguished—responded to this appeal; but their number rarely exceeded fifteen or twenty, and Lady Marian was at length bound to admit that the competitive attractions developed by the enlargement of social life were such as to render a revival of the *salon* impossible, even among acquaintances so carefully chosen as her own.

I may, however, advert to another lady who in a certain sense succeeded where Lady Marian failed; but she succeeded by basing her *salon* on a noticeably different principle—namely, that of inclusion, whereas that of Lady Marian was selection. The passport to her drawing-rooms was fame—even fame of the most momentary kinds—and as fame is the meed of very various activities, not all her own charm was sufficient on some occasions to prevent her company from being a clash of illustrious rivals rather than a *reunion* of friends.

Of a clash of this kind I was once myself a witness, though nobody at the moment divined that there was a clash at all. The scene was not in London, but at the lady's house in the country, where a few guests were staying with her for the inside of a week. Two of these guests were poets; we may call them Sir E. and Sir L. The visit coincided with the time of Tennyson's last illness, the reports of which became daily more alarming. The two poets evinced much becoming anxiety, though this did not interfere with the zeal with which one day at luncheon they consumed a memorable plum tart. Next morning

neither of them appeared at breakfast; and when
both of them remained in their bedrooms for the
larger part of the day I came to the prosaic conclusion that the plum tart had been too much for
them. Next morning came the news of Tennyson's
death. The two bards remained in their cells till
noon, after which they both reappeared like men
who had got rid of a burden. The true secret of
their retirement revealed itself the morning after,
when each of two great newspapers, with which
they were severally connected, was found to contain
long columns of elegy on the irreparable loss which
the country had just suffered—compositions im-
plying a suggestion on the part of each of the
elegists that a poet existed who was not unfit to
repair it. That same day after luncheon the two
competitors departed. Our hostess and the other
guests saw them off at the station, and as the train
went on, the elegists were seen waving independent
adieux, one from a first, the other from a third-
class carriage. The successor to the late Laureate
was Mr. Alfred Austin.

I knew Alfred Austin well; and a few words with
regard to him may not be inappropriate here.
Though his poetry has not commanded any very
wide attention, he had more of true poetry in him
than many people imagine. He had all the qualifications of a really great poet except a sustained
faculty for writing really good poetry. He had a
sound philosophic conception of what the scope and

functions of great poetry are; and it would be possible to select from his works isolated passages of
high and complete beauty. But, if judged by his
poetry as a whole, he seems to have been so indolent
or so deficient in the faculty of self-criticism that
for the most part he suffered himself to be content
with language which resembled an untuned piano,
his performances on which were often calculated to
affront the attention of his audience rather than to
arrest and capture it. He once or twice asked me
to make his works the subject of a critical and comprehensive essay. With some diffidence I consented,
and accomplished this delicate task by picking out
a number of his best and most carefully finished
passages, which showed what he could do if he
tried, and how far by pure carelessness he elsewhere
fell short of the standard which he himself had set.
For example, from his "Human Tragedy" I quoted
the following lines, one of which refers to Rome as
a place where "Papal statues arrogantly wave";
while in another, describing a headlong stream, he
says with the utmost complacency that:

> The cascade
> Bounded adown the cataract.

I pointed out that no conceivable feat was so
absolutely impossible for a statue as that of "waving,"
and that, a cataract and a cascade being practically
the same thing, it was impossible that the former
could manage to bound down the latter. My prac-

tical moral, as addressed to the Laureate, was, "Be just to yourself, and the public will be just to you," and the compliment implied in one part of this criticism did much to mitigate the unwelcome tenor of the other.

Many interesting people I used to meet at the house of Mr. Froude the historian. Among these were two relatives of Mr. Froude's second wife—namely, Henry Cowper, one of the most charming conversationalists of his time, Lady Florence Herbert, and, through her, her well-known husband, Auberon. Auberon Herbert was a most singular character. He represented a movement of thought which has since then taken other directions, and would probably now be associated with some form or other of socialism. In one sense he was certainly no socialist. On the contrary, he was an ardent champion of individual freedom, as opposed to the tyranny of the state. He even contended that all taxation should be voluntary, and actually started a journal, mainly written by himself, in support of this agreeable doctrine. He was, however, yet more pertinacious as an advocate of what is now called "the simple life." His wife shared, though she slightly perhaps tempered, his opinions; and when they first set up house together they insisted that all their household—the domestics included—should dine at the same table. After a week's experience, however, of this regime, the domestics all gave warning, and the establishment was reconstructed on a more conventional footing. This counter-revolution had been accomplished before I knew him, and my intimate acquaintance with him began at a great shooting party given at Highclere Castle by Lord Carnarvon, his brother. Neither I nor he were shooters, and while battues were in progress, and guns were sounding daily at no very great distance, he walked me about the park, declaring that modern castles which stood for nothing but the slaughter of half-tame birds were examples of a civilization completely gone astray. In order that I might see what, shorn of its earlier eccentricities, was his personal ideal of a reasonably ordered life, he asked me to stay with him for a week at his own home, Ashley Arnewood, in Hampshire, on the borders of New Forest. In due time I went. His dwelling among the woodlands was of very simple construction. It was a small farmhouse bisected by a flagged passage giving access to four rooms. On the right as one entered was a kitchen, on the left was an apartment which he dignified by the name of a museum, its sole contents being fragments of ancient British pottery which had been dug up in the neighborhood and were here carefully arranged on a large disused mangle. Beyond, and opposite to one another, were a dining room so limited in size that one end of the table abutted on a whitewashed wall, and a sitting room, luxuriously warm, which was furnished with several deep and remarkably comfortable chairs. The carpets consisted of rough coconut matting, and draughts in the bedrooms were excluded by rough red blankets, which did duty as curtains. The evening repast was almost obtrusively a tea rather than a dinner, though, in deference to my own presumably unconverted appetite, I, and I alone, was provided with some kind of meat. I could not help feeling at times that for my host and hostess alike this practice of "the simple life" represented a sacrifice to their principles rather than a complete enjoyment of them, for on several occasions before bedtime they both confessed to a sensation of acute hunger, and made an expedition to some mysterious region from which they returned with substantial parallelograms of bread.

Through the Antony Froudes I also made acquaintance with Lecky, whose nervous shyness in conversation was in curious contrast to his weighty style as a writer, and also with Dean Stanley and Whyte Melville the novelist. Between the two latter there might seem to be little connection, but I was asked to meet them at a little dinner of four, Whyte Melville being specially anxious to ask the Dean's advice. This was not, however, advice of any spiritual kind. Whyte Melville was thoroughly at home in the social world and the hunting field, and had made himself a great name as an accurate describer of both, but he was now ambitious of achieving renown in a new territory. He was planning a novel, *Sarchedon*, a story of the ancient East, and was anxious to learn from the Dean what historical authorities would best guide the Homer of Melton and Market Harborough in reconstructing the world of Bel and Baylon.

In speaking of novels I am led on to mention an authoress whose fame was concurrent with Whyte Melville's, and whose visions of modern society were not altogether unlike his own visions of Babylonia. This authoress was "Ouida." Ouida lived largely in a world of her own creation, peopled with foreign princesses, mysterious dukes—masters of untold millions, and of fabulous English guardsmen whose bedrooms in Knightsbridge Barracks were inlaid with silver and tortoise shell. And yet such was her genius that she invested this phantom world with a certain semblance of life, and very often with a certain poetry also. In some respects she was even more striking than her books. In her dress and in her manner of life she was an attempted exaggeration of her own female characters. For many years she occupied a large villa near Florence. During that time she visited London once. There it was that I met her. She depicted herself to herself as a personage of European influence, and imagined herself charged with a mission to secure the appointment of Lord Lytton as British Ambassador in Paris. With this purpose in view she called one day on Lady Salisbury, who, never having seen her before, was much amazed by her entrance, and was still more amazed when Ouida, in confidential tones, said, "I have come to tell you that the one man for Paris is

Robert." Lady Salisbury's answer was not very encouraging. It consisted of the question, "And pray, if you please, who is Robert?" In a general way, however, she received considerable attention, and might have received more if it had not been for her reckless ignorance of the complexities of the London world. In whatever company she might be in, her first anxiety was to ingratiate herself with the most important members of it, but she was constantly making mistakes as to who the most important members were. Thus, as one of her entertainers —"Violet Fane"—told me, Ouida was sitting after dinner between Mrs. ——, the mistress of one of the greatest houses in London, and a vulgar little Irish peeress who was only present on sufferance. Ouida treated the former with the coldest and most condescending inattention, and devoted every smile in her possession to an intimate worship of the latter. When, however, she was in companies so carefully chosen that everybody present was worthy of her best attention, and so small that all were willing to give their best attention to *her*, she showed herself, so I was told, a most agreeable woman. Thus forewarned as to her ways, I found that such was the fact. I gave for her benefit a little luncheon party at the Bachelors' Club, the only guests whom I asked to meet her being Philip Stanhope and Countess Tolstoy (now Lord and Lady Weardale), Lord and Lady Blythswood, and Julia, Lady Jersey. Ouida arrived trimmed with the most exuberant furs,

Ouida

which, when they were removed, revealed a costume of primrose color—a costume so artfully cut that, the moment she sat down, all eyes were dazzled by the sparkling of her small protruded shoes. In a word, she quite looked the part, and, perceiving the impression she had made, was willing to be gracious to everybody. As we were going upstairs to the luncheon room, this effect was completed. Lady Jersey laid a caressing hand on her shoulder and said: "You must go first. The entertainment is in honor of you." Ouida was here at her best. No one could have been more agreeable and less affected than she.

Her latter years were overclouded by poverty. This was due to her almost mad extravagance—to her constant attempts, in short, to live up to the standards of her own heroines. Had she acted like a sensible woman, she might have realized a very fair fortune. She had many appreciative friends, who gave her considerable sums to relieve her at various times from the pressure of financial difficulties; but they realized in the end that to do this was like pouring water into a sieve. Somebody gave her £250 in London to enable her to pay her hotel bill; but before a week was over she had lavished more than a hundred in turning her sitting room at the Langham Hotel into a glade of the most expensive flowers. She died, in what was little better than a peasant's cottage, at Lucca. Among the ladies to whom she had been introduced in

London was Winifred, Lady Howard of Glossop. A year or so later Ouida wrote me a letter from Florence, saying, "Your name has been just recalled to me by seeing in the *Morning Post* that you were dining the other night with Lady Howard of Glossop, one of my oldest friends." This is an example of the way in which her imagination enabled her to live in a fabric of misplaced facts, for the person through whom she became acquainted with Lady Howard was none other than myself. The next letter I had from her was to say that she was dedicating one of her later books—a volume of essays—to me. The letter did not reach me till after many delays, and I often regret the fact that before I was able, or remembered, to answer it she was dead.

Another authoress well known to me, of whom I have made mention already, was the beautiful "Violet Fane," who, under that pseudonym, published many volumes of poetry. Her actual name was Mrs. Singleton. She afterward became Lady Currie. I first knew her before my London days began, and I dedicated *The New Republic* to her. She was the center of a group of intimates, of whom those who survive must connect her with many of their happiest hours. No one could have combined in a way more winning than hers the discriminations of fashionable life with an inborn passion for poetry. She was perfect in features, slight as a sylph in figure, and her large dark eyes alternately gleamed with laughter and were grave as though she were listening for a voice from some vague beyond. Many of her phrases, when she was speaking of social matters, were like rapiers with the tip of which, as though by accident, she would just touch the foibles of her nearest and dearest friends, the result being a delicate puncture rather than the infliction of a wound.

She first became known as a poetess by a small volume of lyrics called *From Dawn to Noon*, in which, if, as some say, poetry be self-revelation, her success, according to certain of her censors, was somewhat too complete. The same criticism was provoked by her second volume, *Denzil Place*, a novel in blank verse interwoven with songs. Whatever her censors may have said about it, this, from first to last, was a work of real inspiration. Few who have read it will have forgotten the song beginning:

> You gave to me on that dear night of parting
> So much, so little; and yet everything,

or will have failed to recognize the musical ear of one who has given us the liquid melody of two such lines as these:

> The tremulous convolvulus whose closing blue eye misses
> The faint shadow on the dial that foretells the evening hour.

At all events, whatever her merits as a poetess, she was something like a living poem for a certain group of friends, of whom I happened to be one. This group comprised men such as Wilfrid Blunt,

Lord Lytton, Philip Currie, Hamilton Aidé, Frederick Locker, Clair Vyner, Sir Baldwin Leighton, and others, all of whom had in them a natural appreciation of poetry, while some of them were poets themselves. With a more or less intimate, though loosely formed, group like this my memory associates many small gatherings, which generally took the form of dinners, either at "Violet Fane's" own house in Grosvenor Place, or at Hurlingham, or at the "Star and Garter," or at Vyner's house among its gardens and woods at Combe, where we would linger, forgetful of time, and feeling no inclination to join any larger company.

But of all the worlds which, within the world, were more or less self-cohesive and separate, that in which I felt myself most at home was the Catholic. At any entertainment given at a Catholic house the bulk of the guests—perhaps three-fourths of them—would be Catholics. These would be people so closely connected with one another by blood or by lifelong acquaintance as to constitute one large family. Well-born, well-bred, and distinguished by charming and singularly simple manners, they were content to be what they were, and the Darwinian competition for merely fashionable or intellectual brilliance, however prevalent elsewhere, was, with few exceptions, to them virtually unknown. Yet whenever anything in the way of formal pomp was necessary, they were fully equal to the occasion. The well-known dinners given by Mrs. Washington

Hibbert, at which four-and-twenty guests would be seated round a huge circular table, would fill Hill Street with swaying family coaches, on whose hammercloths crests and coronets maintained an eighteenth-century magnitude which the modern world was abandoning, while on certain ecclesiastical occasions Catholic society could exhibit a stateliness even more conspicuous.

On one of these latter occasions I was, as well as I can remember, the only non-Catholic in the company. This was a great luncheon party given by the then Lord Bute in honor of Cardinal Manning. Lord Bute, who was in many ways the most learned of the then recent converts to Catholicism, was, as is well known, the original of *Lothair* in Lord Beaconsfield's famous novel. Lord Beaconsfield's portrait of him was disfigured, and indeed made ridiculous, by the gilding, or rather the tinsel, with which his essentially alien taste bedizened it; but, apart from such exaggerations, there were elements in it of unmistakable likeness, and the entertainment to which I am now referring was, apart from its peculiar sequel, like a page of *Lothair* translating itself into actual life.

The Butes were at that time living at Chiswick House, which they rented from the Duke of Devonshire. The house is a good example of that grandiose classicality which we associate with the eighteenth century, and the saloon in which the guests were assembled provided them with an appropriate background. They were something like thirty in number, and comprised some of the greatest of the then great Catholic ladies. Lord Beaconsfield himself could not have chosen them better. Indeed his Lady St. Jerome was actually there in person. When I entered there was a good deal of talking, and yet at the same time there was something like a hush. I divined, and divined correctly, that the Cardinal had not yet arrived. The minutes went slowly on; the appointed hour was past. At length a sound was heard which seemed to emanate from an anteroom, and presently a figure was solemnly gliding forward —a figure slight, emaciated, and habited in a long black cassock. This was relieved at the throat by one peeping patch of purple, and above the throat was a face the delicate sternness of which was like semitransparent ivory. The company parted, making way for the great Churchman, and then a scene enacted itself which cannot be better described than in the words written many years previously by the author of *Lothair* himself. "The ladies did their best to signalize what the Cardinal was and what he represented, by reverences which a posture-master might have envied and certainly could not have surpassed. They seemed to sink into the earth, and slowly and supernaturally to emerge."

When the banquet was over, and the guests were taking their departure, our host begged me to remain, so that he and I and the Cardinal might have a little conversation by ourselves. We were presently secreted in a small room or closet, and our little talk must have lasted till close upon six o'clock. I half thought for a moment that this might be a planned arrangement so that then and there I might be received into the Roman fold. Matters, however, took a very different course. Under the Cardinal's guidance the conversation almost immediately— how and why I cannot remember—turned to the subject of Spiritualism, and he soon was gravely informing us that, of all the signs of the times, none was more sinister than the multiplication of Spiritualist séances, which were, according to him, neither more nor less than revivals of black magic. He went on to assert, as a fact supported by ample evidence, that the devil at such meetings assumed a corporeal form—sometimes that of a man, sometimes that of a beautiful and seductive woman, the results being frequent births, in the prosaic world around us, of terrible hybrid creatures half diabolic in nature, though wholly human in form. On this delicate matter he descanted in such unvarnished language that the details of what he said cannot well be repeated here. Of the truth of his assertions he obviously entertained no doubt, and such was his dry, almost harsh solemnity in making them that, as I listened, I could hardly believe my ears. Our host, though a model of strictly Catholic devoutness, was, so he told me with a smile when the Cardinal had taken his departure, affected very much as I was. The impression left on both of us was that, in the

Cardinal's character, there must have been a vein of almost astounding credulity—a credulity which would account for the readiness with which, as a social reformer, he adopted on many occasions the wildest exaggerations of agitators.

I was subsequently invited to call on him at the Archbishop's house in Westminster. During the interview which ensued he revealed intellectual qualities very different from those which had elicited a furtive smile even from a Catholic such as his host at Chiswick. We spent most of the morning in discussing the ultimate difficulties, philosophical, historical, and scientific, which preclude the modern mind from an assent to the philosophy of Catholicism. He displayed on this occasion a broadness and a balance, if not a profundity of thought, in which many theologians who call themselves liberals are wanting. He spoke even of militant atheists, such as Huxley and Tyndall, without any sarcastic anger or signs of moral reprobation. He spoke of their opinions, not as sins which demanded chastisement, but simply as intellectual errors which must be cured by intellectual refutation rather than by moral anathemas, and the personal relations subsisting between him and them were relations—so I have always understood—of mutual amity and respect.

Of another prominent Catholic, Wilfrid Ward, the same thing may be said. As a Catholic apologist he was a model of candor and suavity. He was, moreover, a most agreeable man of the world, among his

134

CARDINAL MANNING

accomplishments being that of an admirable mimic. He was, however, best known as an exponent of Catholic liberalism; and, since I am here concerned only with recollections of social life, to dwell on him longer would carry me too far astray.

Out of this last observation there naturally arises another, which relates to anecdotes or short sketches of individuals as a method of social history. For certain reasons the scope of this method is limited. In the first place, the persons whose doings or sayings are commemorated must be persons who, by their position or reputation, are more or less self-explanatory to the ear of the general reader. They will otherwise for the general reader have very little significance. They must also for the most part be dead, so that their susceptibilities may not be wounded by a too free allusion to their doings. Further, the anecdotes told of them must not be to their disadvantage in any way which would wound the susceptibilities of the living. These mortifying restrictions are, for all those who respect them, a deathblow to the most entertaining, perhaps the most instructive, part of what the memoir-writer has to tell. During the last ten years of his life the late Lord Wemyss amused himself by writing memoirs of his own distinguished activities, and on repeated occasions, when I stayed with him for a week in Scotland, he asked me to run my eye over a number of chapters with a view to seeing if any passages which might give offense had been left in them.

A certain number of such had been already struck out by himself, but I very soon found that a considerable number remained. "God bless my soul!" he exclaimed when I pointed them out to him. "You are perfectly right. Let me have a blue pencil instantly." Lady P——, a witty woman of the widest European experience, attempted a similar task. She, too, asked me to look at what she had written, deploring the fact that all the most amusing parts had passed through the fire to the Moloch of an almost excessive caution. Here again I pointed out to the writer passages which had escaped the sacrifice, and which the living would certainly, even if not justifiably, resent—which they would, indeed, resent in exact proportion to their accuracy.

An example of the results which may be achieved by a memoir-writer who neglects this caution is provided by Augustus Hare. Hare was a man possessed of many accomplishments. Like Hamilton Aidé, he was a very remarkable artist. He was also a great teller of stories, and a master in the craft of improving whatever truth there might be in them. By birth and otherwise he was well and widely connected, and was a familiar figure in many of the best-known houses in England. He was an indefatigable writer of memoirs, and of all such writers he was incomparably the most intrepid. The possibility of offending others, even though they might be his hosts and hostesses, had no terrors for him. I was once staying at a country house in Sussex when a

new book by him appeared, and had just been sent
down from Mudie's. I had twice seen its back on a
table, and meant to have looked at it in my bedroom before dressing for dinner; but whenever I
tried to secure it for my own perusal it had disappeared. I heard someone casually say, "Everybody in the house is reading it." I could not but
wonder why. I managed to secure it at last, and set
myself to find out the reason. It did not take long
to find. Hare, a year before, had been staying in
that very house—a house famous for the material
perfection of its equipments. "The servants here,"
so Hare wrote and printed, "are notoriously more
pampered than those in any other house in England,
and their insolence and arrogance is proportionate
to the luxury in which they live." On another occasion he recorded a visit to Castle ——, the family
name of the owners being C——. He summed up
his gratitude to his entertainers in the following pithy
sentence, "Except dear Lady ——, I never could
stand the C——s." Another of his entries was as
follows. Having migrated from the Stanhopes' at
Chevening to a neighboring old house in Kent, he
wrote, "What a comfort it is, after staying with
people who are too clever, to find oneself with people
who are all refreshingly stupid!" If it were not for
the danger of lapsing into indiscretions like these—
indiscretions of which Hare seemed altogether unconscious—interesting anecdotes might be here in-
definitely multiplied.

Even so, however, such anecdotes, no matter who recorded them, would be simply so many jottings which owed their continuity to the fact that, like the stones of a necklace, they happened to be strung on the thread of a single writer's experiences, and in no two cases would this thread be altogether the same. My own experiences of the social life of London, as I knew it in my earlier days, will perhaps best be described in more general terms. In such terms, then, let me speak of it as, foreshortened by time, it now presents itself to my memory.

For me, in my earlier years, the routine of a London day was practically much as follows. A morning of note-writing—of accepting or refusing invitations—was succeeded by a stroll with some companion among the company—the gay and animated company—which before the hour of luncheon at that time thronged the park. Then, more often than not, came a luncheon at two o'clock, to which many of the guests had been bidden a moment ago as the result of some chance meeting. A garden party, such as those which took place at Sion House or at Osterly, would occupy now and again the rest of an afternoon; but the principal business of every twenty-four hours began with a long dinner at a quarter past eight, or sometimes a quarter to nine. For any young man who took part in the social movement, dinner would be followed by two or by more "At Homes." Then, when midnight was approaching, began the important balls, of which any such young man would show himself at an equal number, and dance, eat quails, or sit with a suitable companion under palm trees, as the case might be; while vigilant chaperons, oppressed by the weight of their tiaras, would ask one another, "Who is the young man who is dancing with *my* daughter?" Finally, if the night were fair, young men, and sometimes ladies, if their houses were close at hand, would stroll homeward through the otherwise deserted streets, while the East, gray already, was being slowly tinged with saffron.

If the life of those who play a part in a London season is to be judged by what they do with themselves during a London season itself, it might be reasonably asked (as it *is* asked by morose social critics) how any sensible people can find such a life tolerable. To this question there are several answers. One is that no society of a polished and brilliant kind is possible unless special talents and graces, wide experience, knowledge, and the power that depends on knowledge, enter into its composition and support it in a peculiar manner which does not prevail elsewhere. This fact, however, will be but partly intelligible unless we remember that it is based on, and implies, another—namely, that the society which is identified with the life of a London season represents for those who figure in it, not life as a whole, but merely one phase of a life of which the larger part is of very different kinds, and which elsewhere exhibits very different aspects.

This observation specially applies to the days when London society was in the main an annual ' assemblage of old-established landed families, whose principal homes were in the country, and whose consequence was derived from their rural, not from their urban, associations. Their houses in the country were constantly filled with visitors. Society, in a certain sense of the word, surrounded them even there. But it was a society differing in its habits, and even in its constitution, from that which formed itself in London, and of the total lives of most of the persons composing it, London life represented not more than a quarter. For me, my own annual life as a Londoner rarely exceeded three months out of twelve. Except for these three months, my habits, as they formed themselves after my father's death, were for a long time these: Of the nine other months I spent about two in Devonshire, where by this time, through inheritance, a new home was open to me—Lauriston Hall, overlooking Torbay, whose waters were visible from the windows through a screen of balustrades and rhododendrons. I generally wintered abroad—for the most part on the Riviera—and the rest of my time was occupied in country visits at home, from the South of England and Ireland to the borders of Sutherland and Caithness.

During the months of the London season my immediate preoccupations, superficially at all events, were, no doubt, those of an idler; but even during such periods, as I presently shall have occasion to mention, serious thoughts beset me almost without cessation. Even experiences of human nature which were flashed on me at balls and dinners, through that species of mental polygamy of which society essentially consists, helped me to mature projects which I executed under conditions of greater calm elsewhere. In the following chapter I shall speak of country houses, describing the atmosphere and aspect of some of those which were best known to me, and which I found most favorable to the prosecution of such serious work as I have accomplished in the way of philosophy, of fiction, and of direct or of indirect politics.

CHAPTER VIII

A Few Country Houses of Various Types—Castles and Manor
Houses from Cornwall to Sutherland

THE pleasantest form of society in country
houses—I speak here for myself—is not to be
found on occasions such as that of a great
shooting party or a party for a country ball, but
rather in gatherings of a smaller and more intimate
kind.

As an illustration of my own views in this respect,
I may mention an incident which may appeal, perhaps, to the sympathies of others whose tastes or
distastes are like my own. I was asked to stay in
Shropshire with some friends whom I knew so intimately that they did not care how they treated
me; and on this occasion they had treated me very
ill. As I was approaching my destination by way
of a little local line, I was surprised at seeing on the
platform of one station after another an extraordinary amount of luggage, together with a number
of footmen and unmistakable ladies' maids. What
could be the meaning of this? At last the question
occurred to me: Can it be possible that some county
ball is impending, and that my dear friends mean to
take me to it? My surmise was but too correct.

"Why," I asked my hostess, "didn't you tell me? I would have come when this ball was over." "Yes," she said, "I know that. That's why I did not tell you. We sha'n't let you off, don't think it." I answered, in tones of resignation: "Well, what must be must be." There the matter dropped, till the night of the ball arrived, and the ladies went upstairs to make themselves ready for the festival. I went upstairs likewise, but my proceedings differed from theirs. I took off my coat, lay down on my bed, and covered myself completely in the folds of a great fur rug. Presently came a voice at the door—that of my hostess—saying, in tones of command: "Are you ready? Be quick! We must be going." "I can't come," I answered. "I'm in bed." My hostess saw that I had got the better of her. I heard her laugh the laugh of confessed defeat. As soon as the sound of her wheels told me she was off the premises, I put on my coat, went down to the library, read a novel by the fire, and when she and her friends returned I had a most charming supper with them at three o'clock in the morning.

The ideal society in country houses is, in my opinion, of a kind more or less fortuitous. It consists mainly of persons connected with their entertainers by family ties or long and intimate friendship. Most of the houses to which I am now alluding—some of them great, others relatively small, but most of them built by the forefathers of their present owners—have been houses which represented for me that old order of things with which I was familiar in my own earliest childhood. Family traditions and associations—elements rooted in the soil of a national and immemorial past—such were the factors by which the life of these houses was dominated. Their influence breathed from old portraits—many of them very bad—on the walls; from old carpets and furniture; from rows of forgotten books; from paths by secluded rivers; from labyrinths of bracken and from the movements of noiseless deer. In such houses, except on rare occasions, the company belonged essentially to the same world as their entertainers. They were a nation within a nation, from which the newly arrived magnates of mere London fashion would be absent, while persons obscure in London would be here in their natural element. Everybody here not only knew everybody else, but had known them, or had at least known all about them, always. In this respect society in such country houses generally bore, and still tends to bear, a strong resemblance to Catholic society in London.

But quite apart from these characteristics which depend on similar antecedents, society in a country house possesses advantages which in a London life are, from the nature of the case, impossible. At a fashionable evening party in London a lady, when she talks to a man, gives him generally the impression, as soon as she has exchanged a word with him, that the one wish of her life is to be talking to somebody else. London conversations, even at dinners, when neither party for an hour or so is able to desert the other, are in any case cut short, like chapters of a novel which are torn away from their context. Country-house conversations are like novels which, if laid down at one moment, can be taken up again the next. The atmosphere of London is one of constant excitement. The atmosphere of a country house is one of interest pervaded by repose. Each night there is a dinner party, but there is no going out to dinner, and there is no separation afterward. What is there comparable in London to the sense of secluded parks, or of Scotch or of Irish hillsides, where society is not absent, but is present only as concentrated in the persons of a few individuals, who at happy moments may be temporarily reduced to two, and where all become new beings in new and undisturbed surroundings?

Further, let me observe this—I have here an eye on my own case in particular—that, for an unmarried man with a literary purpose in life, the enjoyment of such society is heightened by the fact—the very important fact—that at any moment he may shut himself up in his bedroom as soon as the housemaids have done with it, and devote himself to his own avocations like a hermit in an African desert. Of such serious work as I have myself accomplished, I have accomplished a large part in hermitages of this description; and the fact that society was never very far away I have usually felt as a stimulus, and very rarely as a disturbance.

Friends have often suggested to me that even persons whose own acquaintance with country houses is extensive might be interested by a description of some that I have known myself. I have indeed known as many of such houses as most people; but no one person can know more than a limited number of them; and even of this limited number I, in a volume like the present, can mention only a few. I will take them in the order in which for geographical or architectural reasons they most readily recur to my own memory. I may begin with two which deserve to be coupled together on account of the positions which they occupy—namely, the extreme northeast of Great Britain in one case, and the extreme southwest in the other. I allude to Dunrobin Castle in Sutherland, and St. Michael's Mount in Cornwall.

The whole population of the great county of Sutherland is hardly so much as two-thirds of the population of Wimbledon, and, except for some minute portions, was, prior to certain recent sales, a single gigantic property. Dunrobin Castle, with a million silent acres of mountain and moor behind it, looks down from a cliff over the wastes of the North Sea, but is on the landward side sheltered by fine timber. At the foot of the cliff are the flower beds of an old-world garden. The nucleus of the house is ancient, but has now been incrusted by great modern additions, the Victorian regime expressing itself in windows of plate glass. But through the plate glass on one side is visible a pre-historic habitation of the Picts and a cavern in which gypsy mothers are even now brought secretly to give birth to their offspring. On the other side are visible the slopes of a barren hill, inhabited till lately by a witch, who gathered herbs by night under the influence of certain planets, and of whose powers even the doctor at Golspie went in half-acknowledged terror. At dinner two pipers played on a landing outside the dining room. So remote is this great house from any center of modern industry that the carts, dogcarts, and wagonettes used by the estate and the family were built and repaired by a staff of men on the premises. My first visit to Dunrobin was in the days of the Duchess Annie. The duke was away on his yacht, but during my visit he re-turned, and the duchess and I went to meet him at the station—a private station in the grounds. Those were the early days of agrarian agitation in the Highlands—an agitation which was vehemently applauded by the Radical press of London. One Radical correspondent reported in tones of triumph that the duke had been openly cursed by his tenants on his own private platform. The nonsensical nature of such statements is sufficiently illustrated by what happened on the occasion here in question. A num-ber of tenants were gathered together on the plat-form for the purpose of receiving the duke, not with curses, but with welcome; and as soon as he had descended from the train an old woman rushed from the throng and very nearly embraced him. "You dear old woman," he said, laying his hand on her shoulder, "you dear old woman, how glad I am to see you again!"

St. Michael's Mount, though less remote than Dunrobin from the modern world in some ways, is more visibly separated from it in another, being, except at times of low tide, an island. It crowns and incases the summit of a veritable island rock. The entrance to it is by a tower the bases of which seem to descend from above and meet the visitor halfway as he toils up a path apparently made for rabbits. Having mounted a hundred stairs, the adventurer is in a comfortable hall, above which are the dining room, once a monkish refectory, and an ancient church, now used as a private chapel. One door of this hall gives access to a large drawing-room, one of whose walls and whose fireplace have been carved out of the living rock. Another gives access to a billiard room, below which the Atlantic breaks at a depth of two hundred feet, and whose granite balconies are grazed by the breasts of ascending sea birds.

Both these houses, which would constantly suggest to me, when I stayed in them, the celebrated words of Keats:

> Magic casements opening on the foam
> Of perilous seas in faery lands forlorn,

are, it is needless to say, exceptions rather than types. Of the others which I may appropriately mention, a few may be taken as belonging to an exceptional class also, on account of their unusual size; and these I may again divide into genuine and ancient castles, as distinct from modern imitations on the one hand, and what are properly palatial villas of the classical type on the other; the remainder being smaller, though often of great magnitude, and commonly known by such names as "halls," "parks," or "manors."

Of more or less genuine castles I have known a considerable number, many of them much smaller than houses less ambitiously named; but, with the possible exception of Alnwick, the interior of which is undisguisedly modern, there is one which, in point of magnitude and continuity of occupation, forms a class by itself. This castle is Raby, which has never been uninhabited since the days of Stephen, when the first smoke wreaths rose from its kitchen chimney. The house is a huge block, rising at intervals into towers, with a small court in the middle of it, across which carriages drive, having passed through a tunnel of arches, and deposit their occupants in a hall, from which stairs, at both ends of it, lead to the various living rooms, among these being an upper hall more than fifty yards in length. This whole block stands in a walled area, entered by a castellated gateway and encircled by a moat, a portion of which still holds water, and in which the towers reflect themselves. When I stayed there as a guest of the Duke and Duchess of Cleveland, an atmosphere of the past not only pervaded the castle, but seemed to extend itself for some miles into the neighborhood. When I and others who had arrived by the same train issued from the station doors, the carriages awaiting us in the twilight comprised old yellow chariots with postilions, like that of my grandfather in which I had swung myself when a child. I said to Augustus Hare, who happened to be one of the party, "One would think that we all of us were going to Gretna Green." When we approached the castle, whose towers were blots in the November evening, I felt we were approaching a castle in a child's fairy tale. In point of magnitude, combined with ancient and absolutely continuous occupation, there is, so far as my own experience goes, no private dwelling in the kingdom which excels, or even equals, Raby. The duchess kept a great album in which each of her guests was asked to inscribe some record of his or of her visit, which record was to take the form of answers to certain printed questions, or of a sketch, or some original verses. I preferred to take refuge in the last, my own metrical record being this:

Some scoff at what was, and some shrink from what may be
  Or is; but they all must be pleased with a place
Where even what was looks enchanting in Raby,
  And where even what is is redeemed by Her Grace.

Apart from genuine castles of feudal type and origin, the greatest houses I have known, if regarded as architectural structures, are Blenheim, Trentham (the Brentham of Lord Beaconsfield's *Lothair*), and Cliveden. In this class I should, perhaps, include also Sir Robert Walpole's Houghton, where I have stayed as the guest of Cora, Lady Strafford, who occupied it for many years as a tenant, and with singular taste and knowledge so arranged the interior that every chair, sideboard, and table then in common use had been Sir Robert Walpole's own. I wrote my letters one morning in his study, at his own writing table, and using his own inkstand. The walls were lined with books, most of them presents from his contemporaries, and some of them extremely curious. I may mention one in particular. It related to the South Sea Bubble, and contained what was practically a list of the largest commercial fortunes existing then in England.

Other houses which in point of magnitude belong to the same group are Stowe, with its frontage of more than a thousand feet, Hamilton Palace, Wentworth Wodehouse, and Eaton. By those whose knowledge is greater than mine, the list, in any case small, might, no doubt, be extended. I speak here only of those at which I have myself stayed. But, in any case, no one, however wealthy, would think of building on a similar scale now. Their magnitude was useful only in days other than ours, when visitors stayed for a month or six weeks at a time, and brought with them their own carriages and the necessary grooms and coachmen. It is only on very

rare occasions that such houses could be even half
filled to-day; and they dwarf, rather than subserve,
the only possible life that a reasonable man could
live in them. Blenheim impresses a visitor as
though it were built for giants. Alfred Montgomery,
when staying for the first time at Eaton, could not,
on coming downstairs, find his way to the breakfast
room till he encountered a friend who guided him.
"Good God!" he exclaimed as he entered the desired
apartment, "I don't want to eat my breakfast in
a cathedral." Mere magnitude, indeed, beyond a
certain point is not a luxury, but an oppression.
The greatest private dwelling ever erected in England is said to have been Audley End, when its
original builder completed it. James I said of it,
"It is a house fit only for a king"; and before it
could be rendered habitable three-fourths of it had
to be pulled down. Such was the verdict of experience on overbuilding in the past; and though many
conditions have changed, a similar practical criticism
is occasionally being pronounced to-day. Trentham
is practically gone. Hamilton Palace, it is said, will
soon exist no longer.

When, however, we turn to genuine castles, pseudo-
castles, or houses which, large though many of them
are, are small as compared with these, my memory
provides me with examples of them which are scat-
tered all over the kingdom, but of which, since they
are types rather than grandiose exceptions, it will for
the moment be enough to describe a few, others

being reserved for mention in connection with particular circumstances.

Of castles other than the greatest, were I asked to name the most romantic which has been known to me as a visitor, and the most agreeable in the way of an ancestral dwelling, I should, I think, begin with Powis, as it stands with its rose-red walls, an exhalation of the Middle Ages, on a steep declivity among the mountainous woods of Wales—woods full of deer and bracken. Much of its painted paneling had never been, when I stayed there, touched or renovated since the time of the battle of Worcester. In a bedroom which had once been occupied by Charles I there was hardly a piece of furniture which was not coeval with himself. The dining room, as I remember it, had been frescoed by a Dutch artist in the reign of William and Mary.

In respect of mere romantic situation, the English house which I remember as coming nearest to Powis is Glenthorne, the seat of the Hallidays, which not so very long ago was thirty miles from a railway on one side, and seventeen on another. It fronts the Bristol Channel on the confines of Devon and Somerset. I have described it accurately in my novel *The Heart of Life*. In its general aspect it resembles my own early home, Denbury, but in some ways it is quite peculiar. In front of it is an Italian garden, below which are breaking waves, and behind it precipitous woods rise like a wall to an altitude of more than twelve hundred feet. The only approach to the house is by a carriage drive three miles long, which descends to it in zigzags from the upper world of Exmoor.

Hardly less romantic is Ugbrooke, the seat of the Cliffords, about twelve miles from Torquay, associated with the name of Dryden, who was a frequent guest there, and haunted by the Catholicism of a long series of generations. The chapel is approached through, and transmits its incense to, a library which hardly contains a book more recent than the days of the nonjurors, and I have often spent long mornings there examining the files of journals belonging to the epoch of Queen Anne, of the first two Georges, and of Pope. I have kindred recollections of Lulworth Castle in Dorsetshire, where the old religious regime so casts its spell over everything that I should hardly have been surprised if a keeper, encountered in the twilight park, had turned out to be carrying, not a gun, but a crossbow.

Of other houses connected with Catholic memories I may mention two in Yorkshire—Everingham Park and Houghton, then the respective homes of the late Lord Herries and his kinsman, Mr. Charles Langdale. Both were hereditary and absolutely unquestioning Catholics; and, strange to say, a large part of their tenantry were hereditary Catholics also. Each of these houses has a great chapel attached to it, and every Sunday processions of farmers' dogcarts would deposit their occupants at doors the decorations of which plainly showed that for these stalwart Englishmen the Protestant Reformation was no more than a dream.

But putting the question of Catholic atmosphere aside, and reverting once more to castles, I may begin with a mention of Chillingham, sheltered by the shadowy woods and surrounded by the moors of Northumberland.

As compared with Alnwick, Chillingham is a small structure. Apart from some offices added during the nineteenth century, it occupies an area measuring a hundred and twenty feet by a hundred. The outer walls are of enormous thickness, with a tower at each corner; and against these outer walls the rooms which constitute the dwelling, much less massive in their masonry, are built round a small court. They have hardly been altered since the days of Inigo Jones. When I stayed there with Sir Andrew Noble, who for many years was Lord Tankerville's tenant, the whole of the furniture seemed to have grown old with the house. The most modern contents of the bookshelves were the novels of Mrs. Radcliffe, whose faded backs would grow young again in the flickering warmth of fires. Beneath the external windows were the box borders of a garden, and visible on distant slopes were the movements of wild cattle.

Another castle with which I was very familiar was Elvaston, near Derby, where year after year I stayed with the late Lord and Lady Harrington. Originally a red-brick manor house, it was castellated in the days of Wyatt; and though architects of to-day would smile at its artificial Gothic, it may now for this very reason be regarded as a historical monument. It is a monument of tastes and sentiments which have long since passed away. It represents not only a vanished taste in architecture, but sentiments also which are now even more remote. The Earl of Harrington, under whom the Gothic transfiguration was accomplished, seems to have regarded himself as a species of knight-errant. Round the fluted pillars by which the roof of the hall is supported—a hall which he christened "the Hall of the Fair Star"—were strapped imitation lances, and the windows were darkened by scrolls which all bore the same motto, "Loyal to Honor and to Beauty." This Lord Harrington had married a very beautiful wife, for whose pleasure he surrounded the house with a labyrinth of clipped yew hedges, the trees having been brought full grown from every part of England. Animated by a romantic jealousy, he never permitted this lady to stray beyond the park gates, and a little pavilion at the end of a yew avenue contains, or contained till lately, a curious something which is a vivid revelation of his mind. It consists of an image in plaster of Paris of his ladylove, together with one of himself kneeling at her feet and gazing at her, his hands being about to commit his adoration to the strings of a guitar. The Lord Harrington of my time, whose death is a still recent event, was associated with the huntsman's horn rather than with the strings of a troubador, and with the accouterments of the polo-field rather than with spears and lances. Lord Harrington, though his ruling passion was sport, was a man of wide information, expert as a mechanical engineer, and possessed alike in disposition and manner that rare kind of geniality which almost amounts to genius, and made all with whom he came in contact—even the Derbyshire miners—his friends.

The mention of Elvaston carries my thoughts to Cardiff. Cardiff Castle till late in the nineteenth century was mainly, though not wholly, ruinous, and some decades ago it was, at enormous expense, reconstructed by the late Lord Bute. All the lore of the architectural antiquarian was ransacked in order to consummate this feat. Indeed the wealth of detail accumulated and reproduced by him will be held by many people to have defeated its own ends. Ornaments, carvings, colorings, of which ancient castles may severally offer single or a few specimens, were here crowded together in such emphatic profusion as to fill the mind of the spectator with a sense of something novel rather than of anything antique. In a certain spectacular sense Cardiff Castle is large, but for practical purposes it is very much the reverse. I stayed there—and this was my first introduction to Wales—for the Eisteddfod, of which for that year Lord Bute was the president. The house party on the occasion comprised only eight persons, and there was, so I gathered, no room for more. Lord Bute was by temperament a man of extreme shyness, who naturally shrank from obtruding his own person in public, but on this occasion he rose to a full sense of his obligations. He prepared and delivered an address, most interesting and profoundly learned, on Welsh musical history. He and his house party were conveyed to the place of meeting in quasi-royal carriages, preceded and followed by outriders, and for a series of nights he provided the inhabitants of the town with balls, concerts, or entertainments of other kinds. No host could have been more gracious than he. On the last night of my visit there was a gathering practically private. The heroine of this was old Lady Llanover, who, though not a native of Wales, was an enthusiast for all things Welsh. She had brought with her in her train a bevy of her own female domestics, who wore steeple-crowned hats, and also an old butler dressed up like a bard. These were all arranged on a daïs, and sang national melodies; and when the performance was finished Lord Bute, with a charming smile, presented Lady Llanover with a ring. This bore on its large gem an engraving of a Welsh harp, below which was the motto in Welsh, "The language of the soul is in its strings."

Among my fellow guests at the Castle was a singularly interesting personage—Mr. George Clark of Talygarn. Mr. Clark, in alliance with Lord Wimborne, played a prominent part in the development of the Dowlais steel works, and he was at the same time one of the greatest genealogists and heraldic antiquarians of his day. I was intimate with him till his death, and have been intimate with his family ever since.

Apart from St. Michael's Mount, there are two old houses in Cornwall which year after year I visited for some part of December, proceeding thence to a third for a Christmas gathering in Worcestershire, and to a fourth—this was in Yorkshire—for the celebration of the New Year.

The Cornish houses of which I speak were Heligan, near Mevagissy, the home of the John Tremaynes, and Trevarthenick, near Truro, the home of Sir Louis and Lady Molesworth. Pale externally with the stucco of more than a hundred and fifty years ago, neither of these substantial houses has any resemblance to a castle; but the ample rooms and staircases, the dark mahogany doors and the far-planted woods of each represented in some subtle way the Cornish country gentlemen as they were in the days before rotten boroughs were abolished. Within a few miles' radius of Trevarthenick were two little agricultural townlets, hardly more than villages, which together were represented in those days by four members of Parliament. Old Lady Molesworth, Sir Louis's remarkable mother, who when she was ninety-five was as vigorous as most women of sixty, looked on any landowner as a parvenu who had not been a territorial magnate before the days of Henry VIII. When I think of these people and their surroundings I am reminded of an opinion I

once expressed to an artist well known as a luminary
of some new school of painting. When I met him
at the house of a friend he told me that he had
abandoned painting, and was applying his artistic
principles to the manufacture of furniture. He
kindly explained to me in somewhat technical
language what the principles of the new art as applied to furniture were. I apologized for my inability to understand them, and confessed to him
that my own taste in furniture was not so much
artistic as political, and that the kind of chair, for
example, which gave me most satisfaction was one
that had been made and used before the first Reform
bill.

The houses already referred to as successive
scenes of Christmas and New Year visits were
Hewel Grange, Lord Plymouth's, near Bromsgrove,
and Byram, Sir John Ramsden's, about twenty
miles from York.

Hewel Grange, which has taken the place of an
old house, now abandoned, is itself entirely modern.
Of all the considerable houses built in England during
the last thirty years, it is, so far as I know, the most
perfect as a specimen of architecture. Externally
its style is that of the early seventeenth century, but
its great hall is a monument of Italian taste subdued
to English traditions and the ways of English life.
New though the structure is, the red sandstone of
its walls and gables has been already so colored by
the weather that they look like the growth of cen-

turies, and whatever is exotic in the interior carries the mind back to the times of John of Padua.

To pass from Hewel to Byram was to pass from one world to another, though both were saturated with traditions of old English life.   Byram, standing as it does in a territory of absolutely flat deer park, gives, with its stuccoed walls and narrow, oblong windows, no hint of intended art.   Parts of it are of considerable age, but it represents as a whole the dignified utilitarianism of the Yorkshire country gentleman as he was from a hundred to two hundred years ago. Sir John himself, familiar with political office, accomplished as a classical scholar, and endowed with one of the most charming of voices, was of all country gentlemen the most perfect whom it has ever been my lot to know.   He was cradled in the traditions of Whiggism, and to me one of his most delightful attributes was inability to assimilate the spirit of modern Liberalism, whether in the sphere of politics or of social or religious thought.

With Byram my memory associated two neighboring houses—Fryston, then the home of Lord Houghton, and Kippax, that of the Blands.   Fryston was filled with books, and it was in my early days constantly filled with celebrities, generally of a miscellaneous, sometimes of an incongruous, kind.   Sir John Ramsden told me that once, when he had been asked to dine there for the purpose of meeting some bishop whose name he could not read (for Lord Houghton wrote a very illegible hand), the most

reverent of the assembled guests could hardly for-
bear from smiling when their host, having left them
for a moment, came back bringing the bishop with
him.   The bishop was a negro, with a face as black
as his own silk apron.

Kippax, which is close to Fryston, was, in the
eighteenth century, a fairly large, but not notably
large, building, but when Lord Rockingham began
the construction of Wentworth the late Mr. Bland's
ancestor declared that, whatever happened, he would
not be outbuilt by anybody, and that Kippax, in
spite of Wentworth, should be the longest house in
Yorkshire.   He accordingly extended its frontage by
the addition of two wings, which really were for the
most part a succession of narrow outbuildings
masked by classical walls of imposing and balanced
outline, the result being that a dwelling which is
practically of very moderate dimensions confronts
the world with a façade of more than seven hundred
feet.

A house differing in character from any of those
just mentioned is Stanway, where I have stayed as
the guest of the then Lady Elcho. It variegates
with its pointed gables the impending slopes and
foliage of the outlying Cotswold Hills.   It is a beautiful building in itself—but the key to its special
charm was for me to be found in certain pictures,
void of all technical merit, and relegated to twilight
passages—pictures representing, with an obvious
and minute fidelity, scenes from the life lived there

during the times of the first two Georges. One of these shows the milkmaids going home from their work arrayed in striped petticoats, and carrying their milk pails on their heads. Others show members of the family enjoying themselves in the garden or setting out for a ride, while the clergyman of the parish, or the chaplain, is pacing one of the walks in solitary meditation, with a telescope under his arm.

At Lyme, in Cheshire, the ancient home of the Leghs, which owes its present magnificence to Leone, the Georgian architect, by whom Chatsworth was renovated, other pictures of a similar kind abound. In the days of the first Lord Newton I visited Lyme frequently, and was often late for breakfast because as I went through the passages I could not detach myself from a study of these appealing records.

Of houses no less typical of the country life of England I can give a further example without quitting the Cotswolds. I allude to Sherborne—the late Lord Sherborne was one of my earliest friends—with its two principal frontages enriched by Inigo Jones with clusters of Corinthian columns—a house still happily remote from railways and towering chimneys. The late Lady Sherborne, like the Duchess of Cleveland at Raby, kept an album, to which, whenever she could, she extorted a contribution in verse or otherwise from her friends. My own contribution on one occasion was this—it was written at the close of a visit at Whitsuntide:

When June fevers London with riot,
  I regretfully dream of the day
When shadow and sunshine and quiet
  Were alive in your woodlands in May.

I remember your oaks and your beeches.
  I remember the cuckoo's reply
To the ring dove that moaned where the reaches
  Of the Windrush are blue with the sky.

Of country houses which I have known in Scotland I shall speak later, in connection with extraneous incidents. Of such houses in Ireland, of which I have known several, it will be enough to mention one. This is Tullamore in County Down, the home of Strange, Lord Roden and Lady Roden, to the latter of whom I have referred already. It is from my visits at Tullamore that most of my knowledge of Ireland, such as it is, is derived. For many successive years I spent at Tullamore most of the early autumn. There were a few other old friends whom, in addition to myself, Lady Roden was accustomed to ask for similar periods, while the company was constantly augmented by others, mostly Irish, who stayed there for several days. Among these was Mrs. Ronalds—one of the most popular of the American ladies of London, who spent most of her autumn with her daughter, Mrs. Ritchie, at Belfast. More kindly and accomplished entertainers than Lord and Lady Roden it would not be easy to imagine. Tullamore stands among great beech woods and gardens on one side of a valley, at the bottom of which, half hidden by rhododendrons, an amber-colored stream descends in waterfalls to the sea. The slopes opposite to the house are thickly fledged with larches up to a certain height, when they suddenly give place to the wildness of the Mourne Mountains. The house externally is of more or less modern aspect, but within, when I knew it, it was full of fine family portraits, books, and old collections of china, together with certain other objects which appealed to the sense of history rather than to that of art. The Rodens having been among the chief of the Orange families of Ireland, a series of cabinets which stood in a long gallery would be found on examination to contain a collection of engraved wineglasses, each of which bore the inscription "God save King William," or else "To Hell with the Pope." I remember also that a number of fine Dutch mirrors, which were plainly designed for ladies in the act of doing their hair, had been rendered useless for this important purpose by the fact that the whole of their surfaces were covered by delineations of King William on horseback, gesticulating at the battle of the Boyne.

Such sketches of the country houses that have been known to me might be very easily multiplied—houses of which, whenever I think of them, memories come back to me like the voices of evening rooks. But these will be sufficient, so far as England and Ireland are concerned, to illustrate certain portions of my life other than that of London, and I will for the moment turn from those portions to others, which were spent by me for many years not at home, but abroad.

Not long after my Oxford career was ended, a family with which I was closely connected was, in consequence of the illness of one of its members, advised by doctors to pass the winter at Cannes, and, as soon as my friends were settled there, I was asked to go out and join them. A diminutive villa next to their own was secured for me. Its windows opened on an equally diminutive garden, in which orange trees with their golden globes surrounded a spurting fountain, while, rising from the depths of a great garden below—a garden pertaining to a villa built like a Moorish mosque—were the tall spires of cypresses and the yellow clouds of mimosa trees. In this hermitage, which seemed, under southern moons, to open on a world like that of *The Arabian Nights*, I remained for about two months, and wrote there the later portions of my book *Is Life Worth Living?* Social life at Cannes had all the charm and none of the constant unrest of London, and its atmosphere so enchanted me that I spent for many years the best part of my winters on the Riviera, though I subsequently varied my program by a month or so at Pau or Biarritz, and more than once at Florence. On later occasions, of which I shall speak hereafter, I went farther afield, and saw something of what life was like in an old Hungarian castle; in the half-Gothic dwellings and arcaded

courts of Cyprus; in the drawing-rooms of Fifth
Avenue; and also on the shores of Lake Michigan,
along which the great esplanade of Chicago now
extends itself for more than eleven miles.

Of my experiences in foreign countries, just as of
those in Scotland, I shall have to speak again; but I
will first return to those portions of my early life
which, with the exception of an annual few months
in London, I spent for the most part on the Riviera,
in Italy, or in Devonshire, or in country visits at
houses such as those which I have just mentioned,
and I will record what, beneath the surface, my life
and my mental purposes in these often-changed
scenes were.

CHAPTER IX

FROM COUNTRY HOUSES TO POLITICS

First Treatise on Politics—Radical Propaganda—First Visit to the Highlands—The Author Asked to Stand for a Scotch Constituency

THE sketches which I have just given of my purely social experiences may seem, so far as they go, to represent a life which, since the production of *The New Republic*, was mainly a life of idleness. I may, however, say, without immodesty, that, if taken as a whole, it was the very reverse of this. Whether the results of my industry may prove to have any value or not, nobody could in reality have been more industrious than myself, or have prosecuted his industry on more coherent lines.

I have already given some account of *The New Republic*, indicating its character, its construction, the mood which gave rise to it, and the moral it was intended to express. This moral—the fruit of my education at Oxford, and also of my experiences of society before I became familiar with the wider world of London—was, as I have said already, that without religion life is reduced to an absurdity, and that all philosophy which aims at eliminating religion and basing human values on some purely natural substitute is, if judged by the same standards, as absurd as those dogmas of orthodoxy which the naturalists are attempting to supersede. With the purpose of emphasizing this contention in a yet more trenchant way, I supplemented, as I have said already, *The New Republic* by a short satirical romance, *Positivism on an Island*, in the manner of Voltaire's *Candide*. My next work, *Is Life Worth Living?* in which I elaborated this argument by the methods of formal logic, was largely due to that wider knowledge of the world with which social life in London and elsewhere had infected me. The bitterest criticism which that work excited was based on the contention that the kind of life there analyzed was purely artificial, and unsatisfying for that very reason—that the book was addressed only to an idle class, and that from the conditions of this pampered minority no conclusions were deducible which had any meaning for the multitude of average men. Some such objection had been anticipated from the first by myself. I was already prepared to meet it, and my answer was in brief as follows, "If life without a God is unsatisfying, even to those for whom this world has done its utmost, how much more unsatisfying must it be to that vast majority for whom a large part of its pleasures are, from the nature of things, impossible." But a closer and wider acquaintance with the kind of life in question, and the sorrows and passions masked by it, prompted me to translate the argument of the three books just mentioned into yet another form—namely, that of a tragic novel—*A Romance of the Nineteenth Century*.

This book was attacked by the apostles of non-religious morality with a bitterness even greater than that which had been excited in them by *Is Life Worth Living?* And with these critics were associated many others, who, whether they agreed or disagreed with its purely religious tendencies, denounced it because it dealt plainly with certain corruptions of human nature, the very mention of which, according to them, was in itself corrupting, and was an outrage of the decorums of a respectable Christian home. Since those days the gravest reviews and newspapers have dealt with such matters in language far more plain and obtrusively crude than mine, and often displaying a much more restricted sense of the ultimate problems connected with them. Certain critics, indeed—among whom were many Catholic priests, with the experience of the confessional to guide them—took a very different line, and welcomed the book as a serious and valuable contribution to the psychology of spiritual aspiration as dependent on supernatural faith.

Put briefly, the story of the novel is this. The heroine, who is young, but not in her first girlhood, has in her aspect and her natural disposition everything that is akin to the mystical aspirations of the saint; but, more or less desolated by the diffused skepticism of the day, she has been robbed of innocence by a man, an old family friend, and has never been at peace with herself or wholly

170

escaped from his sinister power since. The hero, who meets her by accident, and with whom she is led into a half-reluctant friendship, has at first no suspicion of the actual facts of her history, but believes her troubles, at which she vaguely hints, to be due merely to the loss of religious beliefs which were once her guide and consolation. He accordingly does his best, though deprived of faith himself, to effect in her what Plato calls "a turning round of the soul," and hopes that he may achieve in the process his own conversion also. For aid in his perplexities he betakes himself to a Catholic priest, once a well-known man of the world, and calls her attention to the immortal passage in St. Augustine, beginning, "If to any the tumult of the flesh were hushed, hushed the images of earth and air and heaven." But he feels as though he were the blind endeavoring to lead the blind, and the end comes at last in the garden of a Mediterranean villa, behind whose lighted windows a fancy ball is in progress. The hero, whose dress for the occasion is that of a Spanish peddler, encounters the seducer in one of the shadowy walks and is shot dead by the latter, who believes that his life is being threatened by some genuine desperado; and the heroine, draped in white, like a Greek goddess of purity, witnesses this sudden event, is overcome by the shock, and dies of heart failure on a marble bench close by.

One of the stoutest defenders of this book was Lord Houghton, who, in writing to me with regard to it, mentioned a curious incident. The villain of the piece, Colonel Stapleton, was drawn by me from a certain Lord ——, as to whom I had said to myself the first moment I met him: "This man is the quintessence of selfishness. He is capable of anything that would minister to his own pleasures." "The novel," said Lord Houghton in his letter, "requires no apology. You have made only one mistake in it. The conduct of the colonel in one way would have differed from that which you ascribe to him. For instance," Lord Houghton continued, "I once met Lord X. in Paris, and to my own knowledge what Lord X. would have done on a similar occasion was so-and-so." Lord X. was the very man from whom my picture of the colonel had been drawn.

Some years later I published another novel, *The Old Order Changes*, of which the affection of a man for a woman is again one of the main subjects, but it is there regarded from a widely different standpoint. I shall speak of this book presently, but I may first mention that in the interval between the two a new class of questions, of which at Littlehampton and Oxford I had been but vaguely conscious, took complete possession of my mind, and pushed for a time the interests which had been previously engaging me into the background.

This change was due to the following causes, which partly produced, and were partly produced by, one of the earlier outbreaks in this country of what is now called "social unrest." The doctrines

of Karl Marx, which had long been obscurely fer-
menting in the minds of certain English malcontents,
now began for the first time in this country to be
adopted by a body of such men as the basis of an
organized party—a party which they ambitiously
named "The Social Democratic Federation." The
main object of these persons was the confiscation of
all private capital. Another agitation had been initi-
ated by Henry George, which in this country was
much more widely popular, and which had for its
object the confiscation not of private capital, but
simply and solely of privately owned land. Meanwhile Bright, who was certainly not a Socialist (for
he defended the rights of capital in many of their
harshest forms), had been attacking private landlordism on the ground not that it was in itself an
economic abuse, as George taught, but that in this
country it formed, under existing conditions, the
basis of an aristocratic class. Finally there was
Ruskin, who had, since the days when I first knew
him at Oxford, been attempting to excite sympathy
with some vague project of revolution by rewriting
economic science in terms of sentiment which sometimes, but only on rare occasions, struck fire by
chance contact with the actual facts of life. It is
hardly surprising that such ideas as these, jumbled
together by a mob in Trafalgar Square, took practical form, on a certain memorable occasion, in a
looting of shops in Piccadilly—an enterprise insti-
gated by men one of whom, enlightened by disillu-

sion, has subsequently earned respect as a grave cabinet minister.

As for myself, the most pertinacious conviction which these movements forced on me was that, whatever elements of justice and truth might lurk in them, they were based on wild distortions of historical and statistical facts, or on an ignorance even more remarkable of the actual dynamics of industry, of the powers of the average worker, and of the motives by which he is actuated.

Dominated by this conviction, which for me was verified every time I opened a newspaper, I found myself daily devoting more and more of my time to the task of reducing this chaos of revolutionary thought to order. But what most sharply awakened me to the need for such a work was an incident which, before it took place, would have, so I thought, a tendency to lull my anxieties for a time rather than to maintain or stimulate them.

I had regarded the revolutionary mood as mainly, if not exclusively, an emanation from those hotbeds of urban industry in which the modern industrial system has reached its most complete development, and I pictured to myself the more remote districts of the kingdom—especially the Highlands of Scotland—as still the scenes of an idyllic and almost undisturbed content. As to the rural counties of England, I was, so I think, correct, but, as to the Scottish Highlands, the truth of my ideas in this respect still remained to be tested. To me the

Highlands were thus far nothing more than a name. I was therefore delighted when one morning I received an invitation from Lord and Lady Howard of Glossop, to stay with them for some weeks at Dorlin, their remote Highland home.

Dorlin, which had been bought by Lord Howard from his connection, Mr. Hope Scott, is situated on the borders of a sea loch, Loch Moidart, and of all places in Scotland it then enjoyed the repute of being one of the least accessible. The easiest means of reaching it was by a long day's journey in a rudely appointed cattle boat, which twice a week left Oban at noon, carrying a few passengers, and reached at nightfall the rude pier of Salen, about nine miles from the house. To my unaccustomed eyes the descent from the sleeping car at Oban, with the vision which greeted them of sea and heathery mountain, was like walking into the Waverley Novels. As I followed a barrow of luggage to the pier from which the steamer started, I expected to see Fergus MacIvors everywhere. This expectation was not altogether fulfilled; but at last, when the pier was reached, I knew not which thrilled me most —the smallness and rudeness of the vessel to which I was about to commit myself or the majesty of a kilted being who so bristled with daggers that even Fergus MacIvor might have been afraid of him. Not till later did I learn that the name of this apparition was Jones; but even if I had known it then, no resulting disillusion could have marred the adventurous romance of the voyage which was now awaiting me.

It was a voyage of astonishing and, to me, wholly novel beauty. The islands which we passed, or at which we stopped, wore all the colors of all the grape clusters of the world, until these were dimmed by slowly approaching twilight, when we found ourselves at rest in the harbor of Tobermory in Mull. We waited there for more than an hour, while leisurely boats floated out to us, laden with sheep and cattle, which were gradually got on board in exchange for some other cargo. Then, with hardly a ripple, our vessel was again in motion, its bows pointing to the mouth of Loch Salen opposite. By and by, in the dimness of the translucent evening, our vessel stopped once more—I could not tell why or wherefore, till a splash of oars was heard and some bargelike craft was decipherable emerging out of the gloom to meet us. Into this, as though in a dream, a number of sheep were lowered; and we, resuming our course, found ourselves at last approaching a small rocky protrusion, on which a lantern glimmered, and which proved to be Salen pier.

Gallic accents reached us, mixed with some words of English. With the aid of adroit but hardly distinguishable figures, I found myself stumbling over the boulders of which the pier was constructed, and realized that a battered wagonette, called "the machine," was awaiting me. A long drive among masses of mountain followed. At last a gleam of waters was once again discernible. The road, rough and sandy, ran close to little breaking waves, and then, in the shadow of woods and overhanging rocks, numerous lights all of a sudden showed themselves. The machine with a lurch entered something in the nature of a carriage drive, and I found myself on the threshold of Dorlin—a lodge of unusual size, which seemed to be almost wading in the water. When the door opened I was greeted by an odor of peat smoke. An old London butler conducted me up a flight of stairs, and I was presently in a drawing-room filled with familiar figures. Besides my host and hostess and their then unmarried daughters, were Lady Herbert of Lee, Lord Houghton, the Verulams, and the most delightful of priests, Father Charles Macdonald, famous as a fisherman, inimitable as a teller of stories, and great-grandson of fighters who had died for Prince Charlie at Culloden. One guest at Dorlin, who had left just before my arrival, was the then Lord Lorne, and I was told by Lady Howard that the boatmen who had helped him to land—Catholic Macdonalds all of them—had been heard saying to one another that "not so very long ago no Campbell would have dared to set foot in the Macdonald country." Not far away there were still living at that time two old ladies—Macdonalds—whose small house was a museum of Stuart relics, and who still spoke of the Pretender with bated breath as "the King."

Here, indeed, were conditions closely resembling

those to which I had looked forward. The past was once more present. The modern spirit of unrest had, so it seemed to me, retreated to some incredible distance.

Lord Houghton, Father Charles, one of the daughters of the house, and I invariably beguiled the evenings with a rubber of modest whist. Lord Houghton was to leave on a Monday morning, and as soon as the dinner of Sunday night was over he hurried us to our places at the card table for another and a concluding game. Much to his surprise and annoyance somebody whispered in his ear that Lord Howard, though an excellent Catholic, had always had an objection to the playing of cards on Sundays. "Well," said Lord Houghton, "we must get Lady Herbert to speak to him about it." Lady Herbert, hearing her name, asked what she was wanted to do. Lord Houghton explained, and she, in tones of caressing deprecation, repeated that, as to this matter, Lord Howard was afflicted with a strong Protestant prejudice. "My dear lady," said Lord Houghton, taking both her hands, "what's the good of belonging to that curious superstition of yours if one mayn't play cards on Sunday?" Through her mediation the desired indulgence was granted. The game was played, but Providence nevertheless chastened Lord Houghton, using me as its humble instrument, for I won three or four pounds from him—the largest, if not the only, sum that I ever won at cards in my life.

Such episodes, imported as they were from the social world of England, were not altogether in keeping with the visionary world of Waverley, but they could not dissipate its atmosphere, charged with bygone romance. And yet it was among these "distant dreams of dreams" that my ears became first awake to the nearer sounds of some vague social disturbance of which Ruskin's gospel of Labor, as I heard it at Oxford without any clear comprehension of it, had been a harbinger.

I had been asked, when I left Dorlin, to pay one or two other visits in the Highlands farther north—to the Sutherlands at Dunrobin, the Munro Fergusons at Novar, and the Lovats at Beaufort. My route to these places was by the Caledonian Canal, and in listening to the conversation of various groups on the steamer I several times heard the opinion expressed that, sooner or later, the Highlands were bound to be the scene of some great agrarian revolution. I was well aware that the assailants of landed property, from Marx and George down to the semi-conservative Bright, to whose voices had now been joined that of Mr. Joseph Chamberlain, had pointed to the magnitude of the greater Highland estates as signal types of the abuses to which Highland landlordism is liable; but not till I took that journey on the steamer from Fort William to Inverness had I attached to these arguments more than an academic importance.

In the course of my ensuing visits I talked over

the threatened revolution with persons of much local knowledge, especially with one of the Duke of Sutherland's agents, and Father Grant, the chaplain of the Catholic Lovats at Beaufort. They did not, it appeared to me, take the threatened revolution very seriously, and they showed me how absurdly in error the agitators were as to certain of the facts alleged by them. One of their errors consisted in their gross overestimates of what the practical magnitude of the great Highland properties was, the rent of the Sutherland property being, for instance, no more per acre than the twentieth part of an average acre in England. Father Grant, who was a learned antiquarian, mentioned as a commonplace on revolutionary platforms the statement that in the Highlands no such beings as the private landlord existed prior to the rebellion of 1745, on the suppression of which the government stole their communal rights from the clansmen, turning them into tenants at will, whom the chieftains, now absolute owners, could evict and expatriate as they pleased. No fiction, said Father Grant, himself a crofter's son, could be more absurd than this. It was absolutely disproved, he said, by a mass of medieval charters, in which were assigned to the chieftains by the Scottish Crown the fullest territorial rights possible for lawyers to devise.[1]

At the same time my informants admitted with

---

[1] Father Grant, at my suggestion, published one of these Charters *in extenso* in *The National Review*.

regret that landlordism in the Highlands was liable to special abuses, an instance of which had come to the fore recently. This was the long lease acquired by a rich American of enormous areas which he converted into a single deer forest, evicting certain crofters in the process with what was said to have been signal harshness.

All this information was to me extremely interesting; but I left Scotland wishing that it had been more extensive and methodical. It had, however, the effect of stimulating me in the work to which I was now addressing myself—that is to say, the elaboration of some formal and militant treatise, in which I might not only discredit by analysis the main fallacies common to all the social revolutionaries of the day, but also indicate the main facts and principles on which alone a true science of society can be based. This work took the form of a short treatise or essay, called *Social Equality, or a Study in a Missing Science.* The science to which I referred was the science of human character as connected with the efforts by which wealth and all material civilizations are produced. A French translation of it was soon issued in Paris. I was also asked to sanction what I had no right to prohibit—namely, translations of it into Rumanian and Spanish. My main object was to show that, as applied to the process in question, "social equality" was a radically erroneous formula, the various efforts to which wealth is due being not only essentially unequal in themselves, but only susceptible of stimulation by the influence of unequal circumstances. The Radical doctrines to the contrary, which were then being enunciated with reckless bitterness by Bright, were taken to pieces and exposed, and the claims of mere average labor, as opposed to those of the capitalist, were in general language reduced to their true dimensions. I supplemented this volume by a criticism in *The Quarterly Review* of Henry George's celebrated *Progress and Poverty*, and Henry George himself when he came to London told Lady Jeune (afterward Lady St. Helier), without knowing that I was the author of it, that this criticism was the only reply to himself which was worth being considered seriously. I was conscious, however, of my own limitations, these relating mainly to matters of statistical fact, such as the exact proportion borne in a country like the United Kingdom by the aggregate rental of the landlords to the aggregate income of the capitalists on the one hand and that of the mass of manual workers on the other. I was conscious of being specially hampered in attempting to deal minutely with the statistical fallacies of Bright.

I was still in this state of mind a year after my first visit to Dorlin when I received a letter from Lady Howard asking me to come to them again. I went, and all the charm of my first visit repeated itself; but repeated itself with this difference—that it was no longer undisturbed. The possibility of a revolution in the Highlands had now become a matter of audible discussion even in the remote Macdonald country. The temper of the sparse population was there, indeed, not very violent, but the thought that some sort of disaffection was even there actually alive would often disturb my previous sense of peace, while the Glasgow and Edinburgh newspapers, whether by way of attacking the established order or defending it, were pelting one another with statistical statements in respect of which each party seemed to contradict itself almost as recklessly as it contradicted its opponents. My own growing ambition was to get at definite and detailed information which would either support the agitators or else give them the lie, and would also provide otherwise comprehensive and specific illustrations of the general principles which I had formulated in my late volume. But as to the means by which comprehensive information of this specific kind could be collected I was still more or less at a loss; and from the vague and conflicting character of the statistics adduced it was evident that other people were in the same or in a worse condition. That the required information existed somewhere in the form of official and other records I was convinced. The problem was how to get at these and recast the information in a digested and generally intelligible form.

The necessity for doing this was brought home to me with renewed force by the fact that, when I left Dorlin, I was engaged to stay at Ardverikie with Sir John Ramsden, who was the owner, by purchase, of

one of the greatest sporting territories in the Highlands, a large portion of which he was then planting
with timber. The first stage of my journey from
Dorlin was again Fort William, where I slept, and
whence next morning I proceeded by an old-fashioned
stagecoach to my destination, which lay midway
between Fort William and Kingussie. We had not
gone far before I heard an English voice shouting
something to the passengers near in tones of great
excitement. The speaker, with his black frock coat,
was, to judge from his appearance, a Nonconformist
English minister, who was vaguely pointing to the
mountains on the left side of the road; and at last
I managed to catch a few words of his oratory.
They were in effect as follows: "What was there on
those mountains fifty years ago? Men were on
those mountains then. What will you find there
now? Deer—nothing but deer." This sort of thing
went on for some time, till at last the coachman, a
burly Highlander, turned round on the orator and
said: "I'm thinking you don't know what you're
talking about. In those mountains at which you're
flourishing your hands you won't find a deer all the
way from Fort William to Kingussie." The orator
then, so far as I was able to understand, wandered
away to the question of landed property generally,
and Acts of Parliament passed in the reign of William
and Mary. It seemed, however, that his audience
were not responsive, and he presently began descant-
ing on the ignorance of the Highland people and

their need of more education. Here, again, his eloquence was interrupted by the coachman. "Education," he exclaimed. "What you call education I call the Highland rinderpest." After this the orator was comparatively quiet.

Meanwhile the character of the surrounding landscape changed. We began to see glimpses ahead of us of the waters of Loch Laggan. Presently the loch, fringed with birch trees, was directly below the road. On the opposite side were mountains descending to its silvery surface, some of them bare, some green with larches, and upward from a wooded promontory wreaths of smoke were rising. Then between the wreaths I distinguished a tall gray tower, and something like clustered turrets. Pointing to these, the coachman pulled up his horses, and I understood him to say that at this point I must descend. A man, who had evidently been waiting, came forward from a tuft of bracken. My luggage was extracted from the vehicle and dragged down to a boat, which was, as I now saw, waiting by the beach below; and a row of some twenty minutes took me across the loch and brought me to my journey's end.

Ardverikie is a castellated building. It is something in the style of Balmoral, with which everybody is familiar from photographs. It is surrounded by old-fashioned gardens beyond which rise the mountains. Down one of the graveled paths Lady Guendolen came to meet me, accompanied by her two daughters and Mrs. Arthur Henniker, the younger daughter of Lord Houghton—these, except for Sir John, comprising the whole party. Within were paneled walls, innumerable heads of deer, and two large libraries surrounded by a crowd of books, not many of them new, but all of inviting aspect. The pleasure of meeting old friends under fresh conditions for the time put out of my head the revolutionary orator of the coach. Indeed, the only specially Highland incident talked about was connected with a neighboring minister, who was accustomed to conduct on Sundays a religious service in the dining room, and who on the last of these occasions had unintentionally, but severely, affronted one member of the household. He had begun with calling down the special blessings of the Creator on the heads of all, mentioned seriatim, who were congregated under Sir John's roof. "God bless Sir John," he began. "God bless also her dear Leddyship. Bless the tender youth of the two young leddies likewise. We also unite in begging thee to have mercy on the puir governess."

I had not been many days in the house before I discovered a certain number of books, all more or less modern, dealing with Highland conditions as they had been since the beginning of the nineteenth century. These books were written from various points of view, and some of them were extremely interesting; but in every case there was one thing for which I looked in vain. I looked in vain for

anything in the nature of statistical precision, except
here and there in connection with minor and scat-
tered details. Frequent references were made, for
example, to the decline of the Highland population;
but no attempt had apparently been made by anyone to state by reference to extant official documents
what the total of the alleged decline had been, or
whether or why in some districts it had been greater
or less than in others. The two voluminous works
known respectively as the *Old* and *New Statistical
Accounts of Scotland* were full of significant, but
wholly undigested details. How should I succeed
where so many others had failed? Where should I
find records which would enable me to complete in-
completeness and reduce chaos to some comprehensive order? One afternoon, when I found myself
alone in the house, I was thinking these things over
in one of the silent libraries, and staring again at the
backs of books I had already opened, when, purely
out of curiosity, I dragged at hazard a large and
dusty volume from a row of folios which I had neglected, supposing them to be all atlases. I found
that, instead of an atlas, the volume I had extracted
was a copy of the huge Government Report which is
commonly known by the name of *The New Domesday
Book*. I had heard of this work before, but had
never till now seen it, nor had I realized the nature
of its contents. *The New Domesday Book* was the
result of an official inquiry undertaken some ten
years previously into the number, the extent, and

the rental value of all the landed properties of Great Britain and Ireland. Here, I thought, was at least a large installment of the kind of evidence of which I had felt the want, and during the rest of my visit to Ardverikie I devoted every possible moment to a study of this volume.

Without going into details, it will be enough to mention the broad and unmistakable facts which *The New Domesday Book* disclosed, and which formed a direct counterblast, not to the oratory of the Highland agitators only, but also to the wider assertions of Henry George and of Bright. Henry George, whose statistical knowledge was a blank, had contented himself with enunciating the vague doctrine that in all modern countries—the United States, for example, and more especially the United Kingdom —every increase of wealth was in the form of rent, appropriated by the owners of the soil, most of whom were millionaires already, or were very quickly becoming so. Bright, in dealing with this country, had committed himself to a statement which was very much more specific. The number of persons, he said, who had any interest as owners in the soil of their mother country was not more than 30,000 —or, to put the matter in terms of families, thirty-four out of every thirty-five were "landless." *The New Domesday Book* showed that the number of proprietary interests, instead of being only 30,000, was considerably more than a million; or, in other words, the number of the "landless" as Bright stated it was greater than the actual number in the proportion of thirty-three to one.

Here were these facts accessible in the thousand or more pages of a great official survey. They had doubtless received some attention when that document was issued, but the agitators of the early "'eighties" had forgotten or never heard of them; and Bright, so far as I know, never retracted his own monstrous fallacies. How, then, I asked myself, should the actual facts of this particular case be driven into the heads of the public in a politically effective form? And how should other cognate facts, such as the profits of the business employers, Bright himself being one of them, be dragged effectively into light, compared with the rental of the landlords, and be in a similar way brought home to the public consciousness? Such were the questions which came to possess my mind when luncheons were being eaten among heather by the pourings of some hillside brook, or when deer at the close of the day were being weighed in the larders of Ardverikie.

To these questions a partial answer came sooner than I had expected. On leaving Ardverikie I paid another visit to the Lovats. On joining the train at Kingussie I learned that one of the passengers was Mr. Joseph Chamberlain, who was, as an advanced Radical, to make the following day a great speech at Inverness. Needless to say, this speech turned out to be mainly a vituperation of Highland landlords. I mention it here only on account of one short passage. "The landlords," said Mr. Chamberlain, "have made a silence in the happy glens which once resounded with your industry"—as though every wilderness between Cape Wrath and Loch Lomond had not so very long ago resembled a suburb of Birmingham. This is a curious illustration of how readily even a man of most acute intellect may be led by the need of securing applause at all costs into nonsense which, in calmer moments, he would himself be the first to ridicule.

As an antidote to Mr. Chamberlain's propaganda another meeting was planned under the auspices of a number of the great Highland proprietors, who gathered together to discuss matters at Castle Grant (Lord Seafield's), the ideal home of a chieftain. To this conclave I was taken by my host, Lord Lovat, from Beaufort. Five chieftains were present, supported by five pipers, whose strains might have elicited echoes from the slopes of the farthest Grampians.

Before the public meeting which was planned at Castle Grant took place I had left the Lovats', being called by business to England; but I had not been long in London before an opportunity of political action was offered me, in a manner which I could not resist. My book *Social Equality* had, it seemed, so far achieved its object that a letter presently reached me, written on behalf of a number of students at the University of St. Andrews, asking me whether, could the requisite arrangements be made, I would be willing, at the next election, to stand as Conservative candidate for the St. Andrews Boroughs, as the present member—a Liberal—would before long retire. The proper authorities were consulted, and, the proposal meeting with their approval, I agreed to begin forthwith the needed preliminary work, on condition that if meanwhile some member of a Fifeshire family should be willing to take the place of a stranger such as myself, I should be allowed to withdraw and make room for him.

In the end such a substitute was found, and in due time was elected. Meanwhile, however, I had begun a campaign of speeches which, so I was told, and so I should like to believe, contributed to his ultimate victory. At all events they enabled me to test certain expository methods which other speakers might perhaps reproduce with advantage. As among the subjects discussed by speakers of all parties, the land question generally, and not in Scotland only, continued to hold the most prominent place, I put together in logical form the statistical data relating to it, so far as I had been able to digest them; and having dealt with them verbally in the simplest language possible, I proceeded to illustrate them by a series of enormous diagrams, which were, at the appropriate moment, let down from the cornice like a series of long window blinds. One of these represented, by means of a long column divided into colored sections, the approximate total of the income of the United Kingdom according to current imputations and the enormous portion of it taken as land rent by the owners of more than 1,000 acres as it must have been according to Bright. Another column, which was then let down beside this, represented in a similar way the rental of the larger landlords as it would be according to the principles laid down by Henry George. A third diagram followed, which showed the actual amount of land rent as disclosed by an analysis of *The New Domesday Book*, so that all the audience could see the farcical contrast between the false figures and the true.

As a means of holding attention, and making the meaning of the speaker clear, these diagrams were a great success, and I was invited before long to repeat my exhibition of them at Aberdeen, at Glasgow, and at Manchester. My Fifeshire speeches, moreover, through the enterprise of the *Fifeshire Journal*, having been put into type a day before they were delivered, were printed *in extenso* next morning by many great English newspapers, whereas it is probable that otherwise they would have been relegated to an obscure paragraph.[1] I may, I think, claim for my speeches one merit, at all events—that though many of them were addressed to meetings preponderantly Radical, I so successfully avoided giving offense that only on one occasion, and then for some

---

[1] Another method which I adopted as a supplement to ordinary canvassing was a fortnightly or monthly issue of a printed letter addressed to each voter individually, which dealt with statistics and principles, every letter inviting questions, which would be dealt with in the letter following.

moments only, was I ever interrupted by dissent of a discourteous kind; while, when I delivered my speech on the land question at Manchester, I was, with all hospitable amity, entertained at a banquet by members of a leading Radical club.

Various opportunities, indeed, were at that time offered me of entering, had I been willing to do so, the public life of politics. But various causes withheld me. One of these causes related to the St. Andrews Boroughs in particular. My own home being either in London or Devonshire, frequent journeys to and from the east of Scotland proved a very burdensome duty, and the boroughs themselves being widely separated from one another, the task of often delivering at least one speech in each was, in the days before motors, a duty no less exhausting. Further, I felt that the business of public speaking would interfere with a task which I felt to be more important—namely, that of providing facts and principles for politicians rather than playing directly the part of a politician myself. I was therefore relieved rather than disappointed when a communication subsequently reached me from the Conservative agent at St. Andrews to the effect that the head of an important Fifeshire family was willing to take my place and contest the constituency instead of me. My feelings were confirmed by a totally extraneous incident. The severe reader will perhaps think that I ought to blush when I explain what this incident was.

CHAPTER X

A Venture on the Riviera—Monte Carlo—Life in a Villa at Beaulieu
—A Gambler's Suicide—A Gambler's Funeral

ONE May morning in London, when I had just completed a fortnight of political speaking in Fifeshire, a friend of mine, Ernest Beckett (afterward the second Lord Grimthorpe), came in a state of obvious excitement to see me, and talk, so he said, about something of great importance. He had, it appeared, been spending some weeks in the south of France, and was full of a project the value of which had, so he said, been amply proved by experiment. To me at first sight it seemed no better than lunacy. I could not for some time even bring myself to consider it seriously. This project was to play a new system at Monte Carlo. It was a system founded on one which, devised by Henry Labouchere, had been—such was Beckett's contention—greatly improved by himself, and he and a companion had been playing it with absolutely unbroken success. The two, with only a small capital in their pockets, had won during the course of a week or so something like a thousand pounds—not in a few large gains (for in this there would have been nothing to wonder at), but by a

194

regular succession day after day of small ones. They had tested the system further by applying it, after their departure, to the records, published daily in a Monte Carlo journal, of the order in which colors or numbers had turned up throughout the day preceding at some particular table. Adjusting their imaginary stakes, in accordance with the rules of the system, to these series of actual sequences, the two experimenters had discovered that their original successes were, as a matter of theory, infallibly reproduced. So certain, said Beckett, did all this seem that he would himself be in a position to secure some thousands of pounds of capital for the purpose of renewing the enterprise on a very much larger scale. He would not be able till Christmas to go out to Monte Carlo himself, and for several reasons he desired to remain at first in the background; but the capital in question would, he said, include a sum sufficient to defray the expenses of a few suitable friends, who would set to work meanwhile, and be entitled, as a business matter, to a share of the eventual profits. The coadjutors whom he had in view were myself, the late Lord Greenock, Charles Bulpett, and Charles Edward Jerningham. Moreover, as everything would depend on a correct calculation of the stakes—the amount of which at each coup would vary with the results of the coups preceding—and as this calculation would often be extremely complicated, and have in every case to be made with extreme rapidity, a good deal of preliminary practice on the part of the intending players would be necessary. Would this little group of players be, as he hoped, forthcoming? I still regarded the project as something of the wildcat kind; but I was struck by the undoubted success of Beckett's own experiments, actual and theoretical, so far; and, as the four players would at all events lose nothing, even if they gained nothing, by renewing them, I and the three others at last consented to take part in the venture.

As soon, therefore, as the London season was over we began our preparations, which would necessarily be somewhat lengthy. From the beginning of August up to the end of October we met again and again at Beckett's house in Yorkshire, our proceedings being shrouded in serio-comic secrecy. In order that we might perfect ourselves in the use of our mathematical weapons, each day after breakfast the dining-room table was cleared and covered with a large green cloth divided into numbered spaces, like the green roulette board at Monte Carlo. In the middle of this was placed a large roulette. Rakes were provided of the true Monte Carlo pattern. One of us played the part of croupier, while to each of the others was allotted a certain number of counters indistinguishable in aspect from twenty-franc gold pieces. Each of us made his own calculations on cards provided for the purpose; each day we played solemnly for four hours on end, and then examined the results. We sometimes varied this routine by taking one of the Monte Carlo records, our croupier not turning the wheel, but calling out the numbers or colors seriatim which had actually turned up at the tables on this day or that. The general results were, I must say, most extraordinary. On only two occasions did the operations of an entire day leave any of the players bankrupt or without a substantial gain, though they all started their work at different moments, and the actual details of the staking were in no two cases the same. Throughout a long series of these experimental meetings, the winnings were as a whole about 20 per cent. daily on the total capital risked.

Encouraged by these results, we had no sooner mastered the system as a mathematical scheme than we promptly made arrangements for beginning the work in earnest. We all thought it desirable that, until it was crowned with success, our enterprise should remain unknown to anybody except ourselves. It was therefore settled that our journey should take place at once—that is to say, about the end of October, at which time Monte Carlo would be nearly empty, and we should run least risk of encountering loquacious acquaintances or of having our secret stolen from us by inquisitive and sinister rivals. We accordingly secured in advance—since all the great hotels at the time in question were closed—a suite of four bedrooms and a sitting room at a small establishment called the Hôtel de Russie. Its appointments, when we arrived,

proved to be so simple that the floor of the restaurant was sanded; but the rooms upstairs were
comfortable; and not even at the Hôtel de Paris
could anything better have been found in the way
of wine or cooking.

Accordingly on a certain night we, the four pre-
cursors, were duly assembled on the platform of
Victoria Station; and Beckett, with the air of a
conspirator, appeared at the last moment, thrust
into our keeping certain notes of credit, and gave
us his blessing as we seated ourselves in the continental train. Had we been agents of a plot organized to convulse Europe we could not have been
in a condition of greater and more carefully subdued excitement, though there was not absent from
any of us an underlying sense of comedy. In the
dead of night we were having supper at Calais, and,
scanning the few other travelers who were engaged
in the same task, we were rejoicing in a sense of
having escaped all curious observation, when Jerningham gripped my arm and said: "Did you see the
man who has just gone through the door? Wasn't
he your friend W——?" He had named one of the
most intimate of the Catholic connections of my
family, who was, moreover, the greatest gossip in
Europe. Never would a dear friend have to us been
less welcome than he. Happily, however, I was able
to assure Jerningham that his fears were groundless,
and we settled ourselves in peace among the cushions
of the Paris train without having seen a soul who was

otherwise than a stranger to all of us. Having reached the Gare du Nord at six o'clock in the morning, we scrutinized the faces at the exit with the same gratifying result.

Thus freed from anxiety, we enjoyed at the Hôtel Continental a prolonged sleep, which was haunted by pleasing dreams. By eight o'clock that evening we found ourselves at the Gare de Lyon, disposing our belongings in a compartment of the wagon-lit which ended its course at Ventimiglia. My own arrangements having been made, I was smoking a cigarette in the corridor when a well-known voice over my shoulder was ejaculating my Christian name. I turned round, and there was the very friend whom Jerningham had identified but too correctly at Calais. I took the bull by the horns. I greeted him with the utmost enthusiasm; and when he asked me what I was doing I told him that I and three companions were going to amuse ourselves in the south of France till Christmas, and should—such, I think, was my phrase—have "a look in" at Monte Carlo as one incident of our program. I begged him to come and be introduced to my friends, as soon as our compartment was in order, and I managed meanwhile to inform them as to what had happened. In due time he visited us. He was full of good spirits and conversation, and one of the first facts that he communicated to us was that he was on his way to Monte Carlo himself, to play an infallible system. With sublime presence of mind we expressed a hope that we might meet there, adding that, if we did, he might find that the place had seduced us into trying a little system likewise. He was, however, so much taken up with his own that he had no time or inclination to propound any questions as to ours; and when he got out at Nice he never suspected that, so far as play was concerned, we were more than casual triflers.

When we reached Monte Carlo it was dark. The only vehicle in waiting was the omnibus of the Hôtel de Russie; and into its well of blackness one other passenger followed us. Four hearts were at once set beating by the thought that this man might be a spy, who had already heard of our enterprise, and whose mission was to appropriate or else to thwart our secret. The following day two of us drove into Nice and deposited our notes of credit at one of the most important banks, the manager looking at us with an oddly repressed smile, as though he detected in us a new contingent of dupes. We went back to Monte Carlo armed with two small steel safes, one for such capital as was needed for our immediate purposes, the other for our prospective winnings. Jerningham, who had a curious talent for initiating intimacies everywhere, had meanwhile managed to ascertain from somebody that, if we desired to secure preferential civility from the croupiers, the right thing to do was to make each of them a present of fairly good cigars, gifts of money being naturally not allowed. This was done, and ultimately we began our play feeling as children do when they first put their feet into sea water.

We played in couples, one player calculating the stakes, the other placing them on the table. The couples were to play alternately, one giving place to another as soon as the winnings amounted to fifty pounds. When the total winnings of both reached a hundred pounds we stopped. We played it for that day no longer.

For three weeks the whole thing went like clock-work. We ground out our daily gains—a hundred pounds on an average—as though they were coffee from a coffee mill. But at the beginning of the fourth week the fates were for the first time against us. We lost in the course of a morning about half the sum which it had cost us the labor of three weeks to win. We were not, however, daunted. We re-solved that for the future no couple of players should bring into the rooms more than five hundred pounds, and should this sum be lost we would suspend our proceedings for the day and start afresh next morn-ing. This arrangement being made, our successes began again. A risked capital of five hundred pounds regularly yielded a return of 10 per cent. in not much more than an hour, and we had nearly re-covered the whole of our previous loss when a catastrophe occurred owing to causes which had not come into our calculations. One of our couples, not finding that they were winning as fast as they had hoped to do, completely lost their heads, and

began throwing money on the tables without any
system at all. The result was that in less than a
quarter of an hour every penny which they had
brought with them had disappeared. Beckett, as
the only person who could possibly lose through the
enterprise, was promptly consulted by telegram.
His answer was that he was coming out himself in
a month or so, and begged us to stay where we were,
but to suspend our play till the situation could be
discussed more fully. By this prudent decision on
his part I was not myself displeased; for system-
playing, even when successful, I discovered to be a
very tedious matter.

Meanwhile, in respect of amusements, we four were
by no means derelicts. Empty as Monte Carlo was,
some villas were already occupied, one of these being
Le Nid, of which Laura, Lady Wilton was the mistress—a woman whose hospitalities were no less
agreeable than herself. Having found out enough
about us to show her that we were at least present-
able, she inaugurated an acquaintance with us by
sending a little box to myself, which proved to
contain, on being opened, something in the nature
of a valentine. It contained a spray of mimosa
packed in cotton wool, and lying like an elf among
the petals was a little sleeping bat. Lady Wilton
a week before had appeared as the Evening Star at
a fancy ball at Nice. In return for her valentine I
bought a microscopic puppy, which, packed in cotton
wool and inclosed in a box as the bat was, was trans-

mitted to her by a florist with a card attached to its person, and bearing the words, "From the bat to the Evening Star." Among other friends whom I discovered at Monte Carlo, I may mention a certain family whom I had once known well at Homburg, but had never seen again till now—a father, a mother, and an eminently beautiful daughter. Their home at Monte Carlo was a villa, small, but so curtained with velvet that it looked like a French jewel box. It was smothered in Banksia roses, and it overlooked the sea. By one of its windows the daughter would play the harp.

At length Beckett arrived, bringing his wife with him. Apart from the matter of the system, their coming effected a change which to me was extremely grateful. The Becketts and I before long migrated from Monte Carlo, and took a villa between us for a couple of months at Beaulieu. As for the system, Beckett, who was by no means disheartened, played it himself for many nights in succession, and ultimately admitted that there were defects in it which its late breakdown had revealed rather than caused. Not long afterward he was persuaded into adopting another, commended to him by Butler Johnson, once a prominent Member of Parliament. This system, mechanical rather than mathematical, was based on the assumption that the roulettes used at Monte Carlo were in all probability not accurate implements—that the bearings, unless constantly rectified, would soon be so worn with use that the wheel during a long enough period would bring out certain numbers in more than their due proportion. Hence, anyone backing these—so the argument ran—was necessarily bound in the long run to win. This conclusion, reached by a feat of *a priori* reasoning, was due to the ingenuity of an English engineer called Jaggers, and it was verified by the fact that a system having this mechanical basis was ultimately, with astounding success, played by a syndicate of persons who, before the officials of the Casino managed to detect its nature, had won no less than eighty thousand pounds between them. The secret, however, was found out at last. Before the players were aware of it, the construction of the roulettes was amended. Each was built up of a number of interchangeable parts, the construction of no wheel being for any two days the same. The spell was broken; the players began to lose. One or two of them, suspecting what had actually happened, withdrew from the enterprise and carried off their gains along with them. Less prudent and more sanguine, the rest persisted till all that they had gained was gone. An Italian professor of mathematics, however, declared that, despite the officials, he had discovered how this system might be revived in a new and more delicate form; and Beckett, with renewed hopes, was induced to finance for a time the second experiment out of some of the capital which he had got together for his first. The money, however, melted away as though by a slow hemorrhage; before very long he refused to produce more, and the history of both systems thus came to an end.

But the pleasantness of our life at Beaulieu was sufficient to counterbalance the disappointments inflicted on us by Fortune at the gaming tables. Our fantastic villa was embowered in flowers and foliage. Buginvillæas made a purple flame on the walls. An avenue of palms led down from the house to the flashings of a minute harbor, on which fishing boats rocked their gayly painted prows, while woods of olive made a mystery of the impending hills behind. Friends and acquaintances from Cannes often came to lunch with us, Alfred Montgomery and the Duchess of Montrose among them. Beckett's spirits rose. Singularly sensitive as he always was to poetry, I could hear him (for the walls which divided our rooms were thin) reciting passages from "Paradise Lost" in his tub. Though he had done with systems, he, his wife, and I frequently went to Monte Carlo for dinner, our inducements being mainly the chance of meeting friends whose scrutiny we no longer feared, and the beauty of the homeward drive by the Lower Corniche road. The Prince's palace, pale on its rocky promontory, seemed like some work of enchantment as we swept by in the moonlight, and our horses carried us into strange, fantastic solitudes, with mountainous woods on one side and the waves just below us on the other. In stillnesses broken only by the noise of our own transit, the murmur of the waves was merely a stillness audible, as they whispered along crescents of sand with a sound like a sleeping kiss.

The Becketts, however, had to go back to England some weeks sooner than they expected, and I was left till the expiration of our lease, to occupy the villa alone. It was during the weeks for which I was thus left to myself that a letter reached me from St. Andrews, announcing that if I wished to retire I was honorably free to do so, as a suitable substitute had been found. The news was extremely welcome to me. I had many books with me at Beaulieu, for the most part dealing with economic and social science; and once more, when I was left to myself, the study of these absorbed me, and led me to begin the planning of a kind of political novel, of which I shall speak presently. But my solitude was not enlivened by political speculation only. Two or three times a week I went to Monte Carlo to enjoy the society of the R——s in their villa, which I have already described, and which still remains in my memory as associated with flowers and harp strings. Out of my intimacy with the R——s an incident arose which may be regarded as a fitting conclusion to the drama of Monte Carlo, so far as I myself was concerned with it. The R——s had a friend, Mrs. P——, a not very prosperous widow, who was spending the winter and spring with them. She was far from beautiful, and her manners perhaps were deficient in polish, but her temper was singularly sweet. She was willing to oblige everybody. She

accompanied Miss R—— and myself on many interesting expeditions, and was pleased by our seeking her companionship. Otherwise she was much
alone, and was left to amuse herself; her only
amusement—so I gathered from her chance conversation—being the winning or losing of a five-
franc piece at the tables. One day, when I called
at the villa, I saw by the butler's face that something unusual must have happened. I learned a
few minutes later that Mrs. P—— was dead. The
cause of her death turned out to have been this.
Having begun her exploits at the gambling rooms
with winning or losing a five-franc piece occasionally,
she had, unsuspected by anybody, succumbed by
slow degrees to the true gambler's passion. In
order to gratify this, everything she could sell—and
it was not much—she had sold. Not many hours
ago she had placed her last louis on the table, and
had seen it disappear under the traction of the
croupier's rake. She had nothing left in her bedroom but the clothes which she had worn yesterday,
a hairbrush, and a bottle of laudanum. The bottle
that morning had been found in her hand, empty.
The last incident of my visit to Monte Carlo was
her burial. In the mists of a rainy morning a sur-
pliced English clergyman saw her put out of sight
and mind in a little obscure cemetery. There were
only two mourners. I myself was one; Miss R——,
with her fair hair and her black dress, was the other.
A few days later I left Beaulieu for England by

way of the Italian lakes. I had managed to hire
at Nice a great old-fashioned traveling carriage—
a relic of pre-railway days. By way of a parting
dissipation I picked up the R——s at their villa,
and took them with me as far as San Remo. There
I joined the train, the R——s going back in the
carriage. Next morning I was at Cadennabia, and
Monte Carlo and the system, and Beaulieu and its
Buginvillæas, were behind me.

CHAPTER XI

"THE OLD ORDER CHANGES"

Intellectual Apathy of Conservatives—A Novel Which Attempts to Harmonize Socialist Principles with Conservative

IN spite of the severance of my connection with the St. Andrews Boroughs, I found, when I returned to England from Monte Carlo, that my active connection with politics was not by any means at an end. Politics, as a mere fight over details, or as a battle between rival politicians, appealed to me no more than it had done during my experience of electioneering in Fifeshire; but presently by family events I was drawn once more into the fray. My cousin, Richard Mallock of Cockington, had been asked, and had consented, to stand as Conservative candidate for the Torquay division of Devonshire. His local popularity, which was great, depended mainly on the engaging and somewhat shy simplicity of his manner, on his honesty, which was recognized by all, and on his generosity and sound sense as a landlord. These latter qualities had lately been made conspicuous by his administration of those parts of his property which were now, one after another, being quickly covered with buildings. He was no student, however, of statistics or political theory; as a speaker his practice had been small, and he and his advisers asked me to give what assistance I could.

One night early in July I had, at a large ball in London, spent a most agreeable hour with a companion who was, like myself, no dancer, in watching and discussing with her the brilliantly lighted company. At last, catching sight of a clock, I found myself obliged to go. "I have," I said, "to be at Paddington at five o'clock in the morning. Tomorrow I must speak in Devonshire to a meeting of agricultural laborers." She expressed approval and sympathy, and I presently found myself in the dimness of the still streets, happy in the thought that soon I should be among the smell of meadows and listening to the noise of rooks. The following evening at a village on Richard Mallock's property, his political campaign was to be inaugurated, and I was to be one of the orators.

When the time for the meeting came I found myself erect in a wagon, with a world of apple trees in front of me and a thatched barn behind, and heard myself discussing the program of "three acres and a cow," of which my listeners understood nothing, and I not more than a little. Compared with such an audience the Liberals of St. Andrews were sages. The most intelligent of the Conservative audiences in the constituency were those got together under the auspices of the Primrose League. But Conservatism even with them was no more than a vague sentiment, healthy so far as it went, but incapable of aiding them in controversy with any glib Radical opponent. I tried again and again during the following few weeks to call their attention to the sources from which our national wealth generally, and most of their own food, was derived, and particularly to the economic significance of a town such as Torquay, much of the wealth of which had its origin in foreign countries. In dealing, however, with these matters, I met with no response more encouraging than puzzled smiles; but whenever, for want of something better to say, I alluded to "this great Empire on which the sun never sets," I was greeted with a volume of cheers sufficient, one might almost have thought, to have secured the election of a Conservative candidate on the spot. Besides myself, two other workers were active, who began their political life as Richard Mallock's supporters at Torquay, and who subsequently rose to eminence of a wider kind—George Lane Fox, as Chancellor of the Primrose League, and J. Sandars as secretary and adviser to Mr. Arthur Balfour. But they, so it seemed to me, found it no easier than I did to vitalize the non-Radical or temperamentally Conservative classes with any definite knowledge of the main conditions and forces on which their own livelihood depended, and which Radicals and revolutionaries would destroy. Of this state of mind I remember an amusing illustration.

Many Primrose League meetings, at the time of which I now speak and later, were held at Cockington

Court, which was now a political center for the first time since the days of William and Mary. The proceedings on one occasion were to begin with a few preliminary speeches, delivered from some steps in a garden which adjoined the house. The chair was to be taken by the Duchess (Annie) of Sutherland, who for many years spent part of the summer at Torquay. Her opening speech consisted of five words: "I declare this meeting open." Subsequently George Lane Fox moved a vote of thanks to the duchess "for the very able way in which she had taken the chair." Never did appropriate brevity receive a more deserved tribute. These preliminaries having been accomplished, the business of the day began. The slopes surrounding the house were dotted with various platforms, from each of which addresses were delivered to all who cared to listen. The audience which clustered round one of them was soon of such exceptional size that I joined it in the hope of discovering to what this fact was due. The platform was occupied by two county members, both men of worth and weight, but not even the highest talents which their warmest friends could attribute to them would account, so it seemed to me, for the outbursts of uproarious applause which greeted from time to time the one who was now speaking. In the applauded passages I failed to detect anything more cogent or pungent than the general substance of those which were passed by in silence. I could find no explanation of this perplexing fact till I realized that behind the platform was a tall, greased pole, up which successive competitors were doing their best to climb, the victor's reward being a large leg of mutton at the top of it, and the applause being excited by the feats, not of the orator, but of the acrobats.

The word "acrobats," indeed, represents not inaptly the character which I had from the first imputed to the extreme reformers (whether Radicals or Socialists) as a whole. These extremists were, in my opinion, at once wrong and popular, not because they actually invented either the facts or principles proclaimed by them, but because they practiced the art of contorting facts into any shape they pleased, no matter what, so long as this amounted to a grimace which was calculated to attract attention, and which, in the absence of any opponents who could counter them by detailed exposure, could, by constant repetition, be invested with the prestige of truth. And why was exposure of the requisite kind wanting? Simply because the Conservatives as a whole were so ignorant that they did not know, or so timorous or apathetic that they did not dare to use, the true facts, figures, or principles by the promulgation of which alone the false might be systematically discredited. The need of a scientific Conservatism equipped with these weapons of precision was not so urgent at that time as it has since then become. But I felt it even then. I foresaw how rapidly this need was bound to be aggravated. It had haunted me even at Beaulieu, when I wandered among the sleeping flowers by the light of Mediterranean moons.

The difficulties in the way of formulating a true scientific Conservatism, which the masses shall be able to comprehend, I am the last person to ignore. There is the difficulty of formulating true general principles. There is the difficulty of collecting and verifying the statistical and historical facts, to which general principles must be accommodated. There is the difficulty of bringing moral and social sentiments into harmony with objective conditions which no sentiment can permanently alter. There is the difficulty of transforming many analyses of facts of different kinds into a synthesis moral and rational, by the light of which human beings can live; and, feeling my way slowly, I now attempted to indicate what the nature of such a synthesis would be. In so doing I felt that political problems of life reunited themselves with those which are commonly called religious, and with which, during my earlier years, my mind had been alone engaged.

This attempt at a synthesis was embodied ultimately in the form of another novel, which I have mentioned already, and to which I gave the name of *The Old Order Changes*. The scene of this story, like that of *A Romance of the Nineteenth Century*, was, for the most part, the Riviera, and the story itself was to a very great extent the product of many solitary hours at Beaulieu, during which Monte Carlo and the system became no more than a dream.

The Old Order Changes, moreover, resembles its predecessor in this—that the love interest centers in a woman considered in relation to her higher beliefs and principles; but whereas in *A Romance of the Nineteenth Century* such higher beliefs and principles are those connected with the mysticism of personal virtue, they are connected in *The Old Order Changes* with a sense of social duty, as experienced by a well-born Catholic, to the mass of the common people in respect of their material circumstances.

The heroine, who had come across the writings of modern agitators, in which the masses are depicted as brutalized by an almost universal poverty, most of the fruits of their industry being stolen from them by the rapacious rich, becomes gradually possessed by the conviction that this picture, even if exaggerated, is in the main true. Such being the case, another conviction dawns on her, which troubles her nature to its depth—namely, that the Catholic Church—her own religion by inheritance—will for her have lost all meaning unless it absorbs into the body of virtues enjoined by its doctrines on the rich a corporate sense of their overwhelming obligations to the poor.

She lays bare the state of her mind to a highly connected and highly intellectual priest, Father Stanley (who figures in *A Romance of the Nineteenth Century* also), and asks him if he thinks her wicked. The priest's answer is No. "The Church," he says, "is always extending the sphere of duty as from age to age needs and conditions change. Political economy, as related to the conditions of labor, has indeed in our day become a part of theology—its youngest branch; and as such, I, a priest, have studied it. Every age has its riddle, and this riddle is ours."

He then goes on to explain to her that the relation of the rich to the masses is not so simple as she thinks it. The poverty which agitators ascribe to all mankind, except a small body of plutocrats, is, he says, neither so deep nor so universal as these persons represent it; and, though in part it may arise from a robbery of the many by a rapacious few, this is not the whole of the story. He points out that if a hundred years ago the whole wealth of this country had been divided equally among all, the masses would, as a whole, be poorer than they are now; and that most of the wealth which is monopolized now by the few consists not of abstractions which they perpetrate from a common stock, but of additions to it which they have made themselves by their own talents and enterprise. It is true, he proceeds, that if, having made these additions, the few gave them away instead of retaining them for themselves, as the principles of Socialism would demand, the wealth of the many would be so far increased for the moment; but here comes the practical question. If, of these additions, the few were to retain nothing—if exceptional talent secured no proportionate reward—would these additions, a part of which goes to the mass already, continue to be made by anybody? This might be so if the great leaders of industry had all of them the temperament of monks, whose one passion was not to get, but to give; but to suppose this possible would be merely to dream a dream. "It would be easier," he says, in conclusion, "far easier, to make men Trappists than it would be to make them Socialists."

Animated by this last argument, the heroine is led to dream a dream of her own. Let it be granted, she says to herself, that the leaders of modern industry capable of accepting the Socialist gospel are few, and will always remain few. Still there may be some exceptions; and it may not be unreasonable to expect that, under the influence of the Catholic Church, certain great factories might be assimilated to Trappist or Franciscan monasteries, the profits of which the monks would consecrate to social purposes, voluntarily living the lives of the poorest of the poor themselves. Here, she argues, we should have examples, at all events, by which all might be moved, though all were not fit to follow them.

This outburst of a girl's idealism is considered by the priest with a sympathetic, yet at the same time a cautious, interest. When, turning from the priest, she opens her mind to the hero, he regards some of her ideas as exaggerated; but the affection which he feels for her as a lover makes their appeal deeper.

In *A Romance of the Nineteenth Century*, the hero's love for the heroine resembles the affection of St. Augustine for Monica—a love whose consummation is contingent on a mystical union of both with "the Selfsame, the everlasting One." In *The Old Order Changes* the passion is contingent on a partnership with her in some scheme of idealized political action for the social benefit of the masses. But circumstances soon arise by which the two are estranged. A mischief-maker, quite untruly, informs the heroine's aunts, who are her guardians—Catholics of the strictest type—that the hero is still carrying on an old intrigue with a beautiful Frenchwoman, now living at Nice. This gossip is passed on to the girl. The aunts forbid the hero to have any more communication with her; and the girl herself writes him a cold letter which is tantamount to an abrupt dismissal.

The aunts and the niece leave him to find out the reason for himself, which, since it is quite fictitious, he is unable to do. Having received their letters, and smarting under a sense of wrong, he starts for a walk among the mountains on the slopes of which his house, an old château, is situated. He sprains his ankle, and some strangers bring him home in a carriage. These strangers consist of an American general, who is a Southerner, his attractive wife, and a singularly beautiful daughter. Solitude being for him intolerable, he begs them to become his guests. A few days later they arrive, and round

him, like a naïve Circe, the beautiful daughter un-
designedly weaves her spell. "Under her influence,"
as the words of the novel describe it, "the voices of
men asking for spiritual guidance, the growth of a
democracy uneasily chafing for change, dwindled in
his ears till at last they were hardly audible." This
act of the drama is, however, abruptly interrupted
by family business, which recalls the hero to England. Meanwhile the Catholic heroine and her
aunts learn that he was wholly guiltless of the intrigue at Nice imputed to him, and a kindly mediator
discreetly gives him to understand that if in a week
or two he would meet them at the Italian lakes, all
would be forgotten and forgiven, if indeed there were
anything to forgive. It happens that an Italian
cousin of his has put at his disposal a villa in the
middle of Lago Maggiore; and there his reunion
with the heroine and her Catholic kindred is accomplished. Other friends, who are staying at Baveno,
join the group, Father Stanley among them. In the
chapel of the villa he, by way of a sermon, gives
them a sort of address on the social problems of the
time; and this throughout has reference to the sort of
ideas or projects of which the heroine had already
spoken to him.

He takes for his text the following words from St.
James: "Go to now, ye rich men, weep and howl for
your miseries that shall come upon you. Behold, the
hire of the laborers, which is of you kept back by
fraud, crieth. If a brother or sister be destitute,

and if any of you say to them, 'Depart in peace'; notwithstanding ye give not them those things needful for the body, what doth it profit? To him that knoweth to do good and doeth it not, to him it is sin." The priest then proceeds to the question of what virtue and duty are. "To this," he says, "there are two answers. The first is, that virtue and duty have for their object God. The second answer is, that their object is our fellow men and the health of the social organism, while our inducement to practice them is in part the constant teasing of the tribal instinct or conscience, and in part our imaginative sympathies, as stimulated by a glow of emotion which is consequent on our contemplation of idealized Humanity as a whole. "Within certain limits," he says, "this second answer I take to be entirely right; but if there were nothing further to add, I maintain that it would be right in vain." Summing up the ideas of the heroine, Miss Consuelo Burton, he says that the main duty which the Church to-day enjoins on us is "our spiritual duty to the material conditions of the poor"—our duty to adorn the cottage, though not to destroy the castle. "Duty to the race as a substitute for duty to God is," he says, "worth nothing. It means nothing. But duty to the race regarded as a new and more definite interpretation of our duty to God is a conception which to us Catholics of the present day means everything. Though it relates to material things, it does not supersede spiritual. On the contrary, it represents the spiritual world taking the material world into itself as its minister, and the Catholic who realizes this will find that the echoes of the mass and of the confessional follow him into the street and mix themselves with the clatter of omnibuses. If any of you think that he or she individually can do little, after all, to alter the general condition of things, let them not be thereby disheartened. Let them carry in their minds this divine paradox, that it is far more important to every man that he should do his utmost for Humanity than it ever can be for Humanity that any one man should do his utmost for *it*."

Illuminated by thoughts like these, the hero and the heroine are once more drawn together; and when at night the guests go back to Baveno, and the hero is left in his island villa alone, he betakes himself to a boat, and awaits the approach of the morning. "At last," says the story, "he put the boat about, with thoughts of returning home, and there, far off, beyond the spikes of the mountains, he saw that the sky was pale with the first colors of dawn. There, too, was the star of morning, shining bright with a trembling steadfastness, and he knew that for him a star had risen also. On his spirit descended the hush of the solemn hour, which makes all the earth seem like some holy sanctuary, and there came back to him two lines of Goethe's:

"The woman-soul leadeth us
Upward and on
221

"Meanwhile on the sliding and glassy waters, that moved to left and right at the touch of his dipping oars, there began to flicker a gleam of faint saffron and rose color, and the breeze of the daybreak laid its first touch on his cheek and gently stirred a straying lock of his hair. The lights of Baveno, though still bright, looked belated, and the mounting saffron was clear in the dome over him. Thoughts thronged on his mind of many careers to which his life, with hers, might be dedicated. Visions also, though he knew them too bright to last, floated before him and made his being tingle—visions of great works done among the toiling masses, of comfort and health invading the fastness of degradation, and the fire of faith shining on eyeballs that had long been blind to it."

I am not alluding here to *The Old Order Changes* with a view to discussing its merits or demerits as a novel. I am citing it merely as a record of how my own social philosophy step by step developed itself, the problems of economics and politics being step by step united with those of psychology, of religion, of ambition, and the higher romance of the affections. I am dealing with what took place in my own mind as an example of analogous things which have probably taken place in the minds of most men who, however they may differ otherwise from myself, have been preoccupied in the same way. Thus the emotional optimism with which this novel of mine ends—the vision of the Old Order as capable of being born anew by a sudden reillumination of faith and new acquisitions of knowledge—represents, it has subsequently seemed to me, a mood analogous to that which possessed Lord Beaconsfield when he wrote his romance *Sybil*, or when he seemed to insinuate that all social strife might be ended by doles to the poor, distributed week by week through the almoners of manorial lords.

Of Lord Beaconsfield's visions this is not the place to speak, I am concerned here only with the growth and the defects of my own; and as to the general theory of things which is dramatized in *The Old Order Changes*, its merits and its defects seem to me to be these. As for its merits, if compared with my earlier works, *Is Life Worth Living?* and *A Romance of the Nineteenth Century*—in which no cognizance is taken of social politics whatever—*The Old Order Changes* represents a great extension of thought, social problems being brought to the fore as an essential part of the religious. If compared with *Social Equality*, it represents an extension of thought likewise, in that it shows (as *Social Equality* does not) how these two parts are connected.

It is, however, in two ways deficient. At the time when the book was written, the extremist party in England, though comprising many militant Socialists, was for practical purposes composed mainly of men who were known as extreme Radicals. A prominent representative of this class war was Bright. Another at that time was Mr. Joseph

Chamberlain. Instead of attacking all wealth, like Socialists, most of them were business men who spent their lives in pursuit of it. They denounced it in one form only—namely, land, and land only as the inheritance of aristocratic owners. The extraordinary inconsistency of attitude by which these men were characterized created an animus against them in the minds of many—I myself being one—which, though far from being undeserved, was not sufficiently discriminating. As I pointed out in *Social Equality*—and the same argument was repeated in *The Old Order Changes*—the great modern manufacturer, whatever he may think about old landed families, represents the forces on which the increasing wealth of the modern world depends. And yet in that novel I was more than once betrayed into so far joining the Socialists as to partially accept or repeat their denunciations of the modern manufacturers as persons owing all their wealth to the plunder of those employed by them.

This extreme view is, indeed, corrected more than once by the priest; but it is nevertheless insinuated in certain passages in which the writer, by attributing them to the hero, seems to make it his own. It was not till I had carried my statistical studies farther that I was able to reduce the charge hurled by Socialists against the modern employers to what are their true and their relatively small dimensions.

Meanwhile I felt that in *The Old Order Changes*,

as a synthesis of my previous writings, I had made my profession of faith as clearly as I then could; and not long after its publication I betook myself for a mental holiday to a country where I hoped to discover that modern problems were unknown.

CHAPTER XII

CYPRUS, FLORENCE, HUNGARY

A Winter in Cyprus—Florence—Siena—Italian Castles—Cannes—
Some Foreign Royalties—Visit During the Following Spring
to Princess Batthyany in Hungary

BY the time of which I am now speaking
Richard Mallock was Member for the Torquay division of Devonshire, and I often
still helped him at political and other meetings in
his constituency. Lauriston Hall, Torquay, which
had been for a time my home, was let. I stayed
on such occasions at Cockington, or somewhere else
in the neighborhood. One house at which I often
stayed was Sandford Orleigh, near Newton, belonging to Sir Samuel Baker, the traveler and Egyptian
administrator, with whom I had for years been
intimate. In his cabinets, or on his walls, Sir
Samuel had treasures and trophies from half the
savage or out-of-the-way countries of the world.
One day in his study he took from a shelf a few
pieces of marble—green, streaked with white, and
said to me: "Those are bits of the precious verd
antique. I picked them up among the mountains of
Cyprus, where similar blocks were lying about me
everywhere. Anyone who would bring this marble
down to the sea might make a fortune in no time."

As Sir Samuel talked, the whimsical idea occurred to me of going myself to inspect the particular spot he mentioned, and seeing whether any enterprise of such a kind would be practicable. This idea, like Beckett's idea of his system, was for me at first no more than a plaything, but the very name of Cyprus had always excited my imagination, and the thought of the island having thus by chance been revived in me, I began to feel that a visit to it would be a very charming adventure, and that Sir Samuel's story of the marble, even if it should prove to be a myth, would at least be a plausible excuse for embarking on so long a journey. Moreover, it provided Sir Samuel with an excuse for writing to Sir Henry Bulwer, then governor of the island, and asking him to do what he could in the way of securing accommodation for me during my projected stay. Sir Henry's reply was to the effect that if I would so time my movements as to reach Cyprus in January, the Chief Secretary, Colonel Warren, would receive me as a guest for a month or so, and that during the rest of my stay he would himself entertain me at Government House. Posts to and from Cyprus were at that time extremely slow, and it was not till nearly Christmas that these arrangements were complete. Meanwhile, by Sir Samuel's advice, the specimens of the marble were submitted to a London expert. As I was now bent on going, his verdict, though not very favorable, did nothing whatever to discourage me. What mainly occupied my mind

were thoughts of an island which was unknown to
ordinary tourists, the history of which united the
sway of Byzantine emperors with that •of crusading
kings, of Venetian doges and subsequently of Mos-
lem dynasties, where the mountains were crowned
with castles almost lost in clouds; where the walls
of the marine fortress in which Othello lodged cast
the white reflection of the Lion of St. Mark's on the
waters, and where half the inhabitants prayed with
their faces turned to Mecca and half with their
eyes cast down before jeweled and gilded icons—
an island, moreover, where I could watch and
explore these hybrid scenes and pageants without
any appreciable sacrifice of the comforts and the ease
of London.

In this agreeable frame of mind, I left one evening
the lamps of Charing Cross Station behind me
bound via Brindisi for Alexandria, from which port
an Austrian Lloyd steamer would ultimately bring
me to Cyprus, after a voyage, incredibly slow, of
very nearly a week. On my way out I encountered
several acquaintances—Sir Augustus and Lady
Paget, who were going back to Vienna, and were just
visible in the gloom of the Dover boat; Arthur Paget,
bound for Africa; and also several others, among
whom were Edward Milner and John St. Aubyn,
subsequently Lord St. Levan. The goal of these
last was Damascus. We three slept at Alexandria
on the boat which had brought us from Brindisi,
and were next day rowed across the enormous harbor

to a black craft, the *Diana*, which had just arrived from Trieste, and which by way of Port Said and Jaffa brought us in four days to Beyrout. There, after a day of sightseeing, we had tea with the English consul, whose house was very like a mosque. Milner and St. Aubyn were to sleep that night at a hotel and start for Damascus next morning by diligence. I returned to the ship alone, and I found myself twelve hours later looking at Cyprus from the open roadstead of Larnaca.

I remained in the island for something like three months, as the guest of Sir Henry, Colonel Warren, and other British officials. A year or so afterward I recorded my experiences in a short book called *In an Enchanted Island*. It will here be enough to summarize the various impressions and experiences which are there described in detail.

My impression on landing was one of half-forlorn disappointment. The winter that year in Europe was the coldest within living memory. Even the air of Cyprus had something in it not far from frost, and the treeless hills seemed blighted by the clouded and inhospitable sky. But a day like this proved to be a rare exception. Cyprus, as I knew it in the winter, was for the most part a land of what Englishmen mean by a late spring or an early summer when they dream of it. The evenings were chilly, but the days were warm and shining. They were sometimes, though not often, too warm for refreshment. The greens of the trees glittered, the mountains were scarred with purple, and the midday shadows of arcades were sharp as chiseled jet. My first host, Colonel Warren, had his home in Nicosia, a town in the middle of the island, and twenty miles from the sea. Nicosia lies in a great inland plain, and, as seen from the hilly road which slopes slowly down to it from the south, it resembles the pictures of Damascus with which all the world is familiar. Nicosia, however, has one feature which is in Damascus wanting. Among a forest of minarets is a great cathedral, used as a mosque since the days of the Turkish conquest, but built in the Middle Ages by Christian kings of the house of Guy de Lusignan. The town is a maze of lanes, to which ancient houses turn unwindowed walls, broken only by doors whose high, pointed arches often bear above them the relics of crusading heraldry, and give access to cloistered courts, the splash of secret fountains, and rockwork gay with violets. In a house thus secluded, and entered by such a door, lived Colonel Warren, my host, and under his roof, the morning after my arrival, I first definitely felt that I had left the West behind me, when I found that a noise by which I had been just awakened, and which sounded like the cawing of a rook, was that of the muezzin borne from a neighboring minaret and requesting me to adore Allah.

Colonel Warren was an ardent antiquarian, nor was he altogether insensible to the fascination of business ventures. He was not only eager to tell me whatever he knew of the architectural curiosities of the island, ancient and medieval, but he also offered me every assistance in my quest of the precise spot where, according to Sir Samuel, the green marble was to be found. He at once put me into communication with the owners of mules and carriages, with guides and with other persons whose aid would be necessary for me in reaching and exploring the mountains in whose fastnesses the treasure was concealed. He also introduced me to a charming professor from Edinburgh, who, in some official capacity, was excavating Phœnician tombs, and who, by way of taking a holiday, was willing to be my companion. Accordingly one morning we set out in a carriage which brought us to the foot of the mountains where the rough road, made by the English, ended, and where mules awaited us, on whose very disagreeable backs the rest of our expedition was to be accomplished. Sir Samuel Baker's maps and descriptions provided us with outstanding landmarks, which were more or less unmistakable. The spot which we were seeking lay high up in the clefts of a curious mountain known as "The Five Fingers," and was marked by a ruined church, a cave, and a lonely cypress tree. Our first attempt to find this spot was a failure. Our second attempt was successful. There could be no mistake about it—the lonely cypress was there, the cave and the church also. There, too, after a long search, we discovered fragments of stone—duplicates of Sir Samuel's specimens. But these were fragments only. Nothing could be found that was larger than a large pebble. The potential quarries of which Sir Samuel had spoken were children of his own imagination, and the only good they did us was to illustrate how easily practical men may deceive themselves—even when, like Sir Samuel, they are usually keen observers. We did indeed bring a few specimens back with us, but to the marble quarry as a practical project I had already said "Good-by." Let all disappointed prospectors learn philosophy from me. I said it without regret. I was on the whole relieved—for now I was free to devote myself to those pleasures of imagination which the life and the scenes around me had already begun to stimulate.

Before long each page of my life in Cyprus was like a page from an illuminated missal. I climbed to the mountain castle of St. Hilarion, once occupied by Richard the First. Through the traceries of its windows and from its towers I looked at the snowy summits of Cilicia across sixty miles of sea. I explored its stables, hewn out of the solid rock— stables not for horses, but camels. I examined its cisterns, hanging on the brinks of precipices. While on this expedition, I stayed with one of the judges in a lodge on the mountain side, and spent a night with him looking out on a garden of spices, and comparing the Septuagint version of the Song of Solomon with the English. On another occasion I came in a seaward valley to a beautiful monastery, whose refectory still was perfect, though there was no life in its silence but the life of oleanders peering in at the windows and half hiding from view the foam from which Venus sprang. Often in the early morning, on one expedition or another, I saw groups of peasants moving across dewy plains, their coats as bright as Joseph's, who, with their ass or camel, suggested the Flight into Egypt. When I journeyed for any distance by road my equipage was some old landau, drawn by five horses, and accompanied by three servants, one of these being my own, who spoke very fair English, and who had been born on the slopes of Lebanon. It was in this manner that, when I was staying with Sir Henry, I went from Nicosia to Famaugusta, a distance of fifty miles, which it took ten hours to accomplish. This was how Englishmen traveled in the days of William and Mary. Among the remains of Famaugusta I wandered for several days, its huge walls being still very nearly perfect, though they now inclose little but the huts of some Turkish shepherds, about fifty deserted churches, bright inside with frescoes, and a cathedral so profusely carved that it looks like a hill of flowers.

Within the limits of a day's expedition from Famaugusta were the remains — I was taken to visit them—not entirely ruinous, of the country residence of one of the crusading nobles. I found my way into monasteries still peopled by devotees, and saw in the eyes of many of them monastic faith still shining. In strange churches I studied, behind gilded screens and icons, magnificent copies of the Gospels, and read aloud to a sacristan this passage and that, asking him to read them also, so that I might adjust my pronunciation to his. On one occasion, from a height near Government House, I watched, if I may so express myself, a celebrated icon in action—a jeweled portrait of the Madonna, said to have been painted by St. Luke. On the plain below was the broad bed of a river, dry from continued drought. Unanswered prayers for rain had for some time been frequent and at last this miraculous relic had been brought forth from its hiding place, as a charm which was bound to effect what ordinary prayers could not, and was being carried along the banks of the river by a black procession of monks, who were followed—so it seemed to me—by half the population of the neighborhood. As these companies drew nearer, I gradually distinguished outbursts of distant shouting. I had arrived at the psychological moment. Far off, along watercourses lately dry, a streak of light was advancing like the coils of a silver snake. This was the river, which was actually coming down in flood. Presently, with a rattle of pebbles, it was pouring by below me. In less than an hour the portent died away, but left the memory of a new miracle behind it.

The only thoroughly modern thing in Cyprus at the time of my own visit was Government House, which is not in Nicosia, but outside it. It is built wholly of wood, and was sent out from England—

a mere series of rooms surrounding a court, which was then marked out for a tennis ground. There was only one steam engine in the island, and (needless to say) no railway. These appliances not being there, nobody missed them. I myself thought the absence of railways pleasant rather than otherwise, and steam as an aid to industry was the last thing— so it seemed—that the native population wished for. The Duke of Sutherland, it appeared, had not very long ago thought of buying an estate in the southern part of the island and applying all the methods of science to the cultivation of early potatoes. He would, however, in order to insure success, have had to buy from the neighboring peasants certain way leaves and water rights, and for these they banded together to ask such preposterous prices that the duke, as they half hoped he would do, abandoned an enterprise by which they, then the poorest of the poor, would have been the first persons to benefit.

Sir Henry often discussed with me the economic conditions of Cyprus. The population, he said, comprised no class that in England would be called rich, and very few of the peasants, though mostly their own landlords, lived a life which an English plowman would tolerate. The inhabitants as a whole were certainly exceptionally liable to a class of diseases the cause of which is malnutrition, and I came, as I talked to Sir Henry, to see in Cyprus a very useful refutation of the doctrine that the masses are only poor when a few rich people plunder them.

Meanwhile it was a satisfaction to reflect that nobody in Cyprus could make trouble by holding up the rich to execration, the reason being that there were no rich to execrate, and the charm which the imaginative spectator found in the life around him was not likely to be broken by any very rude awakening. Sir Henry himself was not perhaps sensitive to romance, but he did all he could to aid me in my own quest of it, and until my time for quitting his roof came, one day followed another leaving behind it soothing or exciting memories, the colors of which even now have not lost their freshness.

On my way homeward I went from Cyprus to Florence, to stay with some friends who had a villa there. The time was Easter, but the weather was like a damp winter. I found there many acquaint-ances. Among them was a Madame de Tchiacheff, whom I had known in my boyhood at Littlehampton. Scotch by birth, she had married a well-known Rus-sian, and her house, with its cosmopolitan company, was among the most distinguished in Florence. I and my hostess went to pay a call on "Ouida," whom I knew more or less by correspondence, but the coachman took us by mistake to the Villa Careggi instead. By the kindness of Madame de Tchiacheff I was made known to the Strozzi family, and we visited their monumental palace, which was not then shown to the public. With two other palatial houses I came to be acquainted also—one the home of the Russo-American Bourtolines, the other then occupied by Mr. Macquay the banker. The latter of these houses was specially interesting to myself as having been once the home of the then Austrian Minister, Baron von Hugel, whose younger son my cousin, Miss Froude, married.

The constant question which to me all these great houses suggested was, how were the fortunes made by which they were maintained and built? The Pitti Palace, which would hold the palace of the Strozzi in its court, was built by a private citizen, Luca Pitti, for himself. According to modern requirements it is too large for a king. I often thought that, were I an American millionaire, I would secure the services of a hundred of the most accomplished students of Europe and set them to examine simultaneously the business archives of Florence, and thus provide (as in a short time they might do) a mass of digested materials on which a complete economic history of Florentine wealth might be founded.

From Florence I went for a few days to Siena, where, with a completeness to which Florence offers no parallel, the Middle Ages spectacularly still survive. I visited, while I was there, the great castle of Broglio, which, standing among mountains on the brink of a wooded precipice, lifts into the air its clusters of red-brick towers like tulips. I visited

also Cetinale—a strange classical villa, built by a
Cardinal Chigi, and surrounded by miles of ilex
woods, which are peopled with pagan statues. Returning to Florence, I discovered, with the aid of a
large-scale ordnance map, a building equally strange,
and so little known even to Florentines that our
coachman had never heard of it, and often had to
ask the way. This is Torre a Cona—half medieval
castle and half classical palace. It occupies the
summit of a flat-headed hill or mountain. It is
surrounded by a circular park full of deer and
statues. It is approached by an avenue of cypresses
sixty feet in height, and between these trees, on
either side of the way, are colossal horses rampant,
beneath whose extended forelegs the carriage of the
invader passes. I opened a large door in one wing
of the house, and found myself in a miniature
theater, with its semicircle of boxes decorated in
green and silver.

My own days at Florence, however, were on this
occasion prematurely ended by the breaking of a
drainpipe in the villa of my valued hostess, and my
consequent migration at very short notice to Cannes.
I started at night, and in the small hours of the
morning I had to change trains at Genoa. As I
paced the dark platform, the air was bleak and
wintry, and, looking back with regret to the shining
suns of Cyprus, I took my place at last in another
train, shivering. For a few hours I slept. When
I woke I was less uncomfortable. The air, unless

this was mere fancy, had lost something of its sting. I looked out of the window, and from what I could see in the grayness I guessed that we were somewhere or other between Rappallo and Spezzia. As the light grew slowly clearer the prospects were still bleak, but yet with the following of one chill five minutes on another some change was, it seemed, in progress. The gray air acquired a tinge of purple, the chill turned to warmth, the thin purple turned to a soft, enveloping bloom; and when the train reached San Remo a sunrise worthy of midsummer was shining on a world of roses.

Cannes, though the season was not far from its close, was as yet by no means empty. As I drove to my hotel the streets were alive with carriages, white skirts, and the shining of red sunshades. I was soon asked to participate in a number of forthcoming dissipations, the first of these being a tea party given by Philip Green at his villa, "La Forêt," which was close to my own doors. The company comprised a charming and interesting group of French ex-royalties, and a live German king, who looked like a commercial traveler. This party remains in my mind as though it were a vignette on the last page of a diary, the principal entries in which related to a land of which Catherine Cornaro was the last royal ruler, and whose last democracy was democracy as understood by the doges.

On the whole, my expedition to Cyprus, which, together with its two sequels, had occupied about four months, did for me more than I had ever seriously expected. It was at once a stimulus and a rest. I returned to England in May, pleased with the prospect of enjoying a couple of months of London, after which, in Scotland and elsewhere, I hoped to resume my study of political and social problems, and restate them in forms which politicians might find useful. This labor was, however, often interrupted by the pressure of family business, which would call me back for a week or ten days to Devonshire. When the more urgent details were for the time settled, as they were toward the end of the year, I went once more to Cannes, and subsequently to the Cap d'Antibes, being one of a small party who were to stay at the same hotels and lunch and dine in private. No such arrangement could possibly have prospered better. I had, as I knew I should have, much time to myself, and among my luggage was a boxload of statistical Blue Books, which formed my companions in hours of industrious solitude. We made a number of expeditions to old towns in the hills, one of our frequent companions being Father Bernard Osborne, the Catholic nephew by marriage of Mr. Froude the historian, and son of Rev. Lord Sidney Godolphus Osborne, then the most stalwart choregus of ultraevangelical Protestantism. Another frequent companion was Miss Charlotte Dempster, famous as a writer of novels—especially of one, *Blue Roses*, the scene of which was, oddly enough, Cockington. Miss Dempster, whose mere presence was a monument to her own celebrity, was much given to the cultivation of royalties, and which was to bring to her villa the presence of a reigning sovereign. So important did she deem the occasion that, before the potentate was due, she got together the ladies whom she had honored with an invitation to meet him, and instructed them as to how, in his august presence, they should demean themselves. The instructions had been given, and had been followed by an expectant hush, when sounds in the hall were heard like those of the Second Advent. "Now, ladies," said Miss Dempster, solemnly, "rise." The ladies rose like one man, the portals were thrown open, and a loud voice announced a shy little pink Welshman, Mr. Hugh Price Jones, who had innocently looked in for the purpose of a familiar call.

My original intention, when I joined my friends at Cannes, had been to remain on the Riviera till April, and then go back to England, but I received one morning a letter which suggested a project of a more adventurous kind, the thought of which stirred me as much as my last year's voyage to Cyprus, though it would not geographically take me to any such remote distance.

This came about as follows. Among the country houses of England with which I became familiar soon after leaving Oxford was Eaglehurst, situated on the Solent and immediately facing Cowes. It was then occupied by Count and Countess Edmund

Batthyany, subsequently Prince and Princess. The countess, who had seen much of the diplomatic life of Europe, was a shrewd, kindly, and a most agreeable woman, who spoke English like a native. Her husband, who had been educated at Eton, was English in all his tastes, and at Cowes he was an illustrious character, on account of the many victories of his racing yacht *Kriemhilda*. From the Cowes Week till the middle of September he kept open house at Eaglehurst, where for ten days or a fortnight I had many times been his guest. All kinds and degrees of ornamental and agreeable people, from archdukes downward, flocked to Eaglehurst from The Island, and made day after day a garden party on its lawns. When the count, on the death of his father, succeeded to the family honors, he gave up his lease of Eaglehurst, and the now Prince and Princess took up their abode at the castle of Körmend in Hungary. The Prince subsequently discovered that Vienna was more to his taste. The Princess, however, preferred Körmend, which nothing would induce her to abandon, and there she invited a number of her English friends to visit her. I was one of the number. Her invitation was often renewed, but for this reason or that I had never been able to accept it. I had, indeed, put the matter quite out of my mind when, during my visit at Cannes, I heard from her once again. "I saw, in some paper," she said, "that you were going to be at Cannes for the winter. Come on to me afterward and I will show you a Hungarian spring."

If any country had ever roused in my imagination more interest than Cyprus, that country was Hungary. Of all European countries I gathered that it was the least progressive; that all sorts of impossible things might happen in its enchanted forests; that the rulers were still noble; that the peasants were still contented (a fact which they signalized by kissing their lords' hands), and that nothing was very different from what it had been before the first French Revolution. Here was temptation too strong to resist. I was asked to be a guest at Körmend from April till the end of May. I wrote to say I would come, and when the time arrived I went.

I was happy in having with me an admirable Austrian servant who had been in the country before, and knew more or less of its ways. I found his resources inexhaustible, except on one occasion. I stayed on the way at Vicenza, for the purpose of seeing some of its Palladian palaces, and I asked him, when I reached the hotel, to find some guide or waiter who spoke either French or English. He could find no one who knew a syllable of one tongue or the other. Next morning, however, he had secured an Italian native who spoke and understood German. Here was all I wanted. I spoke English to my servant, he spoke German to the Italian, the Italian spoke to the people of whom I wanted to make inquiries. This arrangement, I found, was productive of great advantages. Having made notes of the palaces I wished to see, I told my Italian in each case to inquire whether an English gentleman, much interested in architecture, might be privileged to visit the interior, of the beauty of which he had heard much. The fact that I was making my rounds with a retinue of two attendants was accepted as such a guaranty of my own good character and importance that I was admitted with the utmost courtesy to stately and interesting interiors, from the portals of which I should otherwise have been driven with suspicion and ignominy.

Having seen what I could at Vicenza, I spent a night at Treviso, whence, having got up before sunrise, I drove in a weeping morning to the wonderful Villa Maser, about twenty miles away—the villa whose halls and chambers are gorgeous from end to end with the frescoes of Paul Veronese, and whose tutelary gods look out over the vastness of the Lombard plains, though their view is slightly impeded by the bulk of a Renaissance church. That evening I ensconced myself in an ill-lit train, which, passing close to Venice and crossing the Austrian frontier, brought me and my servant to a strange little medieval town, where we slept in an arcaded hostelry which would not have seemed strange to Erasmus. I halted here because in the neighboring wonderland is, as I knew from descriptions, a castle more fantastic than any fancy of Albert Dürer's—the high-perched castle of Hoch-Osterwitz. I spent next day in exploring it. It outdid all my dreams. Reached by a corkscrew road which, passing through strange gatehouses, winds upward round an isolated hill resembling a pine-clad sugar loaf, the castle covers the summit. It suggested Tennyson's line to me: "Pricked with incredible pinnacles into heaven." Not so large or terrific as St. Hilarion, it inflicts perhaps on the imagination a yet acuter twinge, for St. Hilarion belongs to an age so wholly dissociated from our own that the distance between them is beyond the reach of measurement. Hoch-Osterwitz, on the other hand, though in consequence of its inconvenient position its owners no longer lived in it, was still not wholly derelict. Its roofs were watertight; a portion of it was occupied by a caretaker; two of its halls were full of neglected armor; and some fragments of ancient furniture survived in a cell-like bedroom which were sufficient for the baron when he came—as from time to time he did—to see the caretaker, a sort of steward, on business. The life of a distant age still smoldered within the ancient walls like a fire not quite extinguished, and the nerves of the present and of the past formed one living and unbroken tissue. A strange example of this fact revealed itself to me when, wandering in a rough courtyard, I noticed a little building which jutted out over a precipice. I opened the door, and discovered a Lilliputian chapel with seats in it for

17

some twenty people. Facing me was an altar
trimmed with decaying lace and supporting a mil-
dewed breviary, and before it, in full armor, with
gauntleted hands outstretched, was the effigy of a
kneeling knight. He had knelt there as an image of
prayer for more than three centuries. When sightseeing was over, and we descended to the world
below, my excellent servant said to me, "Ah, sir,
if these trees could talk, what strange things they
could tell us!" Resuming our journey that evening,
we reached Gratz by midnight, where I slept in a
lofty bedroom of the days of Maria Theresa. By the
following afternoon I was at Körmend, drinking
tea with the Princess, and answering her many
questions—for she was an unappeasable gossip—
about old English friends.

The castle of Körmend lies in a great plain. On
one side of it is a park planted in radiating alleys,
according to the taste of Le Nôtre. On the opposite side its precincts abut on the market place of
a small town, and from the south and north it is
approached by two poplar avenues which together
traverse the Batthyany territory for something like
thirty miles in an absolutely straight line. The
dwelling house is a large, square block, with a courtyard in the middle and a tower at each angle. One
of its frontages forms the side of a forecourt flanked
by grandiose outbuildings—estate offices, stables,
and a great frescoed ballroom. Elsewhere round
the house was a very untidy flower garden, which

half the old women of the little town spent, so it seemed to me, most of their days in weeding—herein reviving my recollections of Dartington Hall and Denbury. Indeed, throughout my whole stay at Körmend country life in Hungary was constantly reminding me of what country life was during my own early days in Devonshire. These likenesses gave piquancy to the points of difference. Körmend, though containing a good deal of English furniture, and a certain amount of valuable, if not very valuable, tapestry, was not well furnished according to English standards. The stonework of the great staircase leading to the principal floor was unpolished and rude, and the walls were rudely whitewashed. My own bedroom, which in many ways was delightful, was reached by a vaulted passage so cold and draughty that the Princess advised me always to wear my hat when I traversed it. There was not a bell in the house, and, if I had not had my own servant with me, who was placed in a room near mine, I should have been helpless. And yet the doors of this dwelling were guarded by a porter in crimson robes, who wielded a staff of office topped by a prince's coronet. Most of the dishes at dinner might have come from some rough farmhouse, but the pastry could hardly have been equaled by the finest *chef* in Paris, while the walls of the circular dining room were daubed with theatrical pillars, so that it looked like a ruined temple on the stage of some company of strolling players in a barn.

Other contrasts and other notable things I discovered as the days went by. The whole of the
lower portion of one side of the house was a museum
of family archives, many of them going back to the
beginning of the fourteenth century, and most of
the attic floor—a kind of museum likewise—was
crowded with precious spoils taken by the Batthyanys from the Turks—jeweled swords and muskets,
horsecloths sewn with emeralds, and pavilions, still
splendid, which once had sheltered Pashas in the
field. Another curiosity was a theater still displaying the scenery which had been painted for some
private performance before the end of the eighteenth
century.

During the first week of my visit the Princess and
I were alone, and considerately for most of the day
she left me to my own devices. I had brought out
with me to Cannes a diary of my life in Cyprus, and,
inspired by my present surroundings, I set myself
to begin a task which more than once I had contemplated—the task of working my notes into a
small coherent book. I very soon found this pursuit
absorbing, and my hostess realized that my entertainment would be far from burdensome to herself.
Meanwhile when we were together I was never
weary of questioning her with regard to Hungarian
life. She told me all sorts of quaint and curious
things. She told me of robbers who still haunted
the forests—of forest gypsies whose lives were a
mixture of theft and music, and who often twanged

their instruments in a tavern near the castle gates. She told me of former Batthyanys and of other castles once possessed by them. She told me how the latest alterations of Körmend had been made to satisfy the whims of a beautiful French mistress whom a Batthyany had brought there from the court of Louis Quatorze. Sometimes she asked to dinner a priest and also one of the agents called Molna, in whom she reposed great confidence. When I was talking with the agent the Princess played the part of interpreter. The priest and I took refuge in bad Latin. I copied his pronunciation, and we both of us threw Ciceronian language to the winds. On the whole we were mutually intelligible, and we differed so favorably from the talkers of the fashionable world that we both of us meant a great deal more than we said. One of the questions as to which I was most anxious for information was whether there were in the neighborhood any other old castles, a visit to which I might find interesting. Neither the Princess, the priest, nor the agent on the spur of the moment had very much to tell me. At all events I found out presently for myself much more than they could tell me.

Adjoining the dining room was a small oval library, the contents of which the Princess had, oddly enough, never been at the trouble of examining. I found that they consisted largely of magnificent French folios, consecrated entirely to descriptions and elaborate engravings of court life in

Paris as it was under Louis Quinze—of royal balls, of banquets and garden fêtes, and of the chief hotels in the Faubourg—not only of their architecture, but of their furniture also, and even of the manner in which the furniture was arranged. Of these pictures some of the most curious were those which represented balls or other great entertainments as they would have appeared to the spectator had the façades of the buildings in which they took place been removed, and the halls, rooms, and even the servants' staircases been revealed in section, like the rooms in a doll's house when the hinged front swings open. In one compartment kitchen boys would be carrying up dishes from below to magnificent footmen on a landing. In another some powdered lady, close to the dividing wall, would be offering her eyes and patches to the homage of some powdered beau. With pictures such as these last the Princess was specially pleased. I brought a number of the great volumes into the drawing-room, and we spent in examining them many pleasant evenings.

But I presently found in the library one which, much humbler in appearance, was to myself of much more immediate interest. It was smaller in size, and its binding was stained and broken. This, too, was full of pictures. As pictures they had no great merit, but together they made up the prize for which previously I had looked in vain. This book, published about the year 1680, consisted entirely of

bald but careful engravings of the principal castles
of Hungary, some of them in ruins, but most of them
still inhabited. This book I showed to the Princess
likewise, having marked the castles which apparently
were not very far from Körmend, and asked her if
they still existed, and whether a visit to any of them
would be practicable. Though she had heard of
some of them, her own knowledge was vague, but
she passed the book on to Molna. Many of these
castles Molna knew by name. Some of them he
had seen, some of them were still inhabited, their
aspect, so he reported, being practically indistinguishable from that represented in the old engravings. He picked out five or six as being well
within the compass of a day's or a two days' expedition. If, said the Princess, I wished to see these
places I might as well begin doing so at once, as she
was before long going to receive some visitors whom
she trusted that I would help her to entertain.
Matters were arranged accordingly. She placed a
carriage and four brisk horses at my disposal, and
under Molna's advice my explorations began.

Most of the great castles of Hungary remained
veritable castles long after castles in England had
been transformed into halls and manor houses.
The reason was that constant wars with the Turks
made it still necessary that every great house should
be a fortress. Thus it came about that the ornaments and luxuries of life—many of them under
French influence—developed themselves within walls

251

approachable only by drawbridges; that boudoirs were neighbored by towers loopholed for musketry; and that under smooth lawns and orangeries rocks were hollowed into caverns in which on occasion regiments of troops could hide. One of the greatest of these great castles, Riegersbourg, was refortified in the days of Pope and Addison. It covers an elevated plateau of which every side is precipitous, and above the entrance arch is a white marble tablet on which, in very bad Latin, the builder, Baron Hammer Purgstall, bewails the fact that the rocks by their irregular shape have caused him to violate the rules of classical architecture. Of such castles I visited as many as I could. In all of them, as though by some enchantment, the present had become the past. The unrest of western Europe in the modern sense was dead. In dining rooms trays of the finest Japanese lacquer formed a background for oaken tables into which the beard of Barbarossa might have grown. Knights in armor kept watch over billiard tables whose green baize had survived the fadings of two hundred years. For me this half-visionary world held the same intoxicating spell that many ears discover in Wagner's music.

The Princess, when I described these scenes to her, showed a genuine though rather faint interest. At all events, before very long my explorations were interrupted by the arrival of some of her promised guests. These—a brother and sister—were in some ways modern enough, but in one way they suggested the period of *Wilhelm Meister*. They brought with them not only their servants. They brought with them also a retinue of two musicians, who emerged from their quarters in the evening, and played to us after dinner. But we had other music besides. The weather by this time had grown rapidly warmer, and, when these performers had retired, we went out on a balcony overlooking the great forecourt, and from some unseen quarter beyond the castle walls came night after night the vibrations of a gypsy band. Nor was this the only sound. From the frondage of the park close by there would come in answer to it the early notes of the nightingales.

The first installment of visitors, with their attendant musicians, having departed, their places were presently taken by a distinguished Hungarian diplomat, Count —— and his wife. When I say of the count, who spoke English perfectly, that one could not distinguish him from a highly placed English gentleman, I am paying him, no doubt, an insular, but I mean it to be a sincere, compliment.

But the Princess had still another guest in reserve, on whose qualities, so I judged from her tones, she set even a higher store. This was a Hungarian lady, young, well born, and married, but unfortunately neglected by her husband, although she was extremely beautiful. As my mind was much engaged with the thoughts of old castles, and also with the composition of my own little work on

Cyprus, I paid no great attention to what the Princess said in praise of this guest whose advent was now approaching. But when the lady arrived I felt that the praise was justified. As she and her husband are by this time beyond the reach both of praise and blame, I may say of her without fear of impertinence that she was a model of innocent beauty, that her conversation was as charming as her expression, and her dresses as charming as her conversation. I am myself not much addicted to cards, but when she proposed in the evenings to teach me the Hungarian game of Tarok I should not have been human had I failed to become her pupil. But I was never long in her company without being conscious of a feeling that she was a woman who, through no fault of her own, had already had a history, or was certain to have one some day. This feeling did not mislead me. A year later it was justified. I learned, by accident, that her history had been short, forlorn, and fatal. Its hidden actualities, reconstructed by my own imagination, I afterward combined in my novel *A Human Document.*

CHAPTER XIII

TWO WORKS ON SOCIAL POLITICS

The Second Lord Lytton at Knebworth—"Ouida"—Conservative
  Torpor as to Social Politics—Two Books: *Labor and the
  Popular Welfare* and *Aristocracy and Evolution*—Letters from
  Herbert Spencer

MY visit to Cyprus one year, and my visit
to Hungary the next, were both of them
retreats from the life of political and even
philosophical thought. They were frank acts of
truancy in the regions of pure romance; where life,
individual and social, is a spectacle to be enjoyed,
not a problem of which thinkers compete in devising
an explanation. But on returning from Hungary to
England the practical affairs of the moment met me
again halfway, at Vienna, where for a day or two I
broke my journey. My acquaintances at Vienna
were few, but they included Sir Augustus and Lady
Paget at the Embassy, whom I had last seen at midnight on the deck of the Dover packet when I was
bound for the shores of Cyprus more than a year
before. Ambassadors, if they know their business,
are necessarily preoccupied with the present, and
when lunching or dining with Sir Augustus it was not
possible to forget it. It was all the more impossible
because on these occasions there was another diplomat present, also an old acquaintance—Sir Henry

Drummond Wolf, who happened to be then on his way home from Persia, and who was voluble on questions of international, and especially of English, politics. So far, however, as my own mood was concerned, this dissipation of romance by realities was a more or less gradual process. Even when I was again in England my inclinations to the life romantic—to what Virgil (I think) calls the "*amor ulterioris ripæ*"—survived for many months the new recall of my mind to the philosophies of prosaic action.

As an illustration of this fact I remember a week-end visit which I paid that summer to Robert, the second Lord Lytton, at Knebworth. The occasion was marked by the coappearance of things romantic and practical in more ways than one. On the day of my arrival one of the first topics discussed was "Ouida," who at that time was in England, and had been staying at Knebworth only the week before. "Ouida's" view of life was nothing if not romantic. Lytton, during the previous spring, had been spending some weeks in Florence. He was quite alone; and "Ouida," who, apart from her affectations, was a very remarkable woman, had had no difficulty in securing his frequent company at her villa, where she fed him at an incredible price with precociously ripe strawberries. On her memory of these tender proceedings she had built up a belief that his nature had been emptied of everything except one great passion for herself, and she had actually come to

Knebworth convinced that a single word from her would tear him from the bosom of his family and make him hers alone. The magic word was said. The expected results had, however, failed to follow— perhaps because the word, or words, had not been very happily chosen. They had been these: "Why don't you leave this bourgeois man-and-wife *milieu* behind you and prove in some Sicilian palace what life may really mean for people like you and I?"

On the occasion of the same visit another meeting between romance and reality was this: Knebworth was originally a dignified but plain structure, built (I should say at a guess) in the time of Charles II; but, as is well known, the first Lord Lytton (the novelist), inspired by the taste of his time, and aided by inexhaustible stucco, metamorphosed it into the semblance of a pinnacled castle or abbey, the old dining room reappearing in the form of a baronial hall. One evening after dinner I, my host, and a certain Admiral B—— happened to be in the hall alone. While the admiral was reading a letter, my host drew me aside and gave me an amusing description of the rise of the admiral's family. His grandfather, having accumulated a substantial fortune as a solicitor, discovered a ruin—a small tower in France—the name of which was identical with his own. This ruin he bought, and declared that it was the cradle from which his own family sprang. He then, having bought an estate in an English county, proceeded to build a Norman castle in ruins, and adjoining this he built a turreted Tudor mansion. Here was a family pedigree translated into terms of stone. The builder crowned his work by the adoption of feudal manners, to which his domestics had so to adapt their own that when a neighbor, who called on him, asked if Mr. B—— was at home, the reply of the footman was, "The right honorable gentleman is taking a walk on the barbican." My host, having finished his story, was for a moment called away. He had no sooner gone than the admiral, coming up to me, jerked his thumb in the direction of the surrounding panels, and said, confidentially, "The whole of this was put up by that man's father."

But in a much more memorable way romance conquered reality one night in the drawing-room. The ladies of the party had disappeared; and by way of doing something Lytton, two other men, and myself became somehow grouped round a card table with our minds made up for whist. At first we put down our cards with promptitude and a semblance of attention, but someone before long made some observation which, though interesting, was wholly irrelevant to the game. The three others put down their cards to listen, and had, when they took them up again, some difficulty in remembering who was to play next. Presently one of them quoted a line of poetry. It was from Coleridge's "Kublai Khan." Somebody else suggested a mild doubt as to whether that poem had, as the author contended, really been composed in a dream. The game once more proceeded, but our host's eyes had already begun to wander, and at last he frankly threw his own cards on the table. Everybody else followed him. Cards were things forgotten. Their place was taken by poetry. Single lines were cited which the authors had dreamed undoubtedly. The most remarkable was dreamed by a brother of Tennyson, after a day spent in examining a bundle of ancient manuscripts. The line—it was Latin—was as follows:

"*Immemorabilium per fulva crepuscula palpans*" —that is to say, "fumbling among the tawny twilights of immemorables." Lord Lytton looked as if he were in a dream himself. Presently he spoke as though his mind were coming back from a distance. "I," he said, "dreamed a poem in India. It has never been written down, but I still can remember every line of it. Listen." The poem, which was full of vague Oriental imagery, was perfectly intelligible, and throbbed with a certain sonority like that of distant gongs; but no sane man would have written it in his waking moments. In that fact lay its charm. The author's voice, naturally low and musical, acquired new tones as he recited it, giving to it the qualities of an incantation; and round us, as though fashioned out of shadows, was the large, dimly lighted drawing-room, which the old novelist had incrusted with impossible heraldries, culminating in escutcheons of pre-Christian Welsh kings.

The pseudo-Gothic revival, of which Knebworth is a late monument, but which was inaugurated by Horace Walpole in the stucco of Strawberry Hill, is, if judged by the strict canons of architectural taste, absurd, but as time goes on and the taste which produced it vanishes the houses in which it embodied itself cease to be mere absurdities. They acquire the rank and dignity of historical documents. They are more than mere architecture. They represent attempts at a reconstruction of life—a new fusion of politics with poetry, romance, and mysticism. Their fault is that this fusion has failed to become actual. And yet these attempts, though largely recorded in stucco, still evoke visions and atmospheres from which many of us are loath to be driven into the wintry actualities of to-day.

For myself, on my return from Hungary, the influence of romance was further protracted by the fact that I for some time was occupied in completing my work on Cyprus; but when this at last had received its finishing touches there was nothing left that could keep other interests at bay. Radical and Socialist oratory was resounding on every side. Doctrines with regard to Labor were again being promulgated in forms so extreme that they reached the verge of delirium, and were yet received with acclamations. Old statistical errors, for the complete refutation of which unimpeachable evidence abounded, were shouted afresh, as though they were not open to question. But in respect of all

facts and principles which lie really at the basis of
things, the Conservative party was, as a whole,
dumb.

I began to say to myself daily, *"Semper ego
auditor tantum? Nunquam ne reponam?"* "Will no
one wake up this unhappily lethargic mass, and by
forcing the weapons of knowledge and reason into
their hands provoke them and enable them to meet
the enemy at the gate?" Every other interest,
philosophic, romantic, religious, fell away from me
for the time. Wherever I was, whether in London or
country houses—for in these respects my habits remained much what they had been—I had with me
the works of economists, statistical reports, multitudes of current speeches, all bearing on industrial
and social questions. At intervals I dealt with one
or another of these in tentative articles contributed to
reviews like the *Nineteenth Century*, till at length I
redigested, rewrote and combined them, thus, after
some three years of effort, producing a succinct book
called *Labor and the Popular Welfare*.

This book, in carefully simplified language, dealt
comprehensively with the fundamental causes to
which the increased wealth of the modern world is
due, and on which the maintenance, to say nothing
of the enlargement, of this modern increment depends. The argument of the book, in its general
outline, is as follows. Without manual labor there
can be no wealth at all. Unless most of its members
are laborers, no community can exist. But so long

as wealth is produced by manual labor only the amount produced is small. In whatever way it may be distributed, the majority will be primitively poor. The only means by which the total product of a given population can be increased is not any new toil on the part of the laboring many, but an intellectual direction of the many by a super-capable few. Here is the true cause of all modern increments of wealth. Let these increments be produced, and it is possible for the many to share in them. It is on securing a share of them that their only hope of an ampler life depends, but it is from the efforts of the few that any increase of their shares must come. The fundamental facts of the case are, indeed, of a character the precise reverse of that which the theories of the Socialists impute to them. In proportion as the wages of labor rise above a given minimum the many are the pensioners of the few, the few are not the plunderers of the many, and those who maintain the opposite are mere intellectual gamins standing on their heads in a gutter.

This thesis I had outlined already in my earlier work, *Social Equality*, but in *Labor and the Popular Welfare* it is urged with more precision, and the general argument is, as in the earlier work it was not, supported by a skeleton of more or less precise statistics. This book, by the advice of a friend, was offered to a celebrated publisher, a pillar of sound Conservatism; but in effect, if not in so many words, he said he would have nothing to do with it, its subject being, in his opinion, unlikely to interest, or its argument to benefit, anyone. It is, I think, not merely an author's vanity which inclines me to regard his decision not so much as a mistaken literary judgment, but as the expression of a temperamental apathy with which many Conservatives are inflicted with regard to social problems. An entire edition of the work was bought soon after its publication by the Central Conservative Office as a textbook for the use of speakers. With a similar object in view, another association, six or seven years later, offered to purchase an entire edition likewise; but I was obliged to decline the proposal, because I had come to recognize that the statistical portions of the work had, in part, become obsolete, and were in part not sufficiently complete. Meanwhile successive editions of it had been sold to the English public. It had many readers in America, and a very large sum was offered me by a Melbourne newspaper for a series of short articles in which its main arguments should be condensed.

My personal concern, however, in these matters was diminished by the fact that the argument of this work, as a whole, soon seemed to me susceptible of a more comprehensive statement. I had already, as I have said before, attempted in my novel, *The Old Order Changes*, to unite the problems of industrial and social politics with those relating to religion and the higher forms of affection, whereas in *Labor and the Popular Welfare* I had confined my attention to pure economics only. I had, indeed, thus confined it in *Social Equality* also. But it now began to dawn on me that, quite apart from the sphere of religion, the philosophy of modern economics could be, and required to be, extended in what for me was a new direction.

A year or two after the publication of *Labor and the Popular Welfare* a work made its appearance which, although it was couched in the driest terms of philosophy, sold as rapidly as any popular novel, and raised its author at once from absolute obscurity to fame. This was *Social Evolution*, by Mr. Benjamin Kidd. Mr. Kidd's style, apart from certain tricks or mannerisms, was, for philosophic purposes, admirable. But no mere merits of style would account for the popularity of a work which consisted, in form at all events, of recondite discussions of evolution as conceived by the Darwinians on the one hand and the disciples of Weismann on the other. The popularity of Mr. Kidd's book was due to the general drift of it. Just as Darwin's theory of evolution, with its doctrine of the survival of the strongest, provided a scientific basis, unwelcome to many, for aristocracy, Mr. Kidd's aim was to show that evolution in its higher forms was in reality a survival of the weakest, and thus provided a scientific basis for democracy—democracy by constant implications being identified with some form of Socialism. To me this book, which I examined with extreme care, seemed, in the practical bearing, a piece of monumental claptrap, though it was claptrap of the highest order, and was for that reason all the more pernicious. Mr. Kidd, in dealing with the facts of social life, seemed to me to be dealing not with facts, but clouds—clouds which suggested facts, as actual clouds may suggest a whale or weasel, but which yet, when scrutinized, had no definite content. To me this book rendered a very valuable service, I found in it an epitome of everything against which my own mind protested; and I soon set myself to prepare a series of tentative studies in which certain of Mr. Kidd's positions were directly or indirectly criticized. If I remember rightly, these were published at intervals in the *Contemporary Review;* and their substance, expanded and digested, appeared by and by in a volume which I called *Aristocracy and Evolution.*

Of this volume, which was a criticism not only of Mr. Kidd, but of Mr. Herbert Spencer also, the fundamental thesis was similar to that of *Social Equality,* and of *Labor and the Popular Welfare*— namely, that in proportion as societies progress in civilization and wealth all appreciable progress, and the sustentation of most of the results achieved by it, depend more and more on the directive ability of the few; and this thesis was affiliated to the main conclusions of evolutionary science generally. It was admitted that, within certain limits, results achieved by the few were absorbed and perpetuated by the many, though the activities of the originators might have ceased, and that a proper definition of evolution pure and simple would be: "The orderly sequence of the unintended." But, at the same time, it was shown that an "orderly sequence of the unintended," though it is a part of what we mean by progress, is a small part only, the major part still requiring the intentional activities of the few, not only for its initiation, but for its sustentation also.

This argument was set forth with great minuteness, and it was shown how many most distinguished thinkers, while admitting its general truth, were constantly obscuring it by formulæ which were, in effect, denials of it. Among the writers thus referred to was Mr. Herbert Spencer, who in one passage described the Napoleonic wars as an incident in the process of evolution and in another passage cited them as examples of the results of the solitary wickedness of one super-capable man. With regard to these issues I received some interesting letters from Mr. Spencer himself. His contention was that I had quite misrepresented his meaning. Economically, at all events, the functions of the super-capable man were in his opinion as important as they possibly could be in mine. I replied that if such were his opinion he very often obscured it, but that I hoped he would acquit me of any conscious unfairness to himself. His first letters were not without a touch of acerbity, but he ended with amicably stating what his actual views were, and saying that if I only amended certain passages

HERBERT SPENCER

relating to himself, he was in entire agreement with my whole argument otherwise.

I never met Mr. Spencer, and of what he may have been in conversation I have not the least conception; but a story is told of him which shows that he must have had a vein of humor in him which his writings do not suggest. His favorite relaxation was billiards. This game he played with more than average skill, but on one occasion, much to his own chagrin, he found himself hopelessly beaten by a very immature young man. "Skill in billiards, up to a certain point, is a sign," he said, "of sound self-training. Too much skill is a sign of a wasted life."

To go back to *Aristocracy and Evolution*, though its sale was equal to some of the works of Herbert Spencer himself, it was by no means comparable to that of the treatise of Mr. Kidd, to which it was designed as a counterblast. Of this the main reason was, I may venture to say, not that it was inferior in point of style or of pertinence, or of logical strength of argument, but that, while appealing, like Mr. Kidd's work, to serious readers only, it appealed to the sentimentalism of a very much smaller number of them—if, indeed, it can be said to have appealed to sentimentalities at all; whereas Mr. Kidd had a semi-Socialist audience ready for him, who lived mainly by sentiment, whose sentimentalities had anticipated his own, and who were only waiting for some one from whom they might learn to sing them to some definite intellectual tune. Moreover, unlike

Labor and the Popular Welfare, which was equally remote from sentimentalism, *Aristocracy and Evolution* did not supply the place of it by providing Conservative thinkers with arguments suitable for immediate use on the platform.

Here we have the old difficulty which has always beset Conservatives when face to face with revolutionaries. The revolutionaries, or, rather, the leading spirits among them—for revolutions are always the work of a small body of malcontents—require no rousing. They welcome any arguments, philosophic or otherwise, which may tend to invest them with the prestige of scientific thinkers; but the Conservatives require to be roused, and roused in two different ways—first, in respect of the principles on which their own position rests, and secondly, in respect of the methods by which those principles can be presented to the multitude in a manner which shall produce conviction. Looking back on *Aristocracy and Evolution*, I now think that, if I could have rewritten it in the light of the above considerations, I should modify, not its argument, but the manner in which this argument was presented. Much of its substance I have incorporated in what I have written since; but, as it stood when I finished it, I felt it so far satisfactory that it expressed all I had then to say as to the subjects of which it treated, and my house of political thought was for the time empty, swept, and garnished. After two years' labor spent on it, though this had been carried on in very agreeable circumstances—in Highland castles and shooting lodges, or at the Rodens' house in Ireland—I felt the need of rest—of forgetting in intercourse with agreeable men and women that anything like disagreeable men existed, who rendered the labors of political thought necessary. My mind, however, instead of resting, was presently driven, or driven back, into activities of other kinds.

CHAPTER XIV

RELIGIOUS PHILOSOPHY AND FICTION

The So-called Anglican Crisis—*Doctrine and Doctrinal Disruption*—
Three Novels: *A Human Document, The Heart of Life, The In-
dividualist*—Three Works on the Philosophy of Religion:
*Religion as a Creditable Doctrine, The Veil of the Temple, The
Reconstruction of Belief*—Passages from *The Veil of the Temple*.

A YEAR or so after the publication of *Aristocracy and Evolution* I found myself taking
by accident quite a new departure. I was
offered and accepted a place on the board of a small
company, and was thus abruptly summoned from
the world of economic philosophy to that of practical
action. The object of the company was to perfect
and introduce an invention which, had it been
properly developed as a mechanism and skillfully
dealt with otherwise, might well have become
popular. The general idea was certainly sound
enough. With regard to this all concerned were
unanimous. But as soon as the project assumed a
minutely practical form all sorts of difficulties arose.
The mechanism was one which might be constructed
in a number of alternative ways, and, according to
the way chosen, the cost of manufacture would
vary very considerably, and its use to the general
public would vary to a degree still greater. Since

the board comprised several engineers, a successful manufacturer of pianos, and a lawyer highly respected in the domain of local government, I imagined that these preliminary difficulties would very soon be solved. I was, however, much mistaken. Each director had some idea of his own, which clashed with the ideas of others, not indeed as to fundamentals, but purely as to incidental details. This rendered concerted action as impossible as it would have been had the differences related not to means, but to ends; and nobody united in himself sufficient technical knowledge with sufficient moral initiative to harmonize these conflicting elements, and thus to render concerted action practicable. The enterprise, in consequence, soon came to an end, certain of the directors bearing most of the loss. But I, at all events, got something for my money in the way of an instructive experience. It was an experience which illustrated by fact what I had previously insisted on as a matter of general theory—namely, that no enterprise undertaken by a number of persons can possibly succeed unless it has some man of exceptional strength at the head of it, who will use the wits of others according to his own judgment; and, further, that this man's strength must be of a very peculiar kind, which has nothing to do with the qualities, moral or intellectual, which make their possessors illustrious in other domains of life.

This taste of business experience did not heighten

my appreciation of the mental leisure which otherwise I now enjoyed. It was a leisure, however, which before very long took the form of activity in a new direction.

The more important questions which agitate the mind of an age, just like those which agitate the mind of an individual, engross and affect it, not simultaneously, but in alternation. One actor recedes for the moment and makes way for another, and the newcomer is an old actor returning. About the time of which I am now speaking there was—on the surface, at all events—a lull in social controversy, and a new outbreak of religious. An illustration of this fact may be found in the extraordinary popularity achieved by a novel purely religious in interest, its name being *Robert Elsmere*, and its authoress Mrs. Humphry Ward. Its religious interest is of a highly specialized kind. It is the story of an Anglican clergyman who starts as an earnest and absolutely untroubled believer in the traditional dogmas which the Church of England inculcates. He is thus at peace with himself till he gradually becomes intimate with a certain distinguished scholar. This scholar, who is the squire of his parish, is the possessor of an enormous library, rich in the writings of continental and especially of German skeptics. Having suggested to Robert Elsmere sundry disquieting arguments, he turns him loose in his library, begging him to use it as his own. The clergyman accepts the invitation. He soon is absorbed in the works of such writers as Strauss and Renan; and little by little their spirit becomes his own. Their eyes become his. Everything which orthodoxy demands in the way of the supernatural disappears. The sacraments become mummeries. Even Christ, in the ordinary sense, no longer lives. The clergyman is left in desolation. How, he asks, can the Church (by which he means the Anglican Church) help him? What evidence, what shred even of probability, have its ministers to support their teaching? They hardly, if closely pressed, know what they mean themselves, and the supernatural teaching of one section of Anglicans contradicts that of the others. The one moral which her hero draws from his studies resolves itself into the words, "Miracles do not happen."

Mrs. Ward's novel was particularly appropriate to the time at which it was published. The question of what a man, as a minister of the English Church, might or might not teach without surrendering his office or without abjuring his honesty was being hotly debated in reviews, in Convocation, and at countless clerical Congresses; but these resulted in no unanimous answer. The English Church, indeed, as a teaching body, was held by many people to be on the very verge of disruption. The situation was precisely similar to that which in my book, *Is Life Worth Living?* I had myself predicted ten years before as inevitable. If Christianity means anything definite—anything more than a mood of precarious sentiment—the only logical form of it is that represented by the Œcumenical Church of Rome. This had been my previous argument, and, stimulated by current events, I felt impelled to re-state it in greater detail and with more pungent illustrations. I found particular satisfaction in analyzing the utterances of dignitaries of the Broad-Church party, such as Farrar and Wilberforce, whose plan for rejuvenating the coherence of the Anglican Church was to reduce all its doctrine which savored of the supernatural to symbols. One of them proposed, for example, to salvage the doctrine of the Ascension by maintaining that its true mean-ing is, not that Christ rose from the earth ver-tically (which would indeed be absurd), but that he disappeared, as it were, laterally, by withdrawing himself somehow or other into the fourth dimension of space. According to another, the statement that Christ on a specified day ascended was merely a symbolical way of saying that about the time in question his work on earth was finished, and that he had, like Sir Peter Teazle, taken leave of his disciples with the words, "Gentlemen, I leave my character in your hands." On the basis of such an exegesis they managed to raise a superstructure of sentiment which had, until it was touched, some likeness to the old fabric, but which a breath of air would dissipate, and unmask the ruins within. Canon Farrar's *Life of Christ* was a work of this description. The work had an enormous sale, and the author, at an Oxford dinner, confided somewhat ruefully to a neighbor that all he got for it himself was not more than three hundred pounds. Another neighbor, overhearing this remark, murmured to somebody else, "He forgets that in the good old days the same job was done for thirty pieces of silver."

A criticism of the clerical rationalists, not dissimilar in its purport, was administered to Jowett by a certain Russian thinker, who knew little as to Jowett's opinions, and had no intention of rebuking them. He was describing, as an interesting event, the development of a religion in Russia which claimed to be Christian and at the same time purely rational. "Was it a good religion?" asked Jowett, with a somewhat curt civility. "No," said the Russian, reflectively, "it was not a good religion. It was schlim-schlam. It was veesh-vash. It was vot you call 'Broad Church.'"

Mrs. Ward, who may fairly be described as the best educated woman novelist of her generation, endeavored, in the disguise of her hero, to found a rationalized Christianity on her own account, and her distinction as a scholar and a reasoner makes this experiment interesting. But the kind of Christianity in which Robert Elsmere takes refuge, and of which he officiates as the self-appointed primate, has no foundation but sentiment and certain *tours de force* of the imagination. As soon as it resolves itself into any definite propositions with regard to objective fact it is evident that these have no authority at the back of them. Without some authority at the back of it, unified by a coherent logic, no religion can guide or curb mankind or provide them with any hopes that the enlightened intellect can accept. It is precisely this sort of authority which, for those who can accept its doctrines, the Church of Rome possesses, and is possessed by that Church alone. Here is the argument in which *Is Life Worth Living?* culminated. The detailed processes by which the authority and the teaching of Rome have developed themselves I had cited in *Aristocracy and Evolution* as an example of evolution in general. In a new volume, *Doctrine and Doctrinal Disruption*, I dealt with it once again, having before me the example of what was then being called "The Great Anglican Crisis." That this book was not written wholly in vain I have sufficient reason to know, for a variety of correspondents assured me that it put into clear form what had long been their unexpressed convictions—certain of these persons—serious Anglicans—having joined, since then, the Church of Rome in consequence.

But the thoughts of which this work was the result were not appeased by its publication. They began to germinate afresh in a kindred, but in a different form. *Doctrine and Doctrinal Disruption* had for its immediate subject a position which was mainly insular—that is to say, the position, not of religion in general, but of the formal interpretations of Chris-

276

tianity which were at that time colliding with complete unbelief in England. But I had from the first —from the days when I was planning *The New Republic* onward—urged that all doctrines pertaining to particular forms of Christianity were merely parts of a wider question—namely, that of the credibility of supernatural religion of any kind, and that this credibility must be tested, not by an examination of religious doctrines as such, or even of religious emotion in the purer and more direct manifestations of it, but in the indirect effects produced by it on the quality of life generally. Thus merely in the capacity of a thinker I felt myself presently impelled to a reconsideration of the contents of the life of the individual; and this impulsion was aggravated by certain domestic dramas which, in one way or another, came to my own knowledge.

In describing my visit to Hungary I mentioned a young and extremely engaging lady, who looked as though she were made for happiness, but whose life, though prematurely ended, had had time since then to become entangled in tragedy. I had often, since I left Hungary, wondered what had become of her; but not till some years later did I learn, quite accidentally, what her story and her end had been. I was told few details, but these sufficed to enable me, by a mere use of the imagination, to reconstruct it, and see in it certain general meanings. Of this reconstructive process the result was my novel, *A Human Document*. It was not, indeed, due to the stimulus of this story alone, and of the philosophic meanings which I read either in or into it. It was partly due, I must confess, to the effects which Hungarian life had on my imagination generally—effects with which the affairs of this lady had nothing at all to do—and to an impulse to reproduce these in some sort of literary form. The castles, the armor, the shepherds playing to their flocks, the wild gypsy music, the obeisances of the peasants, the mysteries of the great forests—all these things, like an artist when he paints a landscape, I longed to reproduce for the mere pleasure of reproducing them. Such being the case, the heroine of my novel and her experiences became unified with the scenes among which I had actually known her.

For this work, as a picture of Hungary and Hungarian life, I am well supported in claiming one merit, at all events. Count Deym, who at that time was Austrian Ambassador in London, told a friend of mine that my picture in these respects could not have been more accurate had I known Hungary for a lifetime. Of its merits as a study of human nature, and an essay on the philosophy of life, it is not my province to speak. I merely indicate the conclusion to which, as an attempt at philosophic analysis, it leads. It leads, although by a quite different route, to the same conclusion as that suggested in *The Old Order Changes* and in *A Romance of the Nineteenth Century*—namely, that in all the higher forms of affection a religious belief is implicit, which connects the lovers with the All, and establishes between them and It some conscious and veritable communion.

The hero gives expression to this conclusion thus: On the evening after that on which the heroine had made herself wholly his the two are together in a boat on a forest lake. She does not regard her surrender as the subject of ordinary repentance. On the contrary, she regards it as justified by the cruelty and neglect of her husband, and yet she is beset by a sense that, nevertheless, she may have outraged something which for some reason or other she ought to have held sacred. Her companion divines this mood, and does what he can to reassure her. "See," he says, "the depths above us, and the depths reflected under us, holding endless space and all the endless ages, and ourselves like a ball of thistledown floating between two eternities. From some of these stars the arrows of light that reach us started on their vibrating way before Eve's foot was in Eden. Where that milky light is new universes are forming themselves. The book of their genesis yet remains to be written. Think of the worlds forming themselves. Think of the worlds shining, and the darkened suns and systems mute in the night of time. To us—to us—what does it all say more than the sea says to the rainbow in one tossed bubble of foam? And yet to us it must say something, seeing that we are born of it, and how can we be out of tune with it, seeing that it speaks to us now?"

The moral of this mysticism is that no affection is

complete unless it is in harmony with some cosmic will which takes cognizance of the doings of the individual, and gives to them individually something of its own eternity; but that, in so far as the two are at variance, the individual must pay the price. In *A Human Document* this price is paid deliberately by the man, and ultimately the woman shares in it, like a character in a Greek tragedy.

This novel was followed by another, *The Heart of Life*, which was more or less constructed on the same lines, and also in response to a similar dual impulse. The scenery and the setting were those of my own early days in Devonshire. The home of the principal actors, as there depicted, is a compound of Glenthorne—I have mentioned its situation already, on the seaward borders of Exmoor—and of Denbury. Several of the characters are clergymen with whom I was once familiar. Mixed with these elements are certain scenes of fashionable life. All these accessories are almost photographically accurate; and the mere pleasure of reproducing them— or, as boys would say, the mere fun of reproducing them—was one of the motives which actuated me in writing this novel and rewriting it—for most of it was written over and over again. The main action, as in *A Human Document*, turned on the nature of the affections and the pangs of unhappy matrimony, these last conducting the two principal personages to a rest in which the heart of life, self-purified, is hardly distinguishable from the content of a Christian child's prayer.

A third novel followed. This novel was *The Individualist*, of which the underlying subject was still the relation of religion to life, but the subject was handled in a spirit less of emotion than of pure social comedy. It was suggested by the movement, then beginning to effervesce, in favor of the rights of women, and by the semi-Socialist hysteria with which some of its leaders associated it, and in which many of them thought that they had discovered the foundations of a new faith. The most prominent character, though she is not in the ordinary sense the heroine, is Mrs. Norham, an ornament of intellectual Bloomsbury. Having certain independent means, she is far from being an opponent of private property as such. Her *bête noire* is the fashionable or aristocratic classes, these being the true Antichrist; and she has founded a church whose main spiritual mission is to instigate an *élite* of the obscure and earnest to despise them. By and by she meets some members of this despicable class herself. Among them is a Tory Prime Minister, who joins with his sister, an exceedingly fine lady, in expressing a respectful and profound admiration of her intellect. Mrs. Norham's philosophy of social religion hereupon undergoes such an appreciable change that she ultimately finds salvation in winding wool for a peeress, the only surviving thorns in her original crown of martyrdom being the loss of some money in a company formed for the production of a perpetual motion, and her discovery that a certain dinner party to which she has been asked is not sufficiently fashionable. This book, though in many respects a mere comedy of manners and characters —among the characters was a South African millionaire and his wife—was under the surface permeated by a serious meaing, being in effect an exhibition of the "fantastic tricks" which those who reject the supernatural are driven to play in their attempts to provide the world with a substitute.

But every general event must have a general cause, for which individuals are not alone responsible; and the fantastic tricks of the people who try to make religions for themselves cannot be due merely to the idiosyncrasies of exceptionally foolish persons. There must be causes at the back of them of a deeper and a wider kind. The first of these causes is obviously the fact that, for some reason or other, multitudes who know nothing of one another are independently coming to the conclusion that supernaturalism, which was once accepted without question as the main content or substratum of human life, rests on postulates which to them are no longer credible. Why is this the case to-day, when it was not the case yesterday? Of these necessary postulates two are the same for all men—namely, an individual life which survives, the individual body, and the moral responsibility of the individual, or his possession of a free will. A third postulate, which is the same for all orthodox Christians, is the miraculous inspiration of the Bible, whatever the precise nature of this inspiration may be. Of these three postulates the last has been discredited all over the world by biblical criticism and scientific comparisons of one religion with another. The first and the second have been discredited by advances in the science of biological physics which has, with increasing precision, exhibited human life and thought as mere functions of the physical organism, the organism itself being, in turn, a part of the cosmic process. If this be the case, what religious significance can attach to the individual as such? His thoughts, his emotions, his actions, are no more his own than the action of a windmill's sails or the antics of scraps of paper gyrating at a windy corner.[1] The first license to men to construct

---

[1] In an early chapter of *The Veil of the Temple* one of the characters describes the situation as follows:

"(For a long time after the death of Hegel) these separate living species seemed radically separated from one another, or connected only as contrivances of the same deity. Thus the different kinds of life—in especial the life of man—seemed to stand up alone above the waters of science, like island peaks above the sea, the objects of a separate knowledge. But all this while the waters of science were rising slowly like a flood, and were signalizing their rise by engulfing from time to time some stake or landmark that a moment before was protruding from them, or by suddenly pouring over a barrier and submerging some new area. No doubt even by this process many people were frightened, but there was no more general panic than there was in the days of Noah. Men from their superior status watched the tide in security. They ate, they drank at their old sacramental altars. They were married before them and given in marriage. But one fine day—as we look back on it now it seems the work of a moment—something happened which, as I often

283

a religion is a license given them by reason to admit the proposition that the individual will is free. The primary obstacle to religious belief to-day is the difficulty of finding in this universe a rational place for freedom—a *"voluntas avolsa fatis."* How is this obstacle to be surmounted?

To this question I attempted an answer in a new philosophical book, *Religion as a Credible Doctrine*, of which the general contention is as follows. If we trust solely to science and objective evidence, the difficulty in question is insuperable. There is no place for individual freedom in the universe, and apologists who attempt to find one are no better than clowns tumbling in the dust of a circus. If they try to smuggle it in through some chink in the *mœnia mundi*, these ageless walls are impregnable, or if here and there some semblance of a gate presents itself, each gate is guarded, like Eden, by science with its flaming swords.

---

amused myself by thinking, would have been for a transhuman spectator the finest stage effect in the world. The gradual rise of the waters gave place to a cataclysm. The fountains of the great deep were broken up when Darwin struck the rock, and an enormous wave washed over the body of man, covering him up to his chin, leaving only his head visible, while his limbs jostled below against the carcasses of the drowned animals. His head, however, was visible still, and in his head was his mind—that mind antecedent to the universe—that redoubtable, separate entity—staring out of his eyes over the deluge, like a sailor on a sinking ship. Then came one crisis more. The waters rose an inch or two higher, and all at once, like a sponge, the substance of his head had begun to suck them up —suck them up into the very home of life and thought; and the mind, sodden all through, was presently below the surface, sharing the doom of limpets, and weeds, and worlds."

The argument of this book, then, is in the main negative. But in dealing with the problem thus it is not negative in its tendency, for it carries the reader to the verge of the only possible solution. For pure reason, as enlightened by modern knowledge, human freedom is unthinkable, and yet for any religion by which the pure reason and the practical reason can be satisfied the first necessity is that men should accept such freedom as a fact. But this argument does not apply to the belief in human freedom only. It applies to all the primary conceptions which men assume, and are bound to assume, in order to make life practicable. If we follow pure reason far enough—if we follow it as far as it will go—not only freedom is unthinkable, but so are other things as well. Space is unthinkable, time is unthinkable, and so (as Herbert Spencer elaborately argued) is motion. In each of these is involved some self-contradiction, some gap which reason cannot span; and yet, as Kant said, unless we do assume them, rational action, and even thought itself, are impossible. If the difficulty, then, of conceiving human freedom is the only difficulty which religious belief encounters, we may trust that in time such belief will reassert itself, and a definite religion of some sort acquire new life along with it.

But religion does not logically depend on the postulate of freedom alone. Moral freedom, in a religious sense, requires, not the postulate of individual freedom only, but also of a Supreme or Cosmic Being, to whose will it is the duty of the individual will to attune itself, and it further requires the postulate that this Being is good in respect of its relations to all individuals equally—that it represents, in short, a multitude of individual benevolences. Nor does the matter end here. Any definite religion postulates some recognized means by which the will of this Being may be made known. I had hardly completed *Religion as a Credible Doctrine* before questions such as these, which there had been hardly touched, began to impress themselves with new emphasis on my mind. My desire was to take these questions in combination, and it seemed to me that this could best be done by adopting a method less formal than that which I had just pursued. I returned accordingly to the methods of *The New Republic*.

In this new work, called *The Veil of the Temple*, the action begins at a party in a great London house, where Rupert Glanville, a politician who has just returned from the East, invites some friends to cut their London dissipations short and pay him a visit at a curious marine residence which a Protestant bishop, his ancestor, had constructed in classical taste on the remotest coast of Ireland. A party is got together, including a bishop of to-day and two ornaments of the Jockey Club, together with some fashionable ladies and a Hegelian philosopher educated at Glasgow and Oxford.

The intellectual argument of the book takes up the threads where *Religion as a Credible Doctrine* dropped them. It begins at the dinner table, where a well-known case of cheating at cards is discussed, and the issue is raised of whether, or how far, a rich man who cheats at cards is the master of his own actions or the pathological victim of kleptomania. One of the lights of the Jockey Club is indignant at the idea that the matter can be open to doubt. "If a gentleman," he says, "is not free to abstain from cheating, what would become of the turf? Eh, bishop—what would become of the Church? What would become of anything?" Thus the question of free will is once again in the air, and the more serious of the guests, as soon as the others depart, set themselves to discuss both this and other questions kindred to it.

Of such other questions the most obvious is this: "How far do educated persons, who are nominally 'professing Christians,' really believe in doctrines of Christian orthodoxy, and more particularly in the authority and supernatural inspiration of the Bible?" Most of them are obliged to confess that at best they are in a state of doubt. On Sunday three Anglican clergymen are imported on a steam launch from a watering place some ten miles off, where they are attending a clerical Congress—an Evangelical, a Broad Churchman, and a Ritualist; and they administer to the company three competitive sermons.

These performances leave confusion worse con-
founded; and the guests during the following days
set themselves to pick their own beliefs to pieces.
At last they come back to the question of free will,
especially as related to science and what is called
scientific materialism. Then the question arises of
"What do we mean by matter?" and then the
question of the possible goodness of a God who, if
he is really the power behind evolution, is constantly sacrificing the unit to the development of
the race or species. This last difficulty is expressed
by one of the disputants in a poem which had been
written many years ago, and which, by request of
the company, he recites. In this poem the man, who
is vowed to abandon every belief for which science
can make no room, is represented by a wanderer
who finds himself at last conducted to a bare region
where no living thing is discernible, but one shining
apparition standing on the brink of a promontory
which juts into a sailless sea. He approaches, and
addresses it thus:

> "Oh, angel of the heavenly glow,
>   Behold I take thine hands and kneel.
> But what is this? Thy brows are snow,
>   Thy hands are stone, thy wings are steel.

> "The radiant pureness of thy face
>   Has not the peace of Paradise,
> Those wings within the all-holy place
>   Were never folded o'er thine eyes.

"And in thine eyes I see no bliss,
　　Nor even the tenderness of tears.
I see the blueness of the abyss,
　　I see the icebergs and the spheres.

"Angel whose hand is cold in mine,
　　Whose seaward eyes are not for me,
Why do I cry for wings like thine?
　　I would leave all and follow thee."

To this the apparition, who is the Spirit of Science, replies:

"Ah, rash one, pause and learn my name.
　　I know not love, nor hate, nor ruth.
I am that heart of frost and flame
　　That knows but one desire—the Truth.

"Thou shalt indeed be lifted up
　　On wings like mine, 'twixt seas and sky.
But can'st thou drink with me my cup,
　　And can'st thou be baptized as I?

"The cup I drink of does but rouse
　　The thirst it slakes not, like the sea;
And lo, my own baptismal brows
　　Must be their own Gethsemane.

"Across the paths where I must go
　　The shuttles of the lightning fly
From pole to pole, and strike, nor know
　　If Christs and kingdoms live or die.

"How wilt thou bear the worlds of fire,
　　The worlds of snow, or dare to mark
On each some ratlike race expire
　　That cannot leave its foundering bark?

"Oh, you, for whom my robes are bright,
    For whom my clear eyes in the gloom
Are lamps—you who would share my flight,
    Be warned in time. I know my doom.

"I shall become the painless pain,
    The soundless sound, as, deaf and dumb,
The whole creation strives in vain
    To sing the song that will not come.

"Till maimed and weary, burnt and blind,
    I am made one with God, and feel
The tumult of the mindless mind
    Torn on its own eternal wheel."

The suppliant replies that he knows from his own experience what such a counsel means, but has found it himself to be no longer practicable. There was a time, he says, when he found the perfect peace in kneeling before the Christian altar, but what is the Eucharist for him who can no longer believe in it? He still is prepared to follow the Spirit of Truth at all costs. "For me," he says:

"For me the kneeling knees are vain,
    In vain for me the sacred dew.
I will not drink that wine again
    Unless with thee I drink it new.

"Give me thy wings, thy wings of steel,
    And I with thee will cleave the skies,
And broken on the eternal wheel
    My God may take his sacrifice."

"And yet," he says in conclusion, "Truth, to those who follow it, may at last bring its own reward."

MEMOIRS OF LIFE AND LITERATURE

"Though storms may blow, though waves may roar,
  It may be, ere the day is done,
Mine eyes shall turn to thine once more,
  And learn that thine and his are one."

The Veil of the Temple winds up, in short, with the indication that, if both are completely thought out, the gospel of Faith is no more irrational than the gospel of scientific negation, and that the former can be a guide to action, whereas, if thought out completely, this is precisely what the latter cannot be.

The Reconstruction of Belief is a synthesis of the main arguments urged or suggested in these two preceding volumes. The necessity of religious belief as a practical basis of civilization is restated. The absurdity of all current attempts on the part of clerical apologists to revindicate it by scientific reason is set forth in detail. The true vindication is shown to reside in the fact that religious belief works, and that scientific negation does not work, and that here we have the practical test by which the validity of the former is to be established, though the process by which this fact will be apprehended by the modern world may be slow.

CHAPTER XV

Summer on the Borders of Caithness—A Two Months' Yachting
Cruise—The Orkneys and the Outer Hebrides—An Unexpected
Political Summons.

DURING the five years occupied in elaborating
these philosophical works I enjoyed two
intervals of relaxation, which in the landscape of memory detach themselves from other
kindred experiences, and one of which—the second—
had a quite unexpected ending.

The first was indirectly connected with the Coro-
nation of King Edward. On a certain evening, while
the event was impending, I found myself sitting at
dinner by a friend, Lady Amherst (of Montreal),
who told me that she and Lord Amherst were shortly
going to a shooting lodge which was close to the
borders of Caithness, and which they rented from
the Duke of Sutherland. For some months past
Lady Amherst had been unwell, and her doctor had
urged her to avoid the crowds of London, for which
reason she and her husband had determined to find
quiet in the north. I told her I thought she was a
very enviable woman, all unusual crowds being to
myself detestable. "If you think that," she said,
"why don't you come with us? A few others will

be there, so we shall not be quite alone." I accepted
the invitation with delight. I said good-by to London on the earliest day possible. In a train which
was almost empty I traveled much at my ease from
King's Cross Station to Brora. Not a tourist was
to be seen anywhere. Except for a few farmers, all
the Highland platforms were empty. I felt like a
disembodied spirit when I found myself at last in
a land of short, transparent nights which hardly
divided one day from another. Uppat, Lord Amherst's lodge, was one of the roomiest on the whole
Sutherland property. Parts of it were old. It had
once been a small laird's castle. Round it were
woods from which came the noise of a salmon river.
Among the woods were walled plots of pasture, and
beyond the woods were the loneliest of all lonely
mountains. In the kitchen was a French *chef*, and
when on my arrival I found Lady Amherst in the
porch, her homespun toilet showed that France
produced artists other than French cooks. To elude
the world without eluding its ornaments—what
more could be prayed for by a mind desiring rest?
Uppat, indeed, in June and July was like a land

> Where all trouble seems
> Dead winds, and spent waves riot
> In doubtful dreams of dreams.

Lord Amherst, as a rule, spent most of the day
fishing. Lady Amherst, I, and two other visitors
very often bicycled. On other occasions we all made

20

our way to purple fastnesses, and lunched where birches lifted their gleaming stems. The only movements discoverable between earth and sky were the sailing wings of eagles, and our own activities below, as we applied mayonnaise sauce, yellower than any primrose, to a sea trout or a lobster. We dined at nearly nine o'clock by a strange, white daylight; and in the outer quiet there was very often discernible a movement of stags' antlers above the wall of a near orchard. We read the newspapers till very nearly midnight without lamps or candles. We watched the blush of sunset, visible, like a dying bonfire, through a gap in the Caithness mountains, and this had not faded completely till it seemed as though someone had lighted beyond a neighboring ridge a bonfire of saffron—the faint beginning of sunrise. No retreat could have been a retreat more complete than this.

Another retreat in the north was vouchsafed to me some years later. I was lunching with my friends, Mr. and Mrs. Saxton Noble, in London, and they told me that, instead of taking, as had been their custom, a country house for the autumn, they had taken a yacht of about five hundred tons, and were going to spend their time in a leisurely cruise round the western coasts of Scotland. I mentioned to them that I had just been reading a very interesting description of Noltland, a curious castle in the remotest island of the Orkneys. We talked of this, which apparently was a very remarkable structure, containing the most magnificent newel staircase in Scotland. Suddenly Mrs. Noble said, "Why won't you join us?" My own plans for the autumn had been mapped out already, and I did not at first take her suggestion seriously. I laughed and said, "Yes, I'll come if you will go as far as Noltland." Both she and her husband at once answered: "Yes. We promise to go to Noltland. Let us take your coming as settled."

Accordingly, toward the end of July we left London by the night mail for Greenock, where the yacht would be found waiting for us. Next morning, in the freshness of a salt breeze, we were transferring ourselves from Greenock pier to a trim-looking motor boat, which was rising and falling on the swish of unquiet waters, while the yacht—a small streak of whiteness—was pointed out to us lying half a mile away. Besides Mr. and Mrs. Noble, our party consisted of their two children, Miss Helen Marhall, and myself. I had with me a Swiss servant; Mrs. Noble had a French maid, together with her London butler, transformed for the time into a mariner by gilt buttons and a nautical serge suit, and the cook was an accomplished *chef* who had once been in the service of the fastidious Madame de Falbe. We were all of us good sailors, so for our prospective comfort everything augured well. Our first few days were spent on the calm waters of Loch Fyne. We then went southward, and, doubling the Mull of Cantyre, had some taste of the turbulence of the open sea. We then turned north, and, protected by the outer islands, followed the mainland placidly until we approached Cape Wrath.

A large part of our time was spent in a succession of lochs. On our way to Oban, and in its harbor, we saw several large yachts; but, except for occasional fishing smacks, after Oban the sea became more and more deserted. Entering one loch after another in the summer evenings, and seeing no human habitations but crofters' cottages, which, except for their wreaths of smoke, were hardly distinguishable from the heather, and hearing no sound at nightfall, when our own engines were still, except the distant dipping of some solitary pair of oars, we felt as though we had reached the beginnings of civilization, or the ends of it. This was specially true of Loch Laxford —the last of such inland shelters lying south of Cape Wrath—Cape Wrath, the lightning of whose lanterns and the boom of whose great foghorns send out warnings to those on "seas full of wonder and peril," which Swinburne's verse commemorates.

Of the peril of these seas our captain had often spoken, and when, leaving the stillness of Loch Laxford, we renewed our northward journey, we soon perceived that his language was not exaggerated. From the mouth of Loch Laxford to Cape Wrath the whole coast might have represented to Dante the scowling ramparts of hell. Of anything in the nature of a beach no trace was discernible. The huge cliffs, rising sheer from the sea, leaned not inward, but outward, and ceaseless waves were breaking in spouts of foam against them. The yacht began to roll and pitch, so that though none of us were sick except Mrs. Noble's maid, we could very few of us stand. We managed, however, to identify the lighthouse and megaphone of Cape Wrath just peeping out of the cliffs, as though they were themselves afraid to meet the full violence of a storm. The skill of the cook, however, and the intrepidity of hunger enabled us to eat our luncheon. We then lay down in our several cabins and slept, till steps on deck and a number of voices woke us. We were soon rolling more disagreeably than ever. But this added annoyance did not last for long. Something or other happened. The motion of the vessel became easier, and at last, peeping into my cabin, Saxton Noble announced that we were back again in Loch Laxford. The megaphones of Cape Wrath had announced that a fog was coming. The captain had fled before it, and we dined that night at a table as stationary and steady as any in any hotel in Glasgow. Next day the weather was clear. We rounded the terrible headland, and were floating at ease that evening on the glassy surface of Loch Erribol. In this half-sylvan seclusion we rested for several days. Thence some eight hours of steaming brought us to the roadstead of Thurso. For several days we lay there while the yacht rocked uneasily, and most of our time was spent in expeditions on dry land. In some ways Thurso was curious. On the one hand, the

shops were excellent. They might have been those
of a country town near London. On the other hand,
the older houses were, as a protection against storms,
roofed with ponderous slabs hardly smaller than
gravestones. At one end of the town was Thurso
Castle, the seat of Sir Tollemache Sinclair, its walls
rising out of the water. At the back of it was a small
wood—the only wood in Caithness. I knew Sir
Tollemache Sinclair well, but unfortunately he was
not at home. He was what is called "a character."
He had strong literary tastes, and firmly believed
that he understood the art of French versification
better than Victor Hugo. The last time I had seen
him was at a hotel in Paris. He was on that occasion in a mood of great complacency, having just
been spending an hour with Victor Hugo at luncheon.
I asked him if, with regard to French versification,
Victor Hugo agreed with him. "No," he replied,
honestly, "I can't say that he did; but he asked me
to lunch again with him whenever I should be next
in Paris."

As soon as the weather was inviting enough we
turned our bows toward the Orkneys, dimly visible
on the horizon some forty miles away, and found
ourselves, on a windless evening, entering Scapa
Flow. We little thought that those then little
visited waters would one day witness the making
of British and German history. Scapa Flow is a
miniature Mediterranean, with the mainland of the
Orkneys on one side and the island of Hoy on the

other. At the northeastern end of it, some ten miles away, a high, red building—a lonely tower—was visible. This was the tower of the great cathedral of Kirkwall. Approaching the Orkneys from Thurso the first things that struck us were certain great structures crowning the mounded hills. These, we discovered afterward were so many great farm-steadings, protected from the wind by cinctures of high walls, many of the Orcadian holdings being at once rich and extensive, and commanding very high rentals.

Kirkwall, in respect of its shops, surprised us even more than Thurso. There were chemists, grocers, booksellers, whose windows would hardly have been out of place at Brighton; but haunting suggestions of the old, the remote, the wild, were tingling in the air everywhere. The huge tentacles of the kraken might have lifted themselves beyond Kirkwall harbor. The beautiful palace of the old Earls of Orkney would have been still habitable if only some local body early in the nineteenth century had not stolen its slates for the purpose of roofing some schoolhouse. Tankerness House, entered by a forti-fied gate, and built round a small court, can have hardly changed since the days of Brenda and Minna Troyle. In the nave of the great cathedral, which took four centuries in building, one would not have been surprised at meeting Magnus Troyle or Norna. The nave is full of the records of old Orcadian notables. These are not, however, for the most part, attached to the walls as tablets. They are attached to the pillars by extended iron rods, from which they hang like the swaying signs of inns. A country without railways and without coal—how peaceful England might be if only it were not for these!

But our peace in a physical sense was very abruptly broken when we quitted Kirkwall en route for the Holy Grail of our pilgrimage, Noltland Castle, which secludes itself on the far-off island of Westray, and, leaving the quiet of Scapa Flow behind us, encountered once more the tumults of the Pentland Firth. But these were nothing in comparison with those that met us as soon as we had rounded the southwest corner of Hoy. The hills of Hoy, so far as we had yet seen them, were of no very great magnitude; but now, as we went northward, they showed themselves as a line of tremendous precipices, which rose from the booming waves to an altitude of twelve hundred feet. This monstrous wall ended where a narrow and mysterious fiord separates Hoy from a low-hilled island north of it. This island gave place to another, and at last, late in the day, our captain told us that we were passing the outer shore of Westray. Consulting our maps, and pointing to the mouth of some new fiord, we asked him if it would not afford us a short cut to our destination. He told us that it was full of hidden rocks and sandbanks, and called our attention to some enigmatic object which rose in midchannel like a deer's horns from the sea. "There," he said, "are the masts of an Icelandic steamer which attempted two years ago to make that passage, and was lost. To reach Westray in safety we must double its farthest promontory." An hour or two later this feat was accomplished. We were once more in smooth water, and found ourselves quietly floating toward something like a dwarf pier and one or two small white houses. By now it was time for dinner, and having dined in a saloon that was hung with jade-green silk, we leaned over the bulwarks and contemplated the remote scene before us. We could just discern by the pier some small tramp steamer reposing. In the little white houses one or two lights twinkled, and presently, not far off, we distinguished a mouse-colored something, the upper outlines of which resolved themselves into high gables. Like Childe Roland when he came to the dark tower, we realized that these were the gables of Noltland Castle. Next morning we explored this building. The main block consisted of a tower unusually large, in the middle of which was a great red-sandstone staircase winding round a newel which culminated in a heraldic monster. This staircase led to a great hall, roofless, but otherwise perfect. Above it had once been bedrooms. On the ground floor were vaulted offices, including a hearth as large as the kitchen of a well-built cottage. Attached to the tower was a court. Ruined chambers surrounded it, in which guests, their retinues, and the servants of the house once slept. Island chieftains once met and reveled here. Here also for a time the most beautiful woman in Europe—Mary Stuart, as a captive—looked out at the sea.

Of the little houses by the pier the largest was a combination of a public house and a store, where we bought a supply of soda water. The store-keeper was a man of slightly sinister aspect. He might have been a character in one of Stevenson's novels. His aspect suggested distant and enigmatic, and perhaps criminal, adventure. He had evidently some education, and spoke of the natives with a sort of detached condescension. I asked him if they were Catholics. He shrugged his shoulders and said: "Some are. In this little island there are four hundred inhabitants, and no fewer than five religions." With the exception of this man's store, the only shop in Westray was locomotive. We met it on a lonely road. It was a kind of glazed cart, the transparent sides of which showed visions of the goods within.

Before leaving Westray we paid a visit to a much smaller island opposite, Papa Westray, with an area of two thousand acres. It was occupied by two farmers, whose average rent was more than ten shillings an acre. On one of these farmers, thus separated from their kind, we called. His farmstead was like a fortified town. His house was larger than many a substantial manse. The sideboard in his spacious dining room was occupied by two expensive Bibles and a finely cut decanter of whisky, but his only neighbors from one year's end to another were apparently his rival, by whom the rest of the island was tenanted, and a female doctor lately imported from Edinburgh, whose business was more closely related to the births of the population than to their maladies.

We had hoped, on leaving the Orkneys, to have gone as far north as the Shetlands, but while we were lying off Westray the weather turned wet and chilly, so we settled on going south again, visiting on our way the islands of the outer Hebrides. The first stage of our journey was rougher and more disagreeable than anything we had yet experienced. Once again we were foiled in our efforts to get round Cape Wrath; and, having spent an afternoon lying down in our cabins, we woke up to find ourselves back again in the quiet of Scapa Flow. Next day we made a successful crossing over sixty miles of sea to Tarbet, a little town crouching on the neck of land which connects the Lewes with Harris. From every cottage door there issued a sound of hand looms. The town or village of Tarbet is in itself neat enough. One of its features is an inn which would, with its trim garden, do honor to the banks of the Thames; but a five minutes' stroll into the country brought us face to face with a world of colossal desolations, compared with which the scenery of Scapa Flow is suburban. The little houses of Westray were, at all events, unmistakably houses. The crofters' huts,

almost within a stone's throw of Tarbet, many of
them oval in shape, are like exhalations of rounded
stones and heather. We felt, as we gravely looked
at them, that we were back again in the Stone Age.
In the island of North Ouist we were visited by the
same illusion. The landing stage was, indeed, a
scene of crowded life; but the life was the life of sea
birds, which were hardly disturbed by our approach.
Leaving North Ouist, we passed the mounded shores
of Benbecula, the island where Prince Charlie once
lived as a fugitive, and where the islanders, all of
them Catholics (as they still are to-day), sang songs
in his honor which, without betraying his name,
called him "the fair-haired herdsman." Far off
on an eminence we could just distinguish the glim-
merings of a Catholic church, in which, with strange
ceremonies, St. Michael is still worshiped. South
Ouist, dominated by the great mountain of Hecla,
likewise holds a population whose Catholicism has
never been broken. Facing the landing stage is an
inn obtrusively modern in aspect, and a little colony
of slate-roofed villas to match; but here, as at Tarbet, a few steps brought us into realms of mystery.
Having strayed along an inland road which wavered
among heaths and peat hags and gray boulders, we
saw at a distance some building of hewn sandstone,
and presently there emerged from its interior a solitary human being. For a moment he scrutinized
our approach, and then, like a timid animal, before
we could make him out, he was gone. When we

reached the building we found that it was a little
Catholic schoolhouse, and that the door was her-
metically closed. I tried the effect of a few very
gentle knocks, and these proved so ingratiating that
the inmate at last showed himself. He was the
schoolmaster—a youngish man, perhaps rather more
than thirty. Finding us not formidable, he had no
objection to talking, though he still was oddly shy.
He told us what he could, in answer to some questions which we put to him. I cannot remember
what he said, but I remember his eyes and the gentle
modulations of his voice. They were those of a man
living in a world of dreams, for whom the outer
world was as remote, and the inner world as pure,
as the silver of the shining clouds that were streaking
the peaks of Hecla. His face was my last memento
of the mystery of the Outer Isles.

The rest of our journeyings lay among scenes
better known to tourists. We visited Skye and
Rum, the latter of which islands was once occupied
as a deer forest by the present Lord Salisbury's
grandfather. Rum is infested by mosquitoes, which
almost stung us to death. Lord Salisbury told a
friend that he protected himself from their assaults
by varnishing his person completely with castor oil.
The friend asked him if this was not very expensive.
"Ah," he replied, "but I never use the best." The
present owner has built there a great, inappropriate
castle. We wondered whether its walls were proof
against these winged enemies. Pursuing our south-

ward course, we watched the Paps of Jura as they rose into the sky like sugar loaves. Plunging through drifts of spray we doubled the Mall of Cantyre, and got into waters familiar to half the population of Glasgow. We lay for a night off Arran. The following day we had returned to our original starting point. We were hardly more than a cable's length from Greenock, and once again we heard the whistling of locomotive engines. At Greenock we separated.

The Nobles were bound for England. I was myself going north to stay once more with Sir John and Lady Guendolen Ramsden. By the West Highland railway I reached the diminutive station of Tulloch, and a drive of twenty miles brought me to the woods, the waters, and the granite turrets of Ardverikie. After two months' acquaintance with the narrow quarters of a yacht there was something odd and agreeable in spacious halls and staircases. Especially agreeable was my bedroom, equipped with a great, hospitable writing table, on which a pile of letters and postal packets was awaiting me. Of these I opened a few which alone promised to be interesting, allowing the others to keep for a more convenient season. By the following morning, which I spent with Lady Guendolen, sketching, I had, indeed, almost forgotten them, and not till the evening did I give them any attention. One of them I had recognized at once as the proofs of an article which I had just finished, before I joined the yacht, on "The Intellectual Position of the Labor

Party in Parliament." The number of this party had been doubled at the last election, and my mind, in consequence, had again begun to busy itself with the question of mere manual labor as a factor in life and politics. I had, indeed, on the yacht been making a rough sketch of a second article on this subject, which would develop the argument of the first.

That night I glanced at the proofs before going to bed, reflecting on the best methods by which the political intelligence of the masses could be roused, reached, and guided. The unopened letters, none of which looked inviting, I put by my bedside, to be examined when I woke next morning. All except one were circulars. One, bearing a business monogram and evidently directed by a clerk, differed from the rest in having a foreign stamp on it. I indolently tore this open, and discovered that it was an invitation from a great political body in New York to visit the United States next winter and deliver a series of addresses on the fundamental fallacies of Socialism.

It was at Ardverikie, many years before, that I had first embarked on a serious study of statistics as essential to any clear comprehension of social principles and problems. By an odd coincidence, it was at Ardverikie likewise that, after years of laborious thought as to political questions which must soon, as I then foresaw, become for politicians the most vital questions of all, I received an invitation to address, with regard to these very questions, a public far wider than that of all Great Britain put together.

CHAPTER XVI

POLITICS AND SOCIETY IN AMERICA

Addresses on Socialism—Arrangements for Their Delivery—American Society in Long Island and New York—Harvard—Prof. William James—President Roosevelt—Chicago—Second Stay in New York—New York to Brittany—*A Critical Examination of Socialism*—Propaganda in England.

THE invitation which I have just mentioned emanated from the Civic Federation of New York—a body established for the promotion, by knowledge and sober argument, of some rational harmony between the employing classes and the employed. Its council comprised prominent members of both, such as Mr. Gompers, the trade-union leader, on one side, and industrial magnates of international fame on the other. It had just been decided to include in their educational scheme the delivery at various centers of special lectures on Socialism, by some thinker from Europe or England who would deal with the subject in a temperate and yet a conservative spirit. It had ultimately been decided that the person who would best suit them was myself. Arrangements were made accordingly, and I have every reason to be grateful to those concerned for the manner in which, on my arrival, they consulted both my judgment and my convenience. The great question to be settled related to the class of audience to whom the lectures should be delivered, and to whose modes of thought they should be accommodated. I said that in my opinion far the best course would be to set the idea of mass meetings altogether aside, and address congregations of the educated classes only. To this view it was objected that the cruder forms of Socialism are sufficiently repudiated by the educated classes already, and that converting the converted would be merely a waste of time. My own reply was that the immediate object to aim at was not to convert the converted, but to teach the converted how to convert others. My position as thus stated was ultimately approved by all; and Mr. Easley, the distinguished secretary of the Federation, took measures accordingly. The best course, he said, would be to arrange with the heads of certain great universities for the delivery of the addresses to audiences of professors and students, other persons being admitted who felt any inclination to attend   These arrangements would take some weeks to complete. Meanwhile, the character of the expected audiences being known, I should have ample time to prepare the addresses accordingly. The universities chosen were Columbia. Harvard, Chicago, Pennsylvania, and Johns Hopkins,

Mr. Easley was so good an organizer that all the details of the program were settled in the course of a few weeks; and, owing to the kindness of American friends in England, I enjoyed meanwhile at New York so many social amenities that I sometimes could hardly tell whether I was in New York or in London. I was provided with a sheaf of introductions by Mrs. Bradley Martin, the Duchess of Marlborough, Lady Cunard, and others, while on my arrival I was to stay for ten days or a fortnight with Mr. Lloyd Bryce, who had been educated at Oxford, where he and I were intimates. He was, for the moment, at his country house in Long Island, and Sandy Hook was still some hundreds of miles distant when a wireless message reached me on board the steamer saying that his secretary would meet me, and be looking out for me when I landed. The secretary was there at his post. He promptly secured a carriage; he escorted me across the city, accompanied me in the ferryboat from the city to Long Island, and saw me into a train, which in less than an hour set me down at Rosslyn, a mile or so from my friend's house. At the station gates there were several footmen waiting, just as there might have been at Ascot or Three Bridges, and several private carriages. One of these—a large omnibus—was my host's. I entered it, followed by an orthodox lady's maid, who was laden with delicate parcels, evidently from New York, and we were off. The country, for the time was January, was covered with deep snow, which clung to the boughs of pine trees and glittered on cottage roofs. A mile or two away from the station we turned into a private drive, which, mounting a parklike slope, with dark pines for its fringes, brought us to Lloyd Bryce's house. It was a house of true Georgian pattern—a central block with two symmetrical wings. Its red bricks might have been fading there for a couple of hundred years. Indoors there was the same quiet simplicity. The grave butler and two excellent footmen were English. The only features which were noticeably not English were the equable heat which seemed to prevail everywhere and the fact that half-drawn portières were substituted for closed doors.

On the evening of my arrival two young men came to dinner. They were brothers, sons of a father who had rented for several years Lord Lovat's castle in the Highlands. Next morning I was sent for a drive in a sleigh. Here, too, I came across things familiar. The coachman was Irish. He had been born on the lands of a family with which I was well acquainted, and I was pleased by the interest he displayed when I answered the questions which he put to me about the three young ladies. A pleasant indolence would, however, have made me more contented with the glow of a wood fire and conversation with an old friend than with any ventures in the chill of the outer air. I was, therefore, somewhat disquieted when I found, a day or two later, that my host had arranged to give me a dinner in New York at the Metropolitan Club, then to take me on to the opera, and not bring me back till midnight. But the expedition was interesting. The marbles, the gilding, the goddesses, the gorgeous ceilings of the Metropolitan Club would have made the Golden House of

Nero seem tame in comparison. The grand tier at the opera was a semicircle of dazzling dresses, though there was not, as happens in London, any obtrusion of diamonds. Here was an example of taste reticent as compared with our own.

Two nights later my host dispatched me alone, to dine at what he described to me as one of the pleasantest houses in New York. I shrank from the prospect of the wintry journey involved, but the dinner was worth the trouble. My entertainers—a mother and two unmarried daughters—belonged to one of the oldest and best known New York families. The house was in keeping with its inmates. It closely resembled an old-fashioned house in Curzon Street. As I drove up to the steps a butler and a groom of the chambers, both sedate with years and exhaling an atmosphere of long family service, threw open tall doors, and admitted me to the sober world within. The room in which the guests were assembled seemed to be lined with books. On the tables were half the literary reviews of Europe. My hostess and her daughters gave me the kindest welcome. I was somewhat bewildered by the number of strange faces, but among them was that of a diplomat whom I had known for many years in London; and the "high seriousness," as Matthew Arnold might have called it, of the men was tempered by the excellence of the dinner, and by the dresses, perfect though subtly subdued, of the women.

Some days later Mr. Easley and an assistant

secretary came from New York to call on me and discuss the arrangements of which I have already spoken. Meanwhile I had secured rooms in the city at the Savoy Hotel, to which in due time I migrated. The day after my arrival Mr. Easley appeared again, and with him Dr. Nicholas Murray Butler, the president of Columbia University. It was arranged that my first addresses should be given there under his auspices, and during the next three weeks I was daily occupied in preparing them. When the day approached which had been fixed for the delivery of the first, Doctor Butler gave a luncheon party at the Metropolitan Club, at which he invited me to meet the editors and other representatives of the weightiest of the New York papers. I explained the general scheme of argument which I proposed to follow, and it appeared, after an interchange of speeches, that it met with general approbation.

This luncheon party and its results struck me as a marked example of the promptitude and businesslike sagacity characteristic of American methods. Every address which I delivered at Columbia University was reported verbatim and fully in the columns of these great journals. The audiences immediately addressed were, from the nature of the case, limited, but my arguments were, in effect, at once brought home to the minds of innumerable thousands, and their main points emphasized by a concert of leading articles. The drastic efficiency of this procedure in

New York and at other centers was sufficiently shown by the countless letters I received from Socialists in all parts of America, most of these letters being courteous, some very much the reverse; but all indicating that I had succeeded in making the writers reflect on problems to which they had previously given insufficient attention.

The composition of these addresses, and the reduction of them to their final form, was a work which, since time was limited, required much concentrated labor; but the labor was lightened by the extraordinary hospitality of friends, who made me feel that, so far as society goes, I had only exchanged one sort of London for another. In my sitting room at the Savoy Hotel, on arriving from Long Island, I found a number of notes inviting me to dinners, to concerts, and various other entertainments. The first of these was a luncheon at Mrs. John Jacob Astor's. Her house was one which might have been in Grosvenor Place; and, for matter of that, so might half the company. I found myself sitting by Mrs. Hwfa Williams. Not far off was her husband, an eminent figure in the racing world of England. There, too, I discovered Harry Higgins, whom I had known in his Oxford days, before his translation from Merton to Knightsbridge barracks; and opposite to me was Monsignor Vay di Vaya, an Austrian ornament of the Vatican, who wore a dazzling cross on a perfectly cut waistcoat, and who, when I last saw him, had been winding wool in the Highlands

314

for Mrs. Bradley Martin. Mrs. Astor, if I may pay her a very inadequate compliment, merely by her delicate presence seemed to turn life into a picture on an old French fan.

My first evening party was, if I remember rightly, a concert at the house of one of the Vanderbilt families. I had hardly entered the music room before my host, with extreme kindness, indicated a lady who was sitting next a vacant chair, and said, "Over there is someone you would like to know." He introduced me to this lady, who was Mrs. Stuyvesant Fish—one of the best-known and important figures in the social world of New York. I was subsequently often at her house. I have rarely been better entertained than I was by her conversation that night during the intervals of the musical program.

This kindness in introducing a stranger to persons likely to be agreeable to him struck me as a distinguishing feature of the New York world generally. I experienced it often at the opera, where the occupants of the grand tier form practically a social club, as well as a mere musical gathering. On one occasion, when I was with Mr. and Mrs. Sloane in their box, Mr. Sloane took me round to the opposite side of the house to present me to a lady whose attractions he praised, and did not praise too highly. I asked him the name of another of singularly charming aspect. Her box was close to his. "Come," he said, "I will introduce you now." Here is one of those graces of social conduct which are, as I have observed already with reference ot London, possible only in societies which are more or less carefully restricted.

There is another matter in which the social world of New York struck me as differing from that of London, and differing from it in a manner precisely opposite to that which those who derive their views from the gossip of journalists would suppose. According to ordinary rumor, fashionable entertainments in New York are scenes of extravagance so wild that they cease to be luxurious and assume the characteristics of a farce. My own short experience led me to a conclusion the very reverse of this. Certain hotels, no doubt, are notoriously overgilded. A story is told of a certain country couple who stayed for a night at one of them. The wife said to the husband, "Why don't you put your boots outside the door to be blacked?" "My dear," said the husband, "I'm afraid I should find them gilt." I speak here of private houses and private entertainments only. The ultrafashionable concert which I mentioned just now is an instance. The music was followed by supper. The company strayed slowly through some intervening rooms to the dining room. It was full of little round tables at which little groups were seating themselves, but when I entered the tables were entirely bare. Presently servants went round placing a cloth on each of them. Then on each were deposited a bottle

of champagne and two or three plates of sandwiches,
That was all. At a corresponding party in London
there would have been soups, soufflés, aspic, truffles,
and ortolans. As it was, the affair was a simple
picnic *de luxe*. To the dinner parties at which I
was present the same observation applies. The New
York fashionable dinner, so far as its menu is concerned, seemed to me incomparably simpler than its
fashionable counterpart in London. The only form
of extravagance, or of what one might call ostenta-
tion, so far as I could see, was what would have
been thought in London the multitude of superfluous
footmen, and in houses like that of Lloyd Bryce even
this feature was wanting. The only dinner which,
within the limits of my own experience, represented
the extravagance so often depicted by journalists—
a dinner which was signalized by monumental plate,
which rose from the table to the ceiling—was at
a house which, despite its magnitude, was practically
ignored by the arbitresses of polite society.

When the delivery of my addresses at Columbia
University was completed I went from New York to
Cambridge and remained there for ten days. Harvard in many ways reminded me of our own Cambridge. The professors, among whom I made many
charming acquaintances, had not only the accent,
but also the intonation of Englishmen. They had
with them more, too, of the ways of the outer world
than is commonly found in the university dons of
England. Notable among these was Prof. William

James, with whom I was already familiar through his singularly interesting book, *Varieties of Religious Experience*—to me very much more interesting than his brother's later novels.

At Harvard, also, I was presented to Mr. Roosevelt, who had come there for the purpose of addressing a great meeting of students. The presentation took place in a large private room, and was a ceremony resembling that of a presentation to the King of England. Some dozen or more persons were introduced to the President in succession, their names being announced by some *de facto* official. With each of these he entered into a more or less prolonged conversation. I observed his methods with interest. In each case he displayed a remarkable knowledge of the achievements or opinions of the person whom he was for the time addressing; and, having thus done his duty to these, he proceeded to an exposition, much more lengthy, of his own. When my turn came he was very soon confiding to me that nothing which he had read for years had struck him so forcibly as parts of my own *Veil of the Temple*, which he had evidently read with care. He crowned these flattering remarks by asking me, should this be possible, to come and see him at Washington before I returned to England; and then, I cannot remember how, he got on the subject of the Black Republic, and of how, in his opinion, such states ought to be governed. On this matter he was voluble, and voluble with unguarded emphasis. I

THEODORE ROOSEVELT

never heard the accents of instinctive autocracy more clearly than, for some ten minutes, I then heard them in his. I wished I could have seen him at Washington, but I had no unoccupied week during which he would have been able to receive me.

From Cambridge I went in succession to Chicago, Philadelphia, and Baltimore. At each of these places I addressed considerable gatherings, and everywhere (except at Philadelphia) I encountered some hostile, though no acrimonious, questioning. At the doors, however, on some occasions a quiet Socialist emissary would offer some tract to the in-goers, in which my arguments were attacked before they had been so much as uttered. Why the temperament of one place should differ from that at another is not easy to say, but at Philadelphia I was not only listened to without question, but at every salient point I was greeted with uproarious applause. Having spent some days at Baltimore, and having accomplished what I had undertaken to do on behalf of the Civic Federation, I returned to New York, and, except for two speeches outside our formal program, I gave myself up for a month to the relaxations of society.

My return to New York was marked by a curious incident, which occurred when I left the ferryboat. The porter whom I secured told me, having looked about him, that there was not a cab available. I pointed to a row of four-wheeled motor hansoms, but none of these, he said, was going out to-night, except one which had been just appropriated. While he was explaining this to me, from the darkness of one of these vehicles a courteous voice emerged, asking where I was going, as the speaker perhaps might be able to drop me somewhere. I told him my destination; he agreed to take me, and I was presently seated at his side, perceiving, indeed, that he was a man and not a woman, but quite unable to distinguish anything else. He presently informed me that he was just back from a golf course. I informed him that I was from Baltimore. "You," he said, "to judge from your voice, must, I think, be English. I have often played golf in England not very far from Chichester." I asked him where, on those occasions, he stayed. He answered, "With Willie James." I told him that I had known Willie James years ago at Cannes. "My own name is James," he said. "Will you think me inquisitive if I venture to ask yours?" I told him, and he at once "placed" me. "I should think," he said, "you must know Baltimore well." I asked him why he thought so. "Well," he said, "in the book of yours that I like best—in *The Old Order Changes*—you introduce an American colonel—a Southerner, and you describe him on one occasion as absorbed in the perusal of the Baltimore *Weekly Sun*. That paper's a real paper, and, because you introduced its name, I thought that you must know Baltimore." The name, so far as I was concerned, was entirely my own invention.

Lloyd Bryce, who knew of my arrival, and who had, during my absence, left Long Island for New York, asked me next day to dine with him. This was the first of a new series of hospitalities. The company was extremely entertaining. It comprised Mr. Jerome, celebrated in the legal world, and at that time especially celebrated in connection with a sensational case which was exciting the attention of the public from New York to San Francisco. This was the trial of Thaw for the murder of Stanford White, of which dramatic incident Evelyn Nesbit was the heroine. She was, at least in appearance, little more than a schoolgirl. She had lived with Stanford White, however, on terms of precocious intimacy. Subsequently Thaw, a rich "degenerate," had married her, but the thought of Stanford White was always ready to sting him into moods of morbid jealousy. He took her one evening after dinner to a roof garden in New York. Stanford White was by accident sitting at a table in front of him. Watching his wife closely, Thaw detected, or thought he detected, signs of a continued understanding between her and her late "protector." Quietly leaving her side, he approached Stanford White from behind and shot him dead with a pistol before the whole of the assembled company. The defense was that his rival had given him outrageous provocation, and that he himself was temporarily, if not chronically, insane. Every attempt was made by the partisans of his wife to enlist public feeling in her favor; to prove that Stanford White was the aggressor, and that her husband's deed was unpremeditated. The trial was protracted, and the story, as it was brought to light, was one which could hardly be equaled outside Balzac's novels. Had the heroine of this drama not been a beautiful young woman, she and her husband would probably have been forgotten in a week. As it was, if any man in the street was seen to be absolutely stationary and absorbed in an evening paper, an observer would have discovered that the main feature of its pages was a portrait of Evelyn Nesbit in some new dress or attitude, with her eyes half raised or drooping, and her hair tied up behind in a black, semichildish bow. Mr. Jerome, with a good deal of pungent humor, told me many anecdotes of the trial, and wound up with an allusion to what he considered the defects of American judges. "In England," he said, "you make men judges because they understand the law. The trouble with us is that here, as often as not, a man will be made a judge because he can play football."

The mention of Stanford White suggests a topic more creditable to himself than his death, and also possessing a different and wider interest. Stanford White, whatever may have been his private life, was the greatest architect in America. Some of the finest buildings in New York are due to his signal genius, and here I am led on to reflections of a yet more extensive kind. My own impression was that architecture in America generally possesses a vitality which to-day is absent from it in older countries. This observation is pertinent to New York more especially. New York being built on a narrow island, it has there become necessary, to a degree hardly to be paralleled elsewhere in the world, to extend new buildings not laterally, but upward. To this living upward pressure are due the towering structures vulgarly called "skyscrapers." These, if properly understood, resemble rather the old campanili of Italy, and suggest the work of Giotto. They make New York, seen from a distance, look like a San Gimignano reconstructed by giants. I am, however, thinking not of the "skyscrapers" only. I am thinking rather of buildings, lofty indeed, but not tower-like, such as certain clubs, blocks of residential flats, or business premises in Fifth Avenue—such, for instance, as those of the great firm of Tiffany. Though metal frameworks are, no doubt, embedded in these, the stonework is structurally true to the strains of the metal which it incases, and the stones of the rusticated bases might have been hewn and put together by Titans. We have more here than an academic repetition of bygone tastes and models. We have an expression in stone of the needs of a new world.

One of the most charming examples of architectural art in New York, lighter in kind than these, and when I was there the most recent, was a new ladies' club, which largely owed its existence—so I was told— to the aid of Mr. J. Pierpont Morgan. Within and without, from its halls to its numerous bedrooms, the taste displayed was perfect. When I was in New York it was just about to be opened, and I was invited to take part in the ceremony by delivering an inaugural address. I took for my subject the Influence of Women on Industry; and the pith of what I had to say was compressed into a single anecdote which I had heard only the day before. My informant had just been told it by one of Tiffany's salesmen. A few days previously the great jeweler's shop had been entered by a couple singularly unlike in aspect to the patrons who were accustomed to frequent it. One of them was a weather-beaten man in a rough pilot jacket; the other was an odd old woman bundled up in a threadbare coat of the cheapest imitation fur. The man, with a gruff shyness, blurted out, "I should like to see a diamond necklace." The salesman with some hesitation put a necklace before him of no very precious kind. The man eyed it askance and said, dubiously, "Is that the best you've got?" The price of this was twenty pounds. The salesman produced another and a somewhat larger ornament. The price of this was forty. The man, still dissatisfied, said, "Have you nothing better still?" "If," said the salesman, by way of getting rid of him, "by better you mean more expensive, I can show you another. The price of that is four hundred." This drama was still repeated, till the salesman, out of pure curiosity, put before him one the price of which was a thousand.

The man, however, again repeated his one unvarying question, "Is that the best you've got?" The salesman, at last losing patience, said, "Well, if it should happen to interest you, I can let you have a look at the most magnificent necklace that money could buy in New York City to-day. The price of that necklace is fifty thousand pounds." He turned to put it away, but the weather-beaten man stopped him. He thrust a hand into the pocket of his rough jacket and extracted from its recesses an immense bundle of notes. He counted out the sum which the salesman named. He clasped the necklace round the old woman's threadbare collar and exclaimed, in a tone of triumph, "Didn't I always tell you that as soon as I'd made my pile you should have the finest necklace that money in New York could buy?" "That necklace," said Tiffany's salesman to my informant, "will never be stolen so long as it's worn like that, for no one in his senses will ever believe it's real." The moral which I drew from this anecdote for the benefit of my fair audience was that women, if not the producers of wealth, are the main incentives to production, that if it were not for them half of the civilized industries of the entire world would cease, and that the Spirit of Commerce, looking at any well-dressed woman, might say, in the words of Marlow, "This is the face that launched a thousand ships"; while the Spirit of Socialism could do nothing but "burn the topless towers." In this way of putting the case there was perhaps some slight exaggeration, but there is in it, at all events, more truth than falsehood.

Another address—it took a more serious form—I delivered by special request to a more comprehensive audience, in which ladies likewise abounded. It was delivered in one of the theaters. The subject I was asked to discuss was a manifesto which had just been issued by a well-to-do cleric in favor of Christian Socialism. The argument of this divine was interesting and certain parts of it were sound. Its fault was that the end of it quite forgot the beginning. He began by admitting that the great fortunes of to-day were due for the most part to the few who possessed to an exceptional degree the talents by which wealth is produced; but talents of this special class were, he said, wholly unconnected with any moral desert. Indeed, the mere production of such goods as are estimable in terms of money was, of all forms of human activity, the lowest, and the men who made money were the last people in the world who ought to be allowed to keep it. The demand of Socialism was, he said, that this gross and despicable thing should be distributed among other people. The special demand of Christian Socialism was that the principal claimant on all growing wealth should be the Church. The fault, he said, of the existing situation was due to the fathers of the Constitution of the United States, who laid it down that one of the primary rights of the individual was freedom to produce as much as he could, and keep it; the true formula being, according to him, that every man who produced appreciably more than his neighbors should be either hampered in production or else deprived of his products. It was not difficult to show, without passing the bounds of good humor, that the arguments of this semienlightened reformer were, in the end, like a snake whose head was biting off its tail.

Except for Monsignor Vay di Vaya, the only cleric whom I met in New York society was one of distinguished aspect and exceedingly charming manners, who was certainly not an apostle of Christian or any other form of Socialism; but an anecdote was told me of another whose congregation, according to a reporter, was "the most exclusive in New York," and had the honor of comprising Mr. J. Pierpont Morgan. This clergyman was one morning surprised by receiving a visit from a negro, who expressed a desire to join his exclusive flock. The shepherd was somewhat embarrassed, but received his visitor kindly. "You are," he said, "contemplating a very serious step. My advice to you is that you seek counsel in prayer; that, if possible, you should see our Lord; that you make quite sure that this step is one of which our Lord would approve; and that in three weeks' time you come and talk again to me." The postulant thanked him, and in three weeks reappeared. "Well," said the clergyman, "have you prayed earnestly, as I advised you?" The negro said that he had. "And may I," said the clergyman, "ask you if you have seen our Lord?" "Yes, sah," said the negro, "I have." "And what," asked the clergyman, "was it that our Lord said to you? Could you manage to tell me?" "What our Lord said to me," the negro replied, "was this: 'I've been trying for eighteen years to get into that church, but I can't. I guess that your trying will come to no more than mine.'"

Meanwhile I had begun, in the intervals between social engagements, to recast my addresses, with a view, as I have said already, to transforming them into a connected book. The first stage in this process was the preparation of an intermediate version of them, which was to be issued as a series of articles in an important monthly journal, these serving as the foundation of the book in its complete form, which was by and by to be issued in America and England simultaneously.

I had arranged to return by the French steamer *Provence*—a magnificent vessel—the largest that the harbor of Havre could accommodate. The restaurant was decorated like a *Salon* of the time of Louis Quinze. The cooking was admirable, the tables were bright with flowers. I was asked to sit at a table reserved for a charming lady, who was bringing with her her own champagne and butter, with both of which she insisted on providing her friends also. My cabin, though small, was perfect in the way of decoration. An ormolu reading lamp stood by the silken curtains of the bed. The washing basin was of pink marble.

MEMOIRS OF LIFE AND LITERATURE

Before returning to England I had settled on spending some solitary months in Brittany, during which it was my object to bring my forthcoming work to completion. I spent a week in Paris, where my French servant rejoined me, whom I had left to enjoy during my absence a holiday, with his family near Grenoble. I never in my life met anyone with more satisfaction.

Paris is notoriously congenial to the upper classes of America; and yet between Paris and New York there is one subtle and pervading difference. Paris has behind it in its buildings and the ways of its people what New York has not—a thousand years of history. The influence of the past is even more apparent in Brittany; and New York became something hardly credible when I found myself in a little hotel—at which I had engaged rooms—an hotel girdled by the ramparts and medieval towers of Dinan. I remained there for six weeks, during which time my book, to which I gave the name *A Critical Examination of Socialism*, was very nearly completed. In spite, however, of my labor, I from time to time found leisure for pilgrimages to moated châteaux, which seemed still to be enjoying a siesta of social and religious peace, unbroken by revolutions and even undisturbed by republics. Of these châteaux one was the home of Chateaubriand. Another, which I traveled a hundred miles to see, was the Château de Kerjaen, its gray gates approached by three huge converging avenues, and the outer walls by which the château itself is sheltered measuring seven hundred by four hundred feet. Though parts of it are habitable and inhabited, Kerjaen is partly ruinous, but its ruin was not due to violence. It was due to an accidental fire which took place when Robespierre was still in his cradle and even in his dreams was "guiltless of his country's blood." Coming, as I did, fresh from the New World, there was for me in Brittany something of the magic of Hungary.

A Critical Examination of Socialism was published a few months after my return to England, where Socialist agitation meanwhile had become more active than ever, and I presently discovered that certain attempts were being made to establish some organized body for the purpose of systematically counteracting it. I put myself in connection with those who were taking, or willing to take, some leading part in this enterprise. The final result was the establishment of two bodies—the Anti-Socialist Union, under the presidency of Col. Claude Lowther, and a School of Anti-Socialist Economics, which, through the agency of Captain (now Sir Herbert) Jessel, was affiliated to the London Municipal Society—a body which, owing to him, was already proving itself influential. All the persons concerned had precisely the same objects, but there were certain disagreements as to the methods which at starting were most imperative. So far as principles were concerned, the Anti-Socialist Union were so completely in agreement with myself that they bought a large · edition of my *Critical Analysis of Socialism* for distribution as a textbook among the speakers and writers whom it was part of their program to employ. There were, however, certain details of procedure in respect of which Captain Jessel's opinions were more in accordance with my own. He and I, therefore, settled on working together, taking the existing machinery of the London Municipal Society as our basis, while the Anti-Socialist Union proceeded on parallel, though on somewhat different, lines. Captain Jessel and I established, by way of a beginning, a school for speakers—mostly active young men—who would speak Sunday by Sunday in the parks and other public places, and attract audiences whose attention had been previously secured by Socialists. These speakers sent in weekly reports, describing the results of their work, which were for the most part of a singularly encouraging kind. But the number of these speakers was small, and, since all their expenses were paid, the funds at our immediate disposal would not enable us to increase it. It appeared to me, therefore, that our work would be best extended by a distribution of literature—leaflets or small pamphlets—simple in style, but coherent in their general import, and appealing not to the man in the street only, but to educated men, even Members of Parliament, also. A start in this direction was made by the publication of skeleton speeches, many of them written by myself, which any orator in the parks or in Parliament might fill in as he pleased, and which was supplemented by weekly pamphlets called "Facts Against Socialism." I found, however, that in preparing these my attention was more and more occupied by industrial and social statistics, and I was, in my colleague's opinion, concerning myself too much with matters which were over the heads of the people.

For several reasons my view of the matter was not quite the same as his. It was, therefore, settled that this statistical work should be prosecuted by myself independently, and in something like two years I issued, at the rate of two or three a month, a series of pamphlets called "Statistical Monographs," addressed especially to Members of Parliament. Three of these pamphlets dealt with the land of the United Kingdom, the number of owners and the acreage and value of their holdings. Two of them dealt with the number and value of the houses which had been annually built during the past ten or fifteen years. Two of them dealt with coal-mining and the ratio in that industry of wages to net profits. Each was a digest of elaborate official figures, which an average speaker, if left to his own devices, could hardly have collected in a twelvemonth, but which when thus tabulated he could master in a couple of days.

Many of these monographs, as I know, were used in practical controversy; but the Conservative party, as a whole—this is my strong impression—was but partly awake to the importance of statistics as a basis of political argument. The use of systematic statistics was at that time left to Socialists, and wild misstatements as to figures formed at that time their principal and most effective weapon. The issue of these monographs was continued till the outbreak of the recent war, when conditions were so suddenly and so completely changed that the then continuance of the monographs would not have been appropriate, even if it had not been rendered impossible. Being, however, unfit for active service, I devoted myself to a volume applicable, so I hoped, to conditions which were bound to arise after the war was over. This volume was *The Limits of Pure Democracy*, to the composition of which I devoted the labor of four years. It has gone through four editions. A translation of it has been published in France. Increased costs of production have rendered a price necessary which would once have been thought prohibitive, but if conditions improve the intention is to reissue it in a cheaper form, when certain of its arguments will be illustrated by events which have taken place since its last page was completed.

Much of the matter contained in the "Statistical Monographs" was condensed by me in a volume called *Social Reform*. This was a study, more minute and extensive than any which I had attempted before, of the income of this country and

333

its distribution among various classes of the population, not only as they were at the beginning of the twentieth century, but also as they were in the earlier years of the nineteenth. My authorities with regard to the latter were certain elaborate but little known official papers showing the results of the income tax of the year 1801. These returns, by means of a minute classification, show the number of incomes from those between £60 and £70 up to those exceeding £5,000, the upshot being that the masses—manual and other wage-workers—were enjoying just before the war an average income per head more than double that which would have been possible a hundred years ago had the entire income of the country—the incomes of rich and poor alike—been then divided in equal shares among everybody. This same general fact had been broadly insisted on in *Labor and the Popular Welfare*. It was here demonstrated in detail by official records, to which I had not had access at the time when I wrote that volume, and of the very existence of which most politicians are probably unaware to-day. *Social Reform* was, however, published at an unlucky moment. It had not reached more than a small number of readers before the war, for a time, put a stop to economic thought, and left men to illustrate economic principles by action, thereby providing fresh data for economic theory of the future.

CHAPTER XVII

THE AUTHOR'S WORKS SUMMARIZED

A Boy's Conservatism—Poetic Ambitions—The Philosophy of
Religious Belief—The Philosophy of Industrial Conservatism
—Intellectual Torpor of Conservatives—Final Treatises and
Fiction.

I BEGAN these memoirs with observing that they
are in part a mere series of sketches and social
anecdotes strung on the thread of the writer's
own experiences, and as such illustrating the tenor
of his social and mental life, but that in part they
are illustrative in a wider sense than this. His
literary activities may be looked on as exemplifying
the moral and social reactions of a large number of
persons, to the great changes and movements in
thought and in social politics by which the aspect of
the world has been affected, both for them and him,
from the middle years of the reign of Queen Victoria
onward. Regarding myself, then, as more or less of
a type, and reviewing my own activities as circumstances have called them into play and as these
memoirs record them, I may briefly redescribe
them, and indicate their sequence thus.

Having been born and brought up in an atmosphere of strict Conservative tradition—conservative in a religious and social sense alike—I had
unconsciously assumed in effect, if not in so many

335

words, that any revolt or protest against the established order was indeed an impertinence, but was otherwise of no great import. Accordingly, my temperament being that of an instinctive poet, the object of my earliest ambitions was to effect within a very limited circle (for the idea of popular literature never entered my head) a radical change in the poetic taste of England, and restore it to what it had been in the classical age of Pope. But, as I left childhood behind me and approached maturer youth I gradually came to realize that the whole order of things—literary, religious, and social—which the classical poetry assumed, and which I had previously taken as impregnable, was being assailed by forces which it was impossible any longer to ignore. Threats of social change, indeed, in any radical sense continued for a long time to affect me merely as vague noises in the street, which would now and again interrupt polite conversation, and presently die away, having seriously altered nothing; but the attack on orthodox religion seemed to me much more menacing, and was rarely absent from the sphere of my adolescent thought. The attacking parties I still looked on as ludicrous, but I began to fear them as formidable; and they were for me rendered more formidable still by the very unfortunate fact that the defenders of orthodoxy seemed to me, in respect of their tactics, to be hardly less ludicrous than their opponents. The only way in which the former could successfully make good their defense was—such was my conclusion—by appeal to common experience: by showing how supernatural religion was implicit in all civilized life, and how grotesque and tragic would be the ruin in which such life would collapse if supernatural faith were eliminated.

Such, as I have explained already, was the moral of my four early books, *The New Republic*, *The New Paul and Virginia*, *Is Life Worth Living?* and *A Romance of the Nineteenth Century*. All these attempts at attacking modern atheistic philosophy were based on a demonstration of its results, and appealed not so much to pure religious emotion as to the intellect, a sense of humor, and what is called a knowledge of the world.

The writing of these works, the first of which I had begun while I was still an undergraduate, occupied about six or seven years. Meanwhile, side by side with the preaching of atheism in religion and morals, a growth had become apparent in the preaching of extreme democracy or Socialist Radicalism in politics, a preaching of which Bright was in this country the precursor, and which first came to a head between the years 1880 and 1900, in the writings of Henry George and the English followers of Marx. What I looked on as the fallacies of these new political gospels seemed to me no less dangerous, and also no less absurd, than those which I had previously attacked in the gospel of atheistic philosophy, and my attention being forcibly diverted from religious problems to social, I devoted myself to the writing of my first political work, *Social Equality* (published 1882), in which all questions of religion were for the moment set aside. In my novel *The Old Order Changes*, published four or five years later, the religious problem and the social problem are united, and an attempt is made to suggest the general terms on which the ideals of a true Conservatism may be harmonized with those of an enlightened Socialism. As a result of my political writings, I was asked, and with certain reservations I consented, to become a candidate for a Scotch constituency.

Between the years 1890 and 1895 I turned again to social politics pure and simple in two books, the first of which was *Labor and the Popular Welfare*, the second being *Aristocracy and Evolution*.

My dealings with social politics being for the time exhausted, I devoted about five years—1895 to 1900—to the composition of three novels, *A Human Document*, *The Heart of Life*, and *The Individualist*, which were studies of the relation of religion to the passions, feelings, and foibles of which for most men the experiences of life consist.

Between the years 1900 and 1907 I published four works on the relation of religious dogmas to philosophy and scientific knowledge—namely, *Doctrine and Doctrinal Disruption*—this volume relating to the Anglican controversies of the time—*Religion as a Credible Doctrine*, *The Veil of the Temple*, and

The Reconstruction of Belief, to which may be added a novel called *An Immortal Soul*.[1]

As a result of the attention excited by these or by certain of these books, I was in the year 1907 invited to visit America and deliver a series of addresses on the Socialist propaganda of the day. These addresses were presently rewritten and published in a volume called *A Critical Examination of Socialism*.

Between that time and the outbreak of the recent war I played an active part, together with other persons, in devising and setting on foot certain schemes of anti-Socialist propaganda in this country. Most of my own efforts I devoted to the collection and promulgation of sound social statistics, especially those relating to the current distribution of wealth, and I may here mention, without even suggesting a name, that I discussed the importance of such statistics with a leading Conservative statesman, who, expressing his sympathy with my views, added at the same time that, so far as the constitution of his own mind was concerned, they were not temperamentally his own. "To me," he said, "columns of figures are merely so many clouds." I answered, "That may be; but they are clouds which, when taken together, make not clouds, but lightning."

---

[1] This work, later in date than the preceding, deals with the religious difficulties arising from the phenomena of multiple personality, a subject which was then being widely discussed in England, on the Continent, and in America.

Anyhow, by the outbreak of war these schemes were suspended, and changed conditions may now make methods other than those which seemed then appropriate necessary. But, as for myself, the first four years of war-time I devoted entirely to the production of a new volume, *The Limits of Pure Democracy*, of which a French translation is being issued, and which may, I hope, prove useful to sober conservatives of more than one school and country, as it aims at establishing a formula acceptable, so far as it goes, to persons who are at present adversaries.

In addition to the works here mentioned, two volumes have been published of *Collected Essays*, on which certain of the works just mentioned are based. I have further published, besides my little book on Cyprus, two short volumes of verse, and a poem of which I shall speak presently, called *Lucretius on Life and Death*. All these works indicate, if taken together, the nature of the fallacies—intellectual, religious, and social—which have in succession provoked them, which have not yet exhausted themselves, and which it has been the ambition of the writer to discredit or modify.

Such have been the activities which, devoted to a continuous and developing purpose, have thus far occupied a writer whose life has been spent in alternations of solitude and the life of society. The latter, so far as he is concerned, resembles that of many other persons to whom society is naturally

agreeable and have had the opportunity of enjoying
it. It is a life which for him has remained substantially the same from his early youth onward,
except for the fact that with time his social experiences have widened, that they have been varied by
travels more or less extensive, and that they might
have been varied also by the vicissitudes of political
publicity had not his disposition inclined him, having
had some taste of both, to the methods of literature
rather than to those of the party platform.

Which method is the best for one who, inspired by
tenacious and interconnected convictions, desires to
make these prevail is a question which different
people will answer in different ways. But let us
make one supposition. Let us suppose that a person, such, for instance, as myself, who has dealt with
ideas and principles in his opinion fallacious (notably
those connected with the current claims of Labor),
should have so succeeded in influencing the thoughts
and the temper of his contemporaries that the
modern strife between employers and employed
should be pacified, and arrangements by sober discussion should render all strikes needless. Nobody
would deny that a person who had brought about
this result had performed what would be, in the
strictest sense, an action—an action of the most
practical and signally important kind, and it would
be no less practical if accomplished by means of
literature than it would be if accomplished by the
ingenuity of cabinets or select committees. Such

being the case, then, the reflection will here suggest itself that literature and action are by many critics of life constantly spoken of as though they were contrasted or antithetic things. It will not be inappropriate here, as a conclusion to these memoirs, to consider how far, or in what sense, this contrast is valid.

CHAPTER XVIII

LITERATURE AND ACTION

Literature as Speech Made Permanent—All Written Speech Not
Literature—The Essence of Literature for Its Own Sake—
Prose as a Fine Art—Some Interesting Aspects of Literature
as an End in Itself—Their Comparative Triviality—No Literature Great Which Is Not More Than Literature—Literature
as a Vehicle of Religion—Lucretius—*The Reconstruction of
Belief.*

IF we go back to the beginning of things, literature, needless to say, is a development of ordinary
speech. It is speech which has been made permanent, partly, indeed, by oral tradition, but
mainly by the art of writing. Without speech no
human co-operation, other than the rudest, would
be possible. Some men at least must speak so as to
organize the tasks of others, and the latter must
understand speech so as to do what the former bid
them. When the Deity determined to confound
the builders of Babel, or, in other words, to render
co-operative work impossible, he did not cut off their
hands, but he virtually took speech away from them,
by rendering the language of each unintelligible to
all the rest. Moreover, in the case of tasks the nature of which is highly complex, it is necessary not
only that the organizers should make use of speech,
but also that what they speak should systematically

343

be written down. The writing down, indeed, is often the most important part of the matter, as in the case of an Act of Parliament or of the delicate and elaborate formulæ on which depends the production of chemicals or of great ships.

If written speech, then, of kinds such as these is literature, literature is obviously not antithetic to action, but is, on the contrary, action in one of its most important forms. To state the case thus, however, is stating no more than half of it. As a matter of fact, laws and chemical formulæ, however carefully written, are not what is meant by literature in the common sense of the word. Though the writing down of speech may in such cases be a form of action, it does not follow that all such written speech is literature. Let us compare the compositions of a child, whether in prose or verse, with a page out of the *Nautical Almanac* or a manual of household medicine. The child's compositions may intrinsically have no literary value, but they nevertheless represent genuine attempts at literature. A page from the *Nautical Almanac* or the manual of household medicine may be, for certain purposes, of the highest value imaginable, but the test of literary beauty would be the last test we should apply to them.

What, then, is the primary difference between written words that *are* literature and written words that are *not*? The primary difference relates to the objects at which severally the writers aim or the motive by which they are impelled to write. The child writes solely because literary composition is a pleasure to him, as for the sake of a similar pleasure another child takes to a piano. The astronomer and the doctor write to help men in navigating ships or mothers in dosing babies. Between written language which is not literature and written language which *is* the initial difference is this: that for the writers written language is, in the first case, something which it is not in the second. In the first case, the writer's concern with language, and the sole interest which written language has for him, are things which have no dependence on the merits of written language as such, except in so far as it is a means of accomplishing ulterior objects, with which otherwise the mere merits of language have nothing at all to do. Sound injunctions to a nurse, provided that their meaning was clear, would have far greater value in a hospital than mistaken injunctions written with a grace or majesty worthy of Plato or Tacitus. In the second case, writing is a feat the successful achievement of which is, for the writer, an object and a pleasure in itself; and how far success is achieved by him depends not alone on the pleasure which he derives from his own performances personally, but also, and we may say mainly, on the quantity of kindred pleasure which his writing communicates to his readers.

These observations become more and more true and pungent in proportion as language becomes a more complex instrument, its progress resembling

the evolution of an organ from a shepherd's pipe.
As it thus progresses, its delicate possibilities of
melody, metaphor, and subtle emphasis increase, and
masters of the literary art enchant with ever new
surprises multitudes who have no capacity for the
literary art themselves. So far, then, as literature
is in this sense literature for its own sake, the contrast between literature and action is, with certain
exceptions, justified. Exceptions, however, to this
rule exist, and these, briefly stated, are as follows.
When a writer writes a book—let us say, for example, a novel—the object of which is to give
pleasure, his primary object in writing it may be
either to please himself or else to make money by
ministering to the taste of others. The importance
of this distinction has been clearly brought out by
Tolstoy, who defines art, and literary art in particular, as a means by which the artist contrives to
arouse in others emotions and interests which he has
experienced in his own person. Such being the
case, then, there are, says Tolstoy, many works
which partake of the nature of literature, but which
are not examples of true literary art. Such, according to him, are our modern detective novels, or any
novels the interests of which depend on the solution
of a mystery, the reason being that the writer is
acquainted with the mystery at starting, and experiences himself no emotion whatever with regard
to it. His sole object is to titillate an emotion in
others which he does not himself share, and from

which, indeed, he is, by the nature of the case, pre-
cluded. This is a criticism which might doubtless
be pressed too far; but it is within limits fruitful,
and, bearing it here in mind, we may say that
literature, if we take it in its pure form and regard
it as an end in itself, is language, as used to express
the personal emotions or personal convictions of the
writer, and is raised by him to such a pitch of beauty,
of strength or of delicacy that it is a source of pleasure
to large classes of mankind apart from all thoughts
of relationship, if any, to ulterior objects.

Thus pure literature, as legitimately contrasted
with action, is a matter of great interest for a large
number of people whom nobody would describe as
literary or as persons of letters otherwise; and I
may, therefore, say something of pure literature as
estimated more particularly by myself.

Let me begin with prose, which, merely as a
pleasurable art, instinct has urged me, from my
earliest days, to cultivate. Of what good prose is I
have always had clear notions; and, whether I have
been successful in my efforts to achieve it or not, my
personal experience of the process may not be without some interest. My own experience is that the
composition of good prose—prose that seems good
to myself—is a process which requires a very great
deal of leisure. True excellence in prose, so I have
always felt, involves many subtle qualities which
are appreciable by the reader through their final
effects alone, which leave no trace of the efforts spent

in producing them, but which without such effort could rarely be produced at all.

As examples of these qualities I may mention a melody not too often resonant, which captivates the reader's attention, and is always producing a mood in him conducive to a favorable reception of what the writer is anxious to convey. Next to such melody I should put a logical adaptation of stress, or of emphasis in the construction of sentences, which corresponds in detail to the movements of the reader's mind—a halt in the words occurring where the mind halts, a new rapidity in the words when the mind, satisfied thus far, is prepared to resume its progress. To these qualities, as essential to perfection in prose, I might easily add others; but these are so complex and comprehensive that they practically imply the rest.

With regard, then, to these essentials, the practice which I have had to adopt in my own efforts to produce them has been more or less as follows. The general substance of what I proposed to say I have written out first in the loosest language possible, without any regard to melody, to accuracy, or even to correct grammar. I have then rewritten this matter, with a view, not to any verbal improvement, but merely to the rearrangement of ideas, descriptions, or arguments, so that this may accord with the sequence of questions, expectations, or emotions which are likely, by a natural logic, to arise in the reader's mind—nothing being said too soon, nothing being said too late, and nothing (except for the sake of deliberate emphasis) being said twice over. The different paragraphs would now be like so many stone blocks which had been placed in their proper positions so as to form a polylithic frieze, but each of which still remained to be carved, as though by a sculptor or lapidary, so as to be part of a continuous pattern or a series of connected figures. My next task would be to work at them one by one, till each was sculptured into an image of my own minute intentions. The task of thus carving each and fitting it to its next-door neighbors has always been, merely for its own sake, exceedingly fascinating to myself, but it has generally been long and slow. Most of my own books, when their general substance had been roughly got into order by means of several tentative versions, were, paragraph by paragraph, written again five or six times more, the corrections each time growing more and more minute, and finally the clauses and wording of each individual sentence were transposed, or rebalanced or reworded, whenever such processes should be necessary, in order to capture some nuance of meaning which had previously eluded me as a bird eludes a fowler.

As an example of this process I may mention a single sentence which occurs in my little book on Cyprus. It is a sentence belonging to a description of certain morning scenes—of dewy plains, with peasants moving across them, and here and there a smoke wreath arising from burning weeds. The effect of these scenes in some poignant way was primitive, and I was able at once to reproduce it by saying that the peasants were moving like figures out of the Book of Genesis. I felt, however, that this effect was not produced by the groups of peasants only. I felt that somehow—I could not at first tell how—some part in producing it was played by the smoke wreaths also. At last I managed to capture the suggestion, at first subconscious only, which had so far been eluding me. I finished my original description by adding the following words, "The smoke-wreaths were going up like the smoke of the first sacrifice."

It may be objected that prose built up in this elaborate way loses as much as it gains, because it is bound to lose the charm and the convincing force of spontaneity. This may be so in some cases, but it is not so in all. I have found myself that, so far as my own works are concerned, the passages which are easiest to read are precisely those which it has been most laborious to write. And for this, it seems to me, there is a very intelligible reason. Half of the interests and emotions which make up the substance of life are more or less subconscious, and are, for most men, difficult to identify. One of the functions of pure literature is to make the subconscious reveal itself. It is to make men know what they *are*, in addition to what spontaneously they *feel* themselves to be, but feel only, without clear comprehension of it. As soon as a writer, at the cost of whatever labor, manages to make these spontaneities, otherwise subconscious, intelligible, the spontaneity of the processes described by him adds itself at last to his description.

A signal example of this fact may be found, not in prose, but in love poems. Most people can fall in love. It takes no trouble to do so, whatever trouble it may bring them. If any human processes are spontaneous, falling in love is one of them. Most lovers feel more than they know until great love poetry explains it to them what they are; but great love poems are great, not because they are composed spontaneously, but because they express spontaneities which are essentially external to themselves. In other words, the achievement of perfection, whether in prose or poetry, is comparable to the task of a piano tuner, who may spend a whole morning in tightening or relaxing the strings, but who knows at once, when he gets them, the minutely precise tones which the laws of music demand.

Whether every reader will agree with me as to these questions or not, they are, at all events, examples of questions purely literary, which are in themselves captivating for large numbers of people, without any reference to ulterior, or what are called practical, objects. To these questions I may add a few others, which have been specially captivating to myself.

One of them is the use of metaphor as an immemorial literary device, especially in the case of poetry. What is the psychology of metaphor? Let us take an instance from Tennyson, who in one of his poems speaks, with very vivid effect, of Mediterranean bays as colored like "the peacock's neck." The color of the bay is at once made present to the reader's mind. But why? A discussion of this question occurs in a dialogue between two of the characters in my novel *The Old Order Changes*. The poet, urges one of them, might, if describing a peacock, have said with equal effect that the peacock's neck was colored like a Mediterranean bay. How is it that we gain anything by comparing one equally familiar thing to another? The secret of the use of metaphor in the poet's art is, says the speaker, this. When the mind is at rest its surface is alive with vivid images which have settled on it like sea birds on a rock, but the moment any one of these detects an approach on our part, in order that we may examine it carefully, its wings are spread, and in a flash it is gone. When, however, we use a simile in order to describe something which is obviously our main concern (say the color of a Mediterranean bay), the thing which we are anxious to describe acts as a kind of stalking-horse, which enables us to approach and capture the thing which we use as an illustration (say the neck of a peacock) before the peacock so much as suspects our neighborhood. We have it alive before us, with all its feathers glittering, and these throw a new light on objects which our direct touch might have frightened away beyond the confines of our field of vision. The more vivid of the two objects communicates its color to the less vivid.

Two other purely literary questions are discussed in *The Veil of the Temple*, the first of these being as follows. One of the speakers calls attention to a criticism which is often and justly made with reference to many, and even to the best of novels, that, while the minor characters are drawn with the utmost skill, the heroes (such as most of Scott's) have often no characters at all. The reason, he says, is that, in most cases, the hero is not so much an individual, with characteristics peculiar to himself, as a certain point of view, from which all the other characters and incidents of the story are drawn. Or else, if some of these are, as very often happens, not drawn from the point of view of the hero, they are drawn from the point of view of some other ideal spectator, on whose position, moral or local, the whole perspective of the story, mental or ocular, depends. Let us take, for example, a typical opening scene of a kind proverbially frequent in the novels of G. P. R. James. Such scenes were proverbially described very much as follows: "To the right lay a gray wall, which formed, to all appearance, the boundary of some great sheep tract. To the left was a wood of larches. Between these was a road, showing so few signs of use that it might have been a relic of some almost forgotten world. Proceeding along this road on a late October evening might have been seen three horsemen, of imperfectly distinguishable, yet vaguely sinister, aspect." In the absence of an ideal spectator, who is tacitly identified with the novelist, his hero, or his reader, such a description would mean very little more than nothing. There would be no left or right unless for a supposed spectator standing in a particular place and looking in a particular direction. The aspect of the horsemen could not be sinister or indistinguishable unless there were an assumed man whose eyes were unable to distinguish it.

The argument here in question will carry us on to certain kindred problems, connected likewise with the novelist's art, which are these: The necessary assumption of the author as ideal spectator being given, a question arises with regard to the range of vision which, in his capacity of spectator, the novelist professes to possess. Many novelists mar the effect of their work—and among these Thackeray is notable—by adopting an attitude which in this respect is constantly vacillating. Sometimes it is one of omniscience, sometimes of blind perplexity. At one time he describes the inmost thoughts of his characters which are suffered or pursued in secret, as though he could see through everything. At another time he will startle the reader with some such question as this: "Who shall dare to say—I certainly cannot—what at that solemn moment the lad's real reflections were?" A partial escape from the sense of unreality which alternations like these produce is to be found in the method which many novelists have adopted—namely, that of dividing the story into so many separate parts, these being told in succession by so many different characters, each recording events as wholly seen from the point of his own unchanged perspective. Such is the method adopted by Wilkie Collins in _The Woman in White_, for example. The danger of this artifice is that it tends to be too apparent. The most logically complete escape from the difficulties which we are here glancing at is to be found, no doubt, in the method of autobiography in a single and undivided form; unless indeed the assumption of absolute omniscience on the author's part can be used with a rigid consistency which it very rarely exhibits.

Another question of a purely literary kind, reflection on which is to me, at least, pleasurable (though many persons of literary taste may, perhaps, regard it as a bore), is the relation of modern prosody to ancient, and more particularly to Latin. It has always seemed to me that the lengthening and shortening of syllables according to their position, as happens in classical Latin, with regard to the syllables that follow them, must always have corresponded with the stresses or absence of stress which would naturally be made apparent by the voice of an ideal reciter; and to me, as to some other people, the question has proved amusing of how far in English verse Latin prosody could be reproduced.

355

Many attempts have been made at deciding this question by experiments. The most remarkable of these are two which were made by Tennyson. One of them, called "Hendecasyllabics," is little more than a trick played with extreme skill, and in no serious sense does it merit the name of poetry. The other, "An Ode to Milton," is no less charming as a poem than as a conquest over technical difficulties. Let us take the first stanza:

> Oh, mighty-mouthed inventor of harmonies,
> Oh, skilled to sing of time and eternity,
> God-gifted organ voice of England,
> Milton a name to resound for ages.

Here the stresses which the meaning of the English verse demands fall exclusively on syllables which would, according to Latin prosody, be long; but there are one or two syllables which in Latin verse would be long (such as "of" in the second line) which invite no stress in the English—which do not, indeed, admit of it—and must for that reason be treated by an English reader as short. Aiming at greater completeness, but otherwise in a manner very much less ambitious, I attempted an experiment of a similar kind myself, consisting of a few hexameters, in which not only do the natural stresses fall, and fall exclusively, on syllables which in Latin would be long, but in which also every syllable would be emphasized by an English reciter with a natural stress corresponding to it. These

356

hexameters were a metrical amplification of an advertisement which figures prominently in the carriages of the Tube Railway, proclaiming the charms of a suburb called Sudbury Town, and remarkable for its surrounding pine woods. The moment I read the words "Sudbury Town" I recognized in them the beginning of a hexameter classically pure; and after many abortive attempts I worked out a sequel—a very short one—as follows:

Sudbury Town stands here. In an old-world region around it
Tall, dark pines, like spires, with above them a murmur of
    umbrage,
Guard for us all deep peace. Such peace may the weary
    suburbans
Know not in even a dream. These, these will an omnibus
    always,
Ev'n as they sink to a doze just earned by the toil of a daytime,
Rouse, or a horse-drawn dray, too huge to be borne by an Atlas,
Shakes all walls, all roofs, with a sound more loud than an
    earthquake.[1]

---

[1] In connection with the above questions, I may mention certain others, all bearing on the relation of prose to poetry. It was said of Plutarch that his sense of sound was so delicate that if it had been necessary for the sake of mere verbal melody, he would have made Cæsar kill Brutus instead of Brutus killing Cæsar. Closely bearing on this criticism is the fact that in old English tragedies from the days of Dryden onward a careful reader will note that, while parts of the dialogue are in blank verse and parts in prose, the writers themselves show, in many cases, a very defective appreciation of where verse ends and prose begins, many passages which are printed as prose being really unconscious verse. An interesting example of this may be found in a passage from Bacon's *Essays*, which Macaulay quotes as an example of the literary altitude to which Bacon's prose could rise. This passage is in reality blank verse pure and simple. It is as follows:

The moral of such experiments seems to me to be this: that even if ancient prosody, such as that of the Virgilian hexameter, could be naturalized completely in English, the emotional effect of the meter would in the two languages be different, and that Anglo-Latin hexameters would, with very rare exceptions, mean no more than successes in a graceful and very difficult game. It is indeed for that very reason that I mention this question here. It is a question of pure literature or of purely literary form. As such, it has proved fascinating to many highly cultivated persons; yet even by such persons themselves it will not be seriously regarded as much better than trivial. But this is not all. From this consideration we are led on to another. If the problems of Anglo-Classical prosody are trivial even for those who happen to find them entertaining, may not all literature, even the highest, when cultivated for its own sake only, be, from certain points of view, a triviality also?

According to differences of taste and temperament, different persons will answer this question

---

> Virtue is like precious odors,
> Most fragrant when they are incensed or crushed.
> Prosperity doth best discover vice.
> Adversity doth best discover virtue.

This passage, with Macaulay's comments on it, may be commended to the notice of those who contend that Bacon could not have written *Shakespeare*, because Bacon's acknowledged verses are of a very inferior kind. If they look in Bacon's prose for verse which was unacknowledged, and which was unintended by himself, they may find reason for modifying this argument.

differently. Since I am not entering here on any formal argument, but am merely recording my own individual views, I should, speaking for myself, answer this question in the affirmative. I may, indeed, confess that the mere artist in literature—the person for whom literature, as such, is the main interest in life—is a person for whom secretly I have always felt some contempt, even though, for myself personally, this magical triviality has been one of life's chief seductions.

The content and significance of such a feeling are presented in concrete form by such institutions as authors' or writers' clubs. In London and in other capitals so many of these have been established, and continue to flourish, that they obviously perform certain useful and welcome functions; but my own criticism would be that to call them clubs for "authors" or "writers" is a misnomer which fails to particularize the real basis of membership. In the modern world, no doubt, all writers, merely as writers, have certain interests in common. They have, in the first place, to get their works published, and the business of publication is a very complex process, which has necessarily a legal and financial side. Questions are inevitably involved of financial loss or gain, and even writers who are indifferent to profit, and are ready to bear a loss, will desire to be treated fairly. They may be ready to bear a loss, but not a loss which is inequitable, and if any gain should ensue, they will desire an equitable share of

it. In connection with such matters, authors' clubs
may perform many useful offices for their members.
In so far, however, as their functions are limited to
offices such as these the proper name for them would
be not clubs, but agencies. On the other hand, in
the modern world authorship to a great extent is a
systematic writing for journals. It has to be performed, in respect both of time and other conditions, in accordance with strict arrangements between the writers themselves and the officials
by whom, whether as editors or owners, these
journals are managed. For this reason persons
who practice journalism—daily journalism in particular—will probably be persons more or less
similar in their habits, and clubs for admission to
which the main qualification consists in the fact of
authorship may provide them with special con-
veniences which they one and all desire. But for
persons whose literary pursuits are carried on in
isolation, and who aim at expressing by authorship
no thoughts or no sentiments but their own, it seems
to me that a club for authors or writers as such represents a conception as wrong as would that of a club
for speakers as such or for politicians as such.
What bond of union would there be between a Tory
and a ferocious Democrat if they neither of them put
pen to paper—if they were not authors at all?
They would keep, so far as was possible, to different
sides of the street. Why, then, should they wish to
meet in a club coffee room and lunch at adjacent

tables, simply because each, besides holding opinions absolutely odious to the other, should, instead of keeping them to himself, endeavor to disseminate them by writing among as many of his fellow creatures as was possible?

It may be said that two such men might very well wish to do so because, though what each expressed was odious to the other in itself, each was a consummate master of literary art in expressing it, and each admired, and was aware of, the presence of this technical mastery in the other. Now, so far as it goes, this, in numerous cases, may be true. Indeed, such an admission is the very point from which the present argument started. Pure literature, as such, is, no doubt, susceptible of consummate beauties, in their natural admiration of which men who are otherwise the bitterest adversaries may agree. What does this admission cover? It applies, in my own opinion, to minor literature only, though masterpieces of minor literature may be in their own way supreme, as Keats has shown us in such poems as "La Belle Dame Sans Merci," but, as applied to literature in its higher and greater forms, the admission fails to be true, because it fails to be adequate. A poem by Keats may be admirable so far as it goes, but really great literature, such as Goethe's "Faust," for example, would possess but a minor value unless there were at the back of it something that is more than literature. In the case of a poem like "Endymion" the poem is greater than the man who writes it. In the case of a poem like "Faust" the man is greater than the poem. Behind the poet stands the man of profound reflection, the man of the world, the philosopher, the passionate or disillusioned lover. He is all of these before he is a literary artist. His writing is only the vehicle by which he communicates what he is in all these capacities to others, and so leaves a practical impression on the thoughts and emotions of the world.

And what is true of verse is more obviously true of prose. Of all prose works which have captured attention by their mere merits as literature, no better example can be given than the great masterpiece of Gibbon. But though Gibbon may be read by many for the sake of his mere literary charm, his place in the world as a great writer depends but in a secondary way on this charm in itself. He lives because this charm was used by him to convey the results of research so penetrating and comprehensive, and guided by a mind so sagacious and powerful, that for the most part these results have stood the test of criticism, however keen and hostile; and in accomplishing this feat Gibbon has rendered a service which is still indispensable to the historical students and historical thinkers of to-day, whereas otherwise his merely literary merits would have been merits displayed in vain or relegated to a literary museum which few men cared to enter.

This conception of pure literature as written language which is mainly appreciated for its own sake, and is for that reason in a relative sense trivial, no doubt widens out again when we come to consider the fact that emotion of some kind is, in the last resort, the one thing which gives value to life. But the fact remains that all the desirable emotions are determined by things which are not in themselves emotions, such as knowledge, intellectual beliefs, and the laws, economic and otherwise, which alone render a civilized society possible; and even the greatest of merely literary charms make great literature only in so far as they endow mankind with fundamental things like these.

Throughout these memoirs there has been constant allusion to the relation borne by literary expression to life in the case of the author himself. I have said already that for mere literature as such, and for its practitioners, I have from my youth onward had a certain feeling of contempt, and I now may explain once more what, at least in my own case, such a feeling really means. It means, not that mere literature at its best is not beautiful and delightful, but that it must, in order to be worthy of a serious man's devotion, be a mere part of some whole, the other part of which is incomparably the larger of the two. It means that literature, in order to be great literature, must at the same time be practically a form of action. I have no ambition to impose this opinion on others. I would merely record it as an opinion on which, since the ending of my early days at Oxford, I have myself by instinct acted. Whatever I have written I have written with one or other ulterior object, to which the mere pleasure of literary opposition as such has been altogether subordinate. Of the nature of these objects I have said enough already, but I may once again define them.

One of them relates to religion, to the quality of the lives and the loves of ordinary men and women as affected by it, and also to metaphysics and science, in so far as they leave, or do not leave, the doctrines of religion credible.

The second of these objects relates to the existing conditions of social and industrial life, more especially to those suggested by the loosely used word "Labor," and the frantic fallacies with regard to these by which the ideas of extreme reformers are vitiated, and from which, instead of meeting them, too many Conservatives shrink in ignominious terror.

With regard to religion, philosophy, science, and the widespread ideas underlying what is vaguely described as Socialism, I have endeavored to discredit, or else to modify, the views which, for something like fifty years, leaders who are called "advanced" have been making more and more widely popular. I have resorted for this purpose to the methods of fiction and of formal argument. The implication of all the writings by which I have attempted to do this is that the mischief, religious, social, and political, which "advanced" thought has done may in time, by a rational development of conservative thought, be undone, and the true faiths be revived on which the sanctities, the stabilities, and the civilization of the social order depend.

I have nevertheless always myself recognized, ever since early enthusiasm felt the chill of experience, that such a counter-revolution must be slow, nor have I ever underrated the obstacles which certain false idealisms now at work in the world may oppose to it. On the contrary, I have always felt that no man is fit to encounter an adversary's case successfully unless he can make it for the moment his own, unless he can put it more forcibly than the adversary could put it for himself, and takes account, not only of what the adversary says, but also of the best that he *might say*, if only he had chanced to think of it.

On this principle I have endeavored myself to act. The process, however, may in some cases be not without the seeming danger that the converter, in thus arming himself for his task, may perform it somewhat too thoroughly, and end by being himself perverted. He must, at all events, go near to experiencing a sense of such perversion dramatically. Of this fact I have myself provided an example in one of my writings, to which I just now alluded, and which herein differs from the rest. Having elsewhere argued in defense of religious faith, as though feeling that, through argument and knowledge, mankind will some day recover it, I wrote the work here in question as a man might write who had himself made a final—even a complacent—surrender to the forces which he had dreamed of dissipating.

This work is a poem called "Lucretius on Life and Death," and was partly suggested by the vogue acquired by Fitzgerald's rendering of the Rubáiyát of Omar Khayyam. The doctrine of Omar is, as everybody knows, a doctrine of voluptuous pessimism. There is no life other than this. Let us kiss and drink while it lasts. The doctrine of Lucretius is to a certain extent similar, but is sterner and more intellectual in its form. I accordingly selected from his great scientific poem, which contains in embryo all the substance of the modern doctrine of evolution, those passages which bear on the meaning of man's existence. I arranged these in logical order, and translated or paraphrased them in the meter with which Fitzgerald has familiarized and fascinated the English ear, so that the philosophy of the Persian and the Roman might be reduced to something like a common denominator. Lucretius is so far a pessimist that, under existing conditions, human life is for him no more than a hideous nightmare; but he is so far an optimist that he looks upon all this misery as due to one removable cause, this cause being the prevalence of one mistaken belief, which a true scientific philosophy will altogether eradicate. The belief in question is a belief in a personal God, who is offended by the very nature of man, and who watches with a wrathful eye by the deathbed of each human creature, in order to begin a torture of him which will last for all eternity. Man's true savior, Lucretius argues, is science, which makes this belief ridiculous by showing clearly that all individual things—human beings included—are nothing but atomic aggregations, which, having been formed for a moment, dissolve and disappear for ever. How, then, can any avenging God be anything more than the distempered dream of children? How could such a God torture men when they die, since as soon as they are dead there is nothing left to torture? Let them cast this incubus of irrational fear behind them, and the mere process of life may then be tolerable enough. It may even, in a sober way, be happy. It certainly need not be, as it now is, miserable; and at all events it will be pleasing as a prelude to the luxury of an endless sleep. Of my own rendering of the great Lucretian message, I may here give a few stanzas as specimens:

> Nothing abides. The seas in delicate haze
> Go off. Those moonèd sands forsake their place;
>   And where they are shall other seas in turn
> Mow with their sands of whiteness other bays.

How, then, the poet asks, shall the individual man be more enduring than these?

> What, shall the dateless worlds in dust be blown
> Back to the unremembered and unknown,
>   And this frail Thou—this flame of yesterday—
> Burn on forlorn, immortal and alone?

What though there lurks behind yon veil of sky
Some fabled Maker, some immortal Spy,
    Ready to torture each poor thing he made?
Thou canst do more than God can. Thou canst die.

Will not the thunders of thy God be dumb
When thou art deaf for ever? Can the sum
    Of all things bruise what is not? Nay, take heart,
For where thou go'st thither no God can come.

And no omnipotent wearer of a crown
Of righteousness, or fiend with branded frown
    Swart from the pit, shall break or reach thy rest,
Or stir thy temples from the eternal down.

In writing this poem I experienced the full sensation of having become a convert to the Lucretian
gospel myself, against which throughout my life it
had been my dominant impulse to protest.

There are, doubtless, many others who experience
this disconcerting vicissitude—for whom the deduc-
tions of science as a moral message are ludicrous,
but for whom its homicidal negations prove in the
end ineluctable. If this is their permanent, if this
is their final condition, they will perhaps deserve
commiseration, but they will hardly deserve castigation, for their attitude is one which will bring its
own castigation with it. I can only hope that I am
entitled to the truly charitable satisfaction of regarding them as a class to which I do not myself
belong, and that the literary industry of a life otherwise idle may prove to be a form of action, or rather

a reaction, which, alike as to religion and politics, will have not been unserviceable to the world.

To sum the matter up, the Lucretian philosophy of life, appealing as it may to men when in certain moods, is one which, when submitted to what Kant calls the "practical reason," shrivels up into an absurdity, and I have shown at length, in my work *The Reconstruction of Belief*, that this becomes only the more apparent when we consider the attempts which have been made by modern thinkers to vivify it by an idea of which in Lucretius there is no trace. Put into language less imposing than his own, the gospel of Lucretius virtually comes to this, that men may eat and drink and propagate their kind in comfort if only they will hold fast to the belief that men, when they die, slip into their burrows like rabbits, and will, though they have done with pleasure, be out of the reach of pain—that whatever they may have done or not done, they will all, as individuals, be as though they never had been. The only enlargement of this gospel which modern thought can suggest is rooted in a transference of men's serious interests in life from the life of the individual to the life of the community or the race, and in the thought that, though the individual perishes, the race will continue and progress.

The answer given to this argument in *The Reconstruction of Belief* is that, even if we suppose such corporate progress to be a reality, it cannot be invested with any practical meaning unless we postu-

369

late the individual, and consider his fortunes first. We have here the Asses' Bridge of all philosophy whatsoever, and until the philosopher has crossed it the philosopher can do nothing but bray. The whole external universe, the race of men included, has for no man any perceptible existence except in so far as it is reflected in the thoughts and the sensations of the individual. The conception of the race is nothing, so far as we can know it, beyond what the individual conceives. Let us suppose it, then, to be in some relative sense true that the human race is undergoing some change always for the better in respect of its material or moral conditions, which change will continue so long as the race exists. In that case the course of Humanity will be comparable to an upward road which the race will be always ascending toward heights of welfare at present hardly imaginable. Such will be the course of the race, but the course of the individuals will be something totally different. It will for each be a progress not *up* such a road, but *across* it, no matter at what altitude this crossing is made. Humanity will always be nothing more than a procession passing from one turnstile to another, the one leading out of, and the other leading into, a something which always must be, for each individual, a nullity. Apart from the individual, nothing which the human race knows as desirable can exist; and, logically and practically alike, the only efficient connection between the individual and the race must first of all be a connection not with the race as such, and not with external nature, but with something which is beyond both, and is not comprehended in either.

The only conceivable human being who will, apart from religion, ever be able to describe himself as coextensive with the human race will, as Nietzsche puts it in one of his most memorable sentences, be the last man left alive when the rest of the human race is frozen. He, and he only, will be able to say truly: "*Homo sum. Humani nihil a me alienum puto.*"

INDEX

Aberdeen, speech at, 192.
Acland, family of, 3.
—— Sir Henry at Oxford, 78.
Aidé, Hamilton, 98, 130.
Alexandria, 228.
Alford, Lady Marian, on society, 119.
America, political visit to, 308.
American architecture, 322.
Amherst, Lord and Lady, 292.
Ardverikie, Sir John Ramsden's lodge, 145, 307.
Aristocracy and Evolution, 265.
Arnold, Matthew, as Mr. Luke in *The New Republic*, 88.
Ashburton, Louisa, Lady, 117.
—— Rawlin Mallock, Whig member for, 4.
Astor, Mr. John Jacob, in New York, 314.
Austin, Alfred, Poet Laureate, 120.

Baker, Sir Samuel, 226–227.
Baltimore, 309, 320.
Batthyany, Prince and Princess, 241–242.
Beaufort Castle (Lord Lovat's), 129.
Beaulieu, villa at, 203.
Beckett, Ernest, second Lord Grimthorpe, 195.
Benbecula, island of, 304.
Bevan, Mr. (the last of the "dandies"), 60.
Bismarck, Countesses Marie and Helen, 55.
Blatchford, Lord, 30.

Blayney, Lord, friend of Cromwell's, 4.
Blenheim, 152.
Blunt, Wilfrid, poet, and breeder of Arab horses, 53, 129.
Boroughs, rotten Cornish, 159.
Breakfast party at Lord Houghton's, 103.
Bright, John, as land agitator; his absurd statistics, 182.
Brittany, visit to, 329.
Broglio, castle of, 237.
Browning, Robert, 71.
Buller, Emma and Antony, 30.
Bulwer, Sir Henry, in Cyprus, 227.
Burdett-Coutts, Miss, at Torquay, 61.
Bute, Lord, original of Lord Beaconsfield's Lothair, 131; at Chiswick, 131; at Cardiff Castle, 151.
Butler, Dr. Nicholas Murray, 313.
Byram, Sir John Ramsden's, in Yorkshire, 161.

Cannes, first visit to, 167; miniature villa at, 167; subsequent visits, 241.
Cardiff Castle, 157.
Carlyle, introduction to, 64.
Carriages, old traveling, 16.
Cary, Mr., of Tor Abbey, and R. Mallock as smugglers, 5.
—— Sir Henry, sells Cockington to R. Mallock, *temp.* Charles I, 4.
Castles, different classes of, 152.

Catholic society in London, 130.

Champernowne family related to Mallocks, 7.

Chelston Cross, built by Mr. W. Proude, 49.

Chillingham Castle, 155.

Civic Federation of New York, 308.

Clark, Mr. George, meeting at Cardiff, 158.

Cleveland, Duchess of, 149.

Cockington Church, 17.

—— Court, 13.

—— Estate, no building leases granted till 1860, 49.

Cockington village, 15.

Conservative party, besetting weakness of, 214, 268.

Conversation, the arts of, 101.

Country houses, description of various, 146–167.

Currie, Philip, afterward Lord Currie, 130.

Cyprus, winter visit to, 227, 235.

Dandies, 63.

Dartington Hall, 12.

—— Parsonage, 10.

Dartmouth as a rotten borough, 50.

De Vere, Aubrey, 54.

Dempster, Miss C., 241.

Denbury Manor, 7.

"Denzil Place," poem by "Violet Fane," 129.

Diagrams, statistical, used at public meetings, 191.

Doctrine and Doctrinal Disruption, 276.

Dorlin, Lord Howard's lodge in the Highlands, 175.

Dreams, poems written in, 259.

Dunrobin, 146.

Eaglehurst, 241.

Eaton, Alfred Montgomery at, 152.

Elvaston Castle, 157.

Erskine, Lady, hostess at Torquay, 54.

Everingham Park, old Yorkshire Catholic house, 154.

Exeter, Henry Philpotts, Bishop of, 31–34.

—— R. Mallock's connection with, *temp.* Elizabeth and James I, 4.

Famaugusta, enormous ruins of, 233.

"Fane, Violet," 130.

Farmer, Devonshire, on free will, 24; on the fall of Jericho, 24.

Fielding, a child's imitation of his novels, 35.

Florence, interesting houses in and near, 236.

Froude, Antony, historian, and Carlyle, 64.

—— Archdeacon, equestrian, dilettante, artist, magistrate, 6.

Froude, Hurrell, leader of Tractarian movement, 6.

—— Mr. and Mrs. William, interesting society at their house, 50.

—— William, his discoveries in naval architecture, 51.

Fryston, 161.

Gaskell, C. Milnes; Lord Houghton's characteristic advice to him, 59.

George, Henry, limitations of his attack on private wealth, 173; his ignorance of statistics, 188.

Georges, Sir Ferdinando: his im-

INDEX

mense landed properties in Maine, 4; Mallock's partner *temp.* Charles I, 4.

Glasgow, the author speaks at, 192.

Glenthorne, its lonely and singular situation, 153.

Governesses, high Tory, 28.

Gratz, 246.

Greenock, Lord, 195.

Grimthorpe, Lord, 194.

Hare, Augustus, his indiscretions as a writer of memoirs, 136.

Harvard, 317–318.

Hatchments in Cockington Church, 17.

Heart of Life, The, 280.

Hebrides, the Outer, 304.

Heligan, the John Tremaynes' house in Cornwall, 159.

Herbert, Auberon, a devotee of "the simple life," 122–124.

—— of Lee, Lady, 177.

Hewel Grange, 160.

Hibbert, Mrs. Washington, 130.

Highlands, the, first visit to, 175.

Hoch - Osterwitz, extraordinary castle of, 245.

Hotels, old-fashioned, private, in London, 94; extravagant gilding of American, 316.

Houghton, Lord, at Torquay, 58; his enormous acquaintance, 59; his dry wit and humor, 60; his social advice to the author, 60; breakfast party given in London by, 103; his remarkable defense of one of the author's novels, 172; in the Highlands, 177.

Houghton, old Catholic house in Yorkshire, 155.

—— Sir Robert Walpole's, in Norfolk, 151.

Howard, Kenneth, 96.

Hoy, island of, its colossal cliffs, 300.

Hugel, Baron von, Austrian diplomat, 237.

Human Document, A, 255–278.

Huxley as Mr. Storks in *The New Republic,* 87–88.

In an Enchanted Island, 229.

Individualist, The, 281.

Ireland, visits in, 164.

Is Life Worth Living? 169.

James, William, at Harvard, 317.

Jerningham, C. E., 200.

Jerome, William Travers, 321.

Jersey, Julia, Lady, 126.

Jowett, as Doctor Jenkinson in *The New Republic,* 88.

Kidd, Benjamin, on Social Evolution, 264.

Kippax, Yorkshire, a product of architectural rivalry, 162.

Kirkwall and its cathedral, 299.

Knebworth, its pseudo - Gothic architecture, 257, 260; "Ouida's" visit to, 256; a night of conversation at, 288.

Körmend, castle of, in Hungary, 246.

Labor and the Popular Welfare, 261.

Land agitation in the Highlands, 180.

—— agitator on Fort William coach, 184.

—— the old basis of London society, 93; decline in rent of agricultural since 1880, 93.

375

Lane Fox, George, 211.

Larnaca in Cyprus, 229.

Laureateship, competitors for, 121.

Library, secret hours in a, 36.

Limits of Pure Democracy, 333.

Literature and action, 341–371.

Literature and utilitarianism, 343.

—— as speech made permanent, 342.

Littlehampton, private tutor at, 39.

Lloyd Bryce, 310.

Long Island, country house in, 310.

Lowther, Mrs. William, 117.

Lucretius on Life and Death, 366.

Lulworth Castle, 154.

Lyme, 163.

Lytton, as contrasted with Carlyle, 65; second Lord, early acquaintance with, 66; his poetry and his generous temper, 67; poem composed by him in a dream, 259.

—— first Lord, at Torquay, 54.

Mallock family, 3–5.

—— Richard, as member for Torquay division of Devonshire, 209; support given him by George Lane Fox and J. Sandars, 211.

Mallocks as members of Parliament for Lyme, Poole, Totnes, and Ashburton, 3.

—— of the eighteenth century: their ecclesiastical patronage, and their patronage of the turf, 5.

Manchester, speech at, on the land question, 192.

Manning, Cardinal, 131.

Marx, Karl, his influence in England about 1880, 173, 179.

Memoirs, difficulties of writing, 135.

Metaphors, the secret of their force in literature, 349.

Molesworth, Sir Louis, 159.

Monte Carlo, 194–208.

Montrose, Duchess of (Caroline), 99.

Morgan, J. Pierpont, 323, 327.

Naval architecture, Mr. Froude's experiments in, 51.

Negro, spiritual ambitions of a, 327.

Nevill, Lady Dorothy, 101.

—— Miss Meresia, her lesson in oratory at Strathfieldsaye, 110.

New Domesday Book, studied by the author at Ardverikie, 187.

Newman, Cardinal, 50.

New Paul and Virginia, The, 90.

New Republic, The, 87.

New York: the opera there a social function, 312; dinner parties in, and other entertainments, 312; good taste in fashionable entertainments, 316; author's address at Columbia University, 313; Evelyn Nesbit and the Thaw trial, 321; ladies' club in, author's address at opening of, 324.

Nicosia, 230.

Noble, Mr. and Mrs. Saxton, 294.

Noltland Castle, in the Orkneys, 301.

Normans and Saxons, 28.

Oban, 175.

Old Order Changes, The, analysis of, 214–217.

Orford, Lord, his views of society, 97.

INDEX

Osborne, Father B., son of a prominent Evangelical, 240.

"Ouida" in London, 126; at Florence, 256; at Knebworth, 256.

Oxford, undergraduate life at, 68; suppers and concerts at, 70–71; Robert Browning and Ruskin at, 71–79; rejection of dogmatic Christianity at, 82; suicide of Balliol undergraduate at, 80; orthodox apologists at, 83; *The New Republic* at, 87.

Paget, Sir Augustus and Lady, 228.

Pater, as Mr. Rose, in *The New Republic*, 88.

Pelham (Lord Lytton's novel), social advice to her son from the hero's mother, 97.

Philpot, Mr., private tutor at Littlehampton, 39; his taste for poetry, 39; the author's happy years under tuition of, 39–49; his professed Radicalism in politics and religion, 43; his fastidiousness in choice of pupils, 43.

Philpotts, Henry, Bishop of Exeter, examples of his polished wit, 32.

Poetry, author's early devotion to, 35–37.

Poor, the rural, of Devonshire, 20–29.

Pope as author's earliest model, 35.

Popoff, Admiral, his visit to Mr. W. Froude at Chelston Cross, 51.

Primrose League meeting at Cockington, humors of the occasion, 211.

Prose, methods of writing good, 347.

Prosody, attempts to write English verse according to Latin, 386.

Provence, the, French transatlantic steamer, 328.

Queen of Holland at Cockington, 17.

Raby Castle, 150.

Ramsden, Lady Guendolen: the author helps her in editing family memoirs, 100; has to reject the most amusing parts, 100.

—— Sir John, an ideal country gentleman, 161.

Reconstruction of Belief, The, 291.

Religion as a Credible Doctrine, 284.

Religion as an element of civilization, 291.

Riegersbourg, castle of, 252.

Roden, Lady, the charm of her conversation, 101.

—— Lord and Lady, in Ireland, 164.

Romance of the Nineteenth Century, A, 169; violent attacks on, 170; analysis of its philosophical purport, 170; defended by Catholic priest and Lord Houghton, 171–172.

Roosevelt, President, author's meeting with, at Harvard, 318.

Ruskin, meeting with, at Oxford, 78; his extreme charm of manner, 79; temperamentally opposed to Jowett, 79; his insistence on the need of definite religious belief, 86;

377

as Mr. Herbert in *The New Republic*, 88.

St. Andrews Boroughs, invitation to stand for, 191.
St. Helier, Lady, and Duke of Wellington, 108.
St. Hilarion, castle of, 232.
St. Michael's Mount (Cornwall), 148.
St. Vincent, first Lord, 14.
Sartor Resartus, Carlyle's, 64.
Savile, Augustus, 96.
Season in London, 138.
Seaton, first Lord, 14.
Sermon, Jowett's, in *The New Republic*, 88; semisocialist, by priest in *The Old Order Changes*, 219.
Servants, Old World, 18.
Shelley, Sir Percy and Lady, 114.
Sherborne House, 163.
—— Susan, Lady, 163.
—— the late Lord, 163.
Shropshire, county ball in, 142.
Sloane, Mr. and Mrs., of New York, 315.
Smuggling by two country gentlemen in Devonshire, 5.
"Social Democratic Federation," 173.
Social Equality, 181.
Socialism, A Critical Examination of, 329.
——, elements of, in *The Old Order Changes*, 222.
Society in London, its traditional basis, 92.
Society in the country, 144.
Somers, Lady, 117.
Somerset, Duchess of, her conversational humor, 100.
Spencer, Herbert, letters from,

about *Aristocracy and Evolution*, 266.
Stanway, picture of life at, in the eighteenth century, 162.
"Statistical Monographs," 333.
Stowe, 151.
Strafford, Cora, Lady, 151.
Suicide, her funeral at Monaco, 207.
Summer on the borders of Caithness, 292.
Sutherland, Duchess (Annie), at Torquay, 212.
Swinburne, admiration of his poetry at Littlehampton, 47; at Jowett's dinner table and afterward, 72; at an undergraduate's luncheon, 74; his humor, 75; recitation of his own verses, 77.
System played at Monte Carlo, 196–197.

Tchiacheff, Madame de, well-known Florentine hostess, 236.
Tennyson, quoted as illustrating the force of metaphor in poetry, 352.
Tiffany's, two queer customers at, 242.
Torquay, extension of, over Cockington and Chelston property, 13–14; winter society at, 54–55.
Torre a Cona, near Florence, 238.
Trevarthenick, Sir L. Molesworth's, 159.
Trevelyans of East Devon, 3.

Ugbrooke, the Cliffords, in Devonshire, 154.

INDEX

Valentines, two living, 202.

Vay di Vaya, Monsignor, 314.

Veil of the Temple, passage on Darwin quoted in, 284; table talk on free will in, 287; verses from, quoted, 288–289; President Roosevelt's interest in, 319.

Verses, three volumes of the author's, 340.

Vicenza, 243.

Villa at Beaulieu, 205.

—— Maser, near Asolo, 244.

Vyner, Clair, 130.

Ward, Mrs. Humphry, 272.

—— Wilfrid, 134.

Wellington, second Duke of, his conversational wit, 105–112; his last Waterloo banquet at Apseley House, 107; as a translator of Horace, 112.

Wemyss, Lord, 135.

Wentworth, Lord, 53, 69.

Westminster, Constance, Duchess of, 99.

White, Stanford, 321–322.

Whyte Melville, 124.

Will, freedom of, 284.

Wilton, Laura, Lady, 202.

Wordsworth, 35.

Wrath, Cape, 296.

Young, Rev. Julian, 54.

THE END